HOW OUR ANCESTORS LIVED

MILTON KEYNES
COUNCIL

A Street Group
Boys dressed in shabby clothes and caps pose by a fountain for an illustration entitled 'Slum life in our great cities'.

$\mathcal{H}$OW OUR ANCESTORS LIVED

A HISTORY OF LIFE
A HUNDRED YEARS AGO

DAVID HEY

the national archives

First edition published in hardback in 2002 by the Public Record Office (1 903365 21 x)

Second edition first published in 2003 by

The National Archives
Kew, Richmond
Surrey, TW9 4DU
UK

www.nationalarchives.gov.uk/

The National Archives was formed when the Public Record Office and
Historical Manuscripts Commission combined in April 2003.

A catalogue record for this book is available from the British Library

ISBN 1 903365 55 4

Cover illustrations: (front) A Day at the Fair, 1898 (TNA: PRO COPY 1/435 A);
(back) Charles Sandy (1841–1925) and his second wife, Olive
(reproduced courtesy of David Hey)

Typeset by Geoff Green Book Design, Cambridge, Cambridgeshire
Printed in the UK by Antony Rowe,
Chippenham, Wiltshire

$\mathscr{C}$ONTENTS

The true state of every nation is the state of common life.

Dr Samuel Johnson,
A Journey to the Western Islands of Scotland (1775)

It is so very large a majority of your fellow countrymen that are of this insignificant stamp. At least eighty out of a hundred of your adult male fellow Britons returned in the last census are neither extraordinarily silly, nor extraordinarily wicked, nor extraordinarily wise; their eyes are neither deep and liquid with sentiment, nor sparkling with suppressed witticisms; they had probably had no hairbreadth escapes or thrilling adventures; their brains are certainly not pregnant with genius, and their passions have not manifested themselves at all after the fashion of a volcano. They are simply men of complexions more or less muddy, whose conversation is more or less bald and disjointed. Yet these commonplace people – many of them – bear a conscience, and have felt the sublime prompting to do the painful right; they have their unspoken sorrows, and their sacred joys; their hearts have perhaps gone out towards their first-born, and they have mourned over the irreclaimable dead. Nay, is there not a pathos in their very insignificance – in our own comparison of their dim and narrow existence with the glorious possibilities of that human nature which they share?

George Eliot, *The Sad Fortunes of the Rev. Amos Barton* (1857)

PREFACE

ON 2 JANUARY 2002 the National Archives released the 1901 census returns for England and Wales to public scrutiny. Because of the 'One Hundred Years Rule' the personal information recorded in the census enumerators' books had remained private up to that point. The official report of 1904 on the statistical findings of the 1901 census had enabled social and economic historians to use a broad brush approach to paint a picture of the society of those times, but the personal information that had been gathered was withheld until a whole century had passed. It is this information that has now been made available to the public at large, including the hundreds of thousands of family and local historians whose previous experience of census enumerators' books had been restricted to those available from 1841 to 1891.

The information about names, relationships, ages, occupations and birthplaces that is recorded for every man, woman and child every 10 years in census enumerators' books is one of the richest sources that the family historian comes across. The National Archives has taken the bold step of making all the data from the 1901 returns available on the internet as well as through traditional outlets. The family historian, or the local historian who is interested in particular communities, now has easy and rapid access to a new source. A further benefit of the electronic age is that he or she can make comparisons with the transcripts of the 1881 census enumerators' books that are available on CD-ROM. One of these days we shall be boring our grandchildren with tales of how we used to make long journeys to distant record offices in order to spend all day toiling at a microfilm reader. Such pleasures have not yet been denied us, but we can all applaud the new way of searching the 1901 census returns as a great advance on previous methods.

When we are immersed in gathering all the personal details of our ancestors from sources such as this it is difficult to sense how the members of our family fitted into their local communities or into society at large. This book, which accompanies the release of the 1901 census returns for England and Wales, tells the social history of the late Victorian and Edwardian period by concentrating on the topics that are of prime concern to

family and local historians: family life, housing, work, movement and so
on. It shows how varied were the life experiences of people from different
parts of the country and of different social classes. Their world is not
entirely unfamiliar to us, for much of it is captured in old photographs, and
parts of the everyday environment survive, but it is a world that is becoming increasingly remote and elusive, full of people dressed in quaint
clothes that were so boringly uniform living in monotonous rows of houses
or run-down cottages. The release of the information contained in the
1901 census enumerators' books will be a great stimulus to new research
into identifying our ancestors and discovering their life-styles in the years
leading up to the First World War, that great turning point in British
history.

I would like to thank Anne Kilminster, Sheila Knight, Aidan Lawes,
Jane Crompton, Kathryn Sleight and Deborah Pownall at the National
Archives for their invaluable assistance and encouragement in writing and
producing this book. They have been an excellent team to work with.

CHAPTER ONE

AN UNEQUAL SOCIETY

WHEN QUEEN VICTORIA died on 22 January 1901, her body lay in state for 10 days at Osborne House before it was brought by rail to London and then on to Windsor for the funeral service in the Albert Memorial Chapel. People knelt in the fields as the train passed through the countryside or packed the streets of the capital city to see the funeral procession. The *Salford Reporter* claimed that upon news of her death strong men could scarce restrain their grief, whilst wives and mothers broke down completely. No-one was in any doubt that her death, coming as it did at the end of the century, marked the passing of an era. Two months after her funeral a census of the United Kingdom was taken and three years later a full report on its findings was published. The census enumerators' books for England and Wales that have just been released for public scrutiny after the lapse of a hundred years provide a rich source of information about the state of the two countries at the close of her reign and about her subjects, who as she grew older had come to hold her in high regard.

It had not always been so. *The Times*, commenting on the death of the queen, noted the striking change in public attitudes towards the monarchy that had occurred during the second half of her long reign. Her predecessors, George IV and William IV, had been poorly regarded. When George IV died in 1830, *The Times* wrote, 'There never was an individual less regretted by his fellow-creatures than this deceased King'. When William IV died in 1837, *The Spectator* observed that, 'His late majesty, though at times a jovial and, for a king, an honest man, was a weak, ignorant, commonplace sort of person'. After the death of Prince Albert in 1861, Victoria's withdrawal from public life as 'the Widow of Windsor' made her increasingly unpopular. The turning point came in June 1872, when Disraeli made his famous Crystal Palace speech, in which the Crown was raised as the symbol of Imperial Britain. Four years later Victoria accepted the new title of Empress of India. Her longevity also helped to turn popular opinion. The Golden Jubilee of her reign was celebrated in public throughout the land in 1887, her Diamond Jubilee 10 years later. So impressive were these celebrations that a south Yorkshire miner, known to everyone in later life as Dai Reckless, was actually christened Diamond

Diamond Jubilee Celebration
The inhabitants of the Pennine town of Alston gather in their market place for a formal photograph on the occasion of Queen Victoria's Diamond Jubilee in 1897. One obviously had to wear a hat, bonnet or cap to be properly dressed.

Jubilee Reckless in that year. In the late-Victorian and Edwardian era London was transformed from the squalid, fog-bound city that Dickens had portrayed so well into an imperial capital, as grandiose as Paris or Vienna. Edward VII, who came to the throne in 1901 at the age of 59, enjoyed the pomp and display that was created to enhance the aura of the monarchy. Photographs of royal visits to provincial cities show triumphal arches and mock castle gateways, huge displays of flags and bunting, bands leading the processions and enormous crowds lining the streets, ready to sing 'God Save the King' or 'Rule Britannia'. When the Prince and Princess of Wales came to Bradford to unveil a statue of Queen Victoria three years after her death, over 50,000 people gathered in the city centre to watch the event and to listen to a massed choir of 3,000 school children. Every school had a large map of the world which showed Britain's extensive dominions and colonies painted in red. The British were prominent members of a select band of the richest and most powerful nations on earth. That this was so was a continuing matter of national pride, even amongst the millions of Victoria's subjects who were living in wretched poverty.

Wealth and Poverty

At the beginning of the twentieth century the Prime Minister sat in the House of Lords, though he was the last to do so. The Marquis of Salisbury, leader of the Conservative Party, was approaching the end of his third term of government, from 1895 to 1902. His country seat, Hatfield House, which his ancestor, Sir Robert Cecil, chief minister to Elizabeth I and James I, had built three centuries earlier, was the frequent scene of political gatherings, for the great aristocratic country houses still played a major role in national politics. Although Britain was reputedly one of the world's great democracies, the majority of its population had no say in such matters. Only two-fifths of the adult population, with no women at all, had the right to vote at general elections. The franchise was not given to all men until 1918 and all women until 10 years later. Long after Salisbury was succeeded by his fellow Conservative, Arthur James Balfour, aristocrats remained prominent members of the Cabinet and a powerful force in political life.

A parliamentary enquiry into the ownership of land in 1872–73, published as *Return of Owners of Land* (1875) and analysed by John Bateman in *Great Landowners of Great Britain and Ireland* (1883), had shown how much of the countryside was dominated by great estates at the height of the Victorian era. Thus the Marquis of Bath at Longleat owned 55,000 acres, the Earl of Pembroke at Wilton owned 42,244 acres, or some five per cent of the whole county of Wiltshire, nearly three-quarters of Rutland was owned by just six men, and Nottinghamshire's five largest owners the Dukes of Portland and Newcastle, Earl Manvers, Lord Middleton and A.W. Savile – controlled 27 per cent of the county's acres between them. Bateman's analysis revealed that 400 peers or peeresses owned 5,728,979 acres or 17.4 per cent of the total land in Great Britain and that the top 1,288 commoners owned 8,497,6999 acres or 25.8 per cent. Between them, this tiny elite of 1,688 owners of substantial estates of at least 3,000 acres owned 43 per cent of the entire acreage of the country. In 1872–73 four-fifths of the land of Great Britain was owned by a mere 7,000 proprietors. By far the most extensive estate was the 186,000 acres of the Duke of Northumberland, though the great majority of it consisted of moorland. Next came the Duke of Devonshire with 139,000 acres, the Duke of Cleveland with 104,000 acres and the Duke of Bedford with 86,335 acres. Ten owners had 60,000 or more acres and another 49 had more than 30,000 acres. Most of the greater owners held land in different parts of the country, where each of their scattered estates was centred on a country house. The Duke of Devonshire had nine houses: Chatsworth House and Hardwick Hall (Derbyshire), Holker Hall (Lancashire), Bolton Abbey (Yorkshire), Compton Place (Sussex), Devonshire House and Chiswick House (London), Beaufort House (Newmarket) and Lismore Castle

In 1872–73 four-fifths of the land of Great Britain was owned by a mere 7,000 proprietors.

(Ireland). At the other end of the scale, nearly one-quarter of the land was in the hands of owners who possessed between one and 300 acres. Probably not more than 10 per cent of this was owner-occupied. Of course, the great majority of the population owned no land at all.

Most of the great estates that Bateman classified in the 1870s had been substantial two centuries earlier, though they had not always remained in the hands of the same family. Though few opportunities arose for upward social mobility into the top ranks, the risk of downward mobility was an ever-present threat. In the late nineteenth century landowners were hit by the great agricultural depression, which caused rents and land values to fall considerably. Duties on the death of a landowner, introduced in 1894, added to the burden, so that a number of large estates went on to the market before the First World War. Some aristocrats remained very rich despite these problems, however, especially when they owned urban land or if minerals could be mined under their estates. The Earl of Derby's annual income increased from £163,000 in 1876 to £300,000 in 1900. In Victoria's reign the Grosvenors, Marquesses of Westminster since 1831, Dukes since 1874, were reputed to be the richest family in Europe because of their ownership of Belgravia, Mayfair and Pimlico in London's fashionable West End. The Russells, Dukes of Bedford since 1694, were incredibly wealthy because they owned large parts of Bloomsbury, St Pancras, Covent Garden and St Martin's. A small number of towns were wholly, or mostly, owned by a single landlord, such as the Lowthers at Whitehaven, the Earl of Scarbrough at Skegness, and the Duke of Devonshire at Eastbourne.

Many aristocratic titles were of no great antiquity. Over 300 men had been raised to the peerage between 1830 and 1895. The Earl of Wharncliffe, for example, was descended from a medieval Yorkshire gentry family, the Wortleys, through an illegitimate daughter and subsequently through other heiresses. Eighteenth- and nineteenth-century owners of the Wortley estates were known as Wortley-Montagu and as Stuart-Wortley. In 1826 James Archibald Stuart-Wortley was made the first Baron Wharncliffe; 50 years later, his successor was made the first Earl of Wharncliffe. The apparent antiquity of the titles of Victorian peers could be deceptive. One of the richest men, Lord Armstrong of Cragside, had made his fortune in armaments on Tyneside. By the end of Victoria's reign the wealth of the old aristocratic landowners was matched by that of newly-rich men with financial and industrial interests who did not invest in land. Together, these very rich families – new and old – formed a formidably wealthy group. On the eve of the First World War the top 1 per cent of British society owned 69 per cent of the nation's capital, a higher concentration than at any other time in modern British history.

In many parts of rural England the dominance of aristocratic and gentry families was immediately apparent not only in the great country

Edensor
The estate village that was built in the 1840s on the opposite bank of the River Derwent to Chatsworth House. The houses, which were built in a variety of styles taken from pattern books, provided superior accommodation for the estate workers.

houses but in estate cottages, schools, almshouses, hospitals and other public buildings, and in the restored or rebuilt parish churches. No estate village is more redolent of the Victorian era than Edensor, which the sixth Duke of Devonshire had rebuilt in his great park at Chatsworth, after completing the grandiose extensions to his house and before turning his attention to his architectural gardens on the hillside reaching up to the moors. Edensor (pronounced Ensor) was originally a separate manor on the opposite bank of the River Derwent to Chatsworth, but it became the principal estate village for the great house. The small part of the village that could be seen from Chatsworth had been removed when 'Capability' Brown landscaped the park in the 1760s for the fourth Duke of Devonshire. The rest was entirely remodelled around 1839–40 to designs by John Robertson of Derby, under the supervision of Joseph Paxton, for the sixth duke. The designs of the houses were based on illustrations in contemporary pattern books and ranged from Norman to Tudor and Jacobean. The medieval church was rebuilt in Early English Gothic style by Sir George Gilbert Scott between 1868 and 1870 with a spire that would not have been out of place in a populous town. The houses were constructed using the highest-quality local stone and they provided spacious accommodation that was a world apart from the thatched, mud-walled hovels which were the homes of the rural poor in some other parts of England. The various census returns confirm that these excellent houses were built for workers on the Chatsworth estate, such as farm labourers, gardeners, joiners and the house porter, as well as for the land agent and the clerk of works. Many of the women worked as servants, housemaids and cooks.

Few estate tenants were housed as commodiously as the parishioners of Edensor. In 1903 the Bedfordshire village of Ridgmont, which stands two or three miles north-east of Woburn Abbey, the seat of the Duke of

Bedford, was soon to be rebuilt. The Bedford estate owned much but not all of the land and managed it efficiently, yet in that year a social investigator, H. P. Mann, found that 34 per cent of the villagers were so poor that they were unable to get enough to eat and another 7 per cent fell below the poverty line when times were hard. Half of the poor were children under the age of 16. The major reasons for this debilitating poverty were large families and the death, desertion, ill-health or old age of the wage-earner, but Mann showed that not all the blame could be heaped on the poor themselves. He proved that half the families that had sunk below the poverty line were the victims of irregular work and low wages. Allotments and pig-fattening helped, but they were no substitute for poor rates of pay. Whereas the annual income of the Duke of Bedford was about £100,000, his farm labourers earned just £50 a year.

At the time of the 1881 census Ridgmont was a large village, with its main streets, a lower end, and a few thatched cottages arranged around yards. The land was a mixture of sand and clay, half of it devoted to wheat, barley and beans and half laid down as permanent grass. The new church of All Saints had been built in 1855 in the decorated Gothic style, with a tower and spire, to serve a small parish of 2,308 acres. A large Baptist chapel and a handsome Wesleyan one provided alternate venues for worship. The Nonconformist British school rivalled the National school of the Anglicans, and in the middle of the village The Bedford Agricultural Institute (founded by the county council in 1896) provided educational courses for both men and women. Several families lived in cottages that the Bedford estate had built in the 1860s. Outwardly, all seemed well.

The birthplaces of the 149 male heads of households who were recorded in the 1881 census show that 87, or 58 per cent, had been born in Ridgmont, another 11 nearby in Lidlington, 6 in neighbouring Husborne Crawley, and 27 in 17 other places in Bedfordshire, all within a few miles of Ridgmont. Altogether, 131 men, or 88 per cent of the householders, had been born in Bedfordshire. The rest included five men from Buckinghamshire and two from Northamptonshire. The 10 who had come from further afield comprised the vicar (from Scotland), the Baptist minister (from Shropshire), the farmer of Manor Farm, a retired farmer, a retired butcher, two grocers, a railway signalman, a groom and a gamekeeper, but not the 67 agricultural labourers who formed 45 per cent of the male householders or the 9 general labourers and 3 shepherds. One of the labourers was a 77-year-old widower, born at Husborne Crawley, who was listed as 'Ag. Lab. Local Preacher Wesleyan'. The other householders included a long list of local tradesmen, including the hosts of the *Red Lion*, the *White Hart*, and the *Rose and Crown*. Anyone who has tried to analyse occupations from census enumerators' books will have come across the difficulty of placing certain individuals in an appropriate category, but what are we to make of Charles Gosling, born in Ridgmont in 1830, who

*W*hereas the annual income of the Duke of Bedford was about £100,000, his farm labourers earned just £50 a year.

informed the enumerator that he was a draper, grocer, baker, and assistant dressmaker, with seven acres of land? The labourers and tradesmen made a poor contrast to the farmers, one of whom had 600 acres at Park Farm (employing 18 men and 7 boys), another had 365 acres at Manor Farm (15 men and 5 boys), a third had 413 acres (14 men and 7 boys), and a fourth had 375 acres (11 men and 5 boys). The others comprised a farmer and dealer with 51 acres, the vicar with 13 acres, a retired farmer, the farm manager at Manor Farm (294 acres; with 14 men and 8 boys), a farm foreman, and a foreman of fences and drains on the Bedford Estate.

The occupations of 92 Ridgmont men and boys who were not heads of households included 61 agricultural labourers, 6 general labourers, 2 farm servants, 2 grooms, a shepherd, a milkman, etc. The total male workforce amounted to 241, of whom 128, or 53 per cent, were agricultural labourers. In 1881 vital contributions to family incomes were also still coming from the earnings of women and girls. The large number of 172 female occupations that were recorded in Ridgmont included 98 lacemakers (or 57 per cent) and 23 straw plaiters, straw hat or bonnet makers, etc. (or 13 per cent). No doubt many of the 'scholars' who were enumerated also made some contribution through these old Bedfordshire hand crafts. The other women and girls comprised 12 dressmakers, 2 needlewomen, a seamstress, 8 domestic or general servants, 6 housekeepers, 3 cooks, a housemaid, a nursemaid, 3 laundresses, 2 washerwomen, 2 charwomen, the caretaker of the reading room, a monthly nurse, the post mistress, 2 schoolmistresses, the governess at the vicarage, a scholar monitor at the school, a tradesman's widow, a woman who held a life interest in property, and 2 sisters who lived off the interest of money. In general, the opportunities for females were as limited as those on offer for the men, but they were nevertheless able to make a vital contribution to family incomes. Ridgmont was a working-class village, whose population was overwhelmingly local in origin, and whose standard of living was largely dependent on farm work and hand crafts.

Twenty years later, Ridgmont families were suffering from the poverty that Mann was soon to uncover in his survey. The villagers were as deeply rooted in the local countryside as before: 74 of the male heads of household had been born in Ridgmont, another 41 had been born elsewhere in Bedfordshire (mostly in the neighbouring villages) and 17 came from beyond the county boundary; 62 of the wives and widows had been born and bred in Ridgmont, 53 in other parts of Bedfordshire and 19 in more distant places. But the village's population had declined steadily from the 999 recorded in 1851 to 746 in 1881 and 591 in 1901, and the neighbouring communities of Eversholt and Husborne Crawley declined in similar proportions during the same period. The debilitating effects of the agricultural depression were forcing families to leave. The 1901 census returns named a greatly reduced workforce of 33 farm labourers, 13 general

A Street Group
Boys dressed in shabby clothes and caps pose by a fountain for an illustration entitled 'Slum life in our great cities'.

labourers and 22 other estate workers (horse keepers, stockmen, shepherds, etc) among the heads of household, and 23 farm labourers, 8 other labourers and 10 estate workers among the sons and boarders. The irregular work and low wages that these men obtained was only part of the story of Ridgmont's decline, however, for now the women and girls had little opportunity to add their earnings to the family budget. The 98 lacemakers of 1881 had dwindled to 22 (and only seven of these were under the age of 40), while the 23 straw bonnet makers had no work at all. The farming depression, the severe decline of lacemaking, the total disappearance of straw plaiting and the limited opportunities for domestic service or other employment forced families to leave for the towns or else face unrelenting poverty. A few years after Mann's survey, the Bedford estate responded belatedly to this crisis, so that visitors to the village now see some substantial brick estate cottages, inscribed with a B and the dates 1910 and 1911 in their gables, where once the labourers had been inadequately housed and paid.

Social investigators found the same debilitating poverty in some of England's major cities. Charles Booth, sensing that official statistics on poverty in London were substantially defective, conducted his own investigations, using techniques that provided accurate measures. In *Life and Labour of the People of London* (1892–97) he demonstrated that 30.7 per cent of the inhabitants were living in poverty and that, of these, only 0.9 per cent were responsible for their plight. The main causes of poverty were low wages and irregular employment. Booth advocated state aid for the honest poor, particularly in the form of old age pensions.

The East End of London was, of course, notorious for its poverty, so Booth's sombre findings could perhaps be regarded as untypical of the nation as a whole. But in 1901 the young Seebohm Rowntree, second son of Joseph, the Liberal, Quaker chocolate-manufacturer, published *Poverty: A Study of Town Life*, a thorough house-to-house survey which revealed that poverty was nearly as widespread in the ancient cathedral city of York as it was in the capital. In the autumn of 1899 he and his investigators had visited 11,560 families living in 388 of the city's streets, sampling 46,754 of York's 75,812 inhabitants. Rowntree concluded that 27.84 per cent of York families lived in poverty, a figure that was only a little lower than the 30.7 per cent in London. Though no social scientist would now try to measure poverty to two decimal points, the magnitude of the problem was made clear. In many ways, York was a typical English town, with heavy industry (railways) as well as light industry (confectionery). Booth's findings could no longer be dismissed as exceptional. Rowntree had visited the London slums and thought they were larger in extent but otherwise no worse than York's.

Rowntree separated poverty into two categories. He described families as enduring primary poverty when the four basic requirements of food, fuel, shelter and clothing were not met from income, no matter how carefully family budgets were managed. Secondary poverty occurred when families had the necessary income to cover the basic necessities, but did not have the money to meet irregular but essential expenditure, such as on medicine. Rowntree concluded that 15.46 per cent of wage earners, or 9.91 per cent of York's population, were living in primary poverty and 17.93 per cent in secondary poverty. Nearly 28 per cent of York's population were living below the nutritional standard which he calculated was necessary to maintain physical health. More than half of all the children of working men were poorly fed. As Peter Laslett has written in *The World We Have Lost*,

> These were the scrawny, dirty, hungry, ragged, verminous boys and girls who were to grow up into the working class of twentieth-century England. This was the generation that was to man the armies of the First World War, although they were inches shorter and pounds lighter than they would have been if they had been properly fed and cared for.

Rowntree's most important finding was that poverty was cyclical, arriving at three points in life: during childhood; when a newly-married couple had to raise young children; and when people were old and sick. At other times, on a typical worker's wage, provided that the number of children was not above the national average of four, and if almost nothing was spent on drink and other pleasures, it was just possible to feed the whole family adequately. But many working-class families spent up to six shillings a week – a sixth of their income – on buying as many as 36 pints of beer and so a large number of families fell into secondary poverty. Rowntree was nevertheless certain that the most important cause of poverty was low wages: 'The wages paid for unskilled labour in York are insufficient to provide food, clothing and shelter adequate to maintain a family of moderate size in a state of bare physical efficiency.' And the well-being of a household depended on the father keeping in work. Rowntree's considered judgement was that 'in this land of abounding wealth, during a time of perhaps unexampled prosperity', the fact that probably more than one-fifth of the population were living in poverty should cause 'great searchings of heart'.

In his survey, special attention was paid to the Walmgate district, in the north-eastern part of the city of York, which had once been 'peopled by a very different class' but was now the most notorious slum. Irish immigrants had swollen the tightly-packed population. Here, Rowntree observed the chief characteristics of slum life:

Nearly 28 per cent of York's population were living below the nutritional standard which he [Rowntree] calculated was necessary to maintain physical health.

THE NEW YEAR'S GIFT.

A *Punch* cartoon of 6 January 1909 celebrates the introduction of Old Age Pensions.

the reckless expenditure of money as soon as obtained, with aggravated want at other times; the rowdy Saturday night, the Monday morning pilgrimage to the pawn shop, and especially that love for the district, and disinclination to move to better surroundings, which, combined with the indifference to the higher aims of life, are the despair of so many social workers.

On a 500-yard stretch between Walmgate Bar and Fossgate Rowntree counted 20 pubs, 4 off-licence shops and a club.

People in all parts of the land had a deep fear of the poverty that awaited them in old age. The one thing they all tried to save for was the cost of their funeral. Even now, a hundred years later, some older people dislike having to go into hospital – even where the buildings are new – because so many of them are on the sites of former workhouses. Booth's and Rowntree's surveys and the example of the laws of insurance against old age and infirmity that Germany had introduced in 1889 greatly influenced the Liberal government which was elected with a massive majority in 1906. Their most enduring measure was the introduction of old age pensions on 1 January 1909, at the rate of five shillings a week to persons over 70 years of age. Only those old people who had an income of less than £31.10s. a year, who had no criminal convictions, and who had never received support from the Poor Law were eligible. The destitute still went to the workhouse. Nevertheless, almost half a million people qualified. In *Lark Rise to Candleford* Flora Thompson remembered the wondering reaction of old people:

> When the Old Age Pensions began, life was transformed for such aged cottagers. They were relieved of anxiety. They were suddenly rich. Independent for life! At first when they went to the Post Office to draw it, tears of gratitude would run down the cheeks of some, and they would say as they picked up their money, 'God bless that Lord George (for they could not believe that one so powerful and munificent could be a plain 'Mr.') and God bless *you*, miss!' and there were flowers from their gardens and apples from their trees for the girl who merely handed them the money.

The pensionable age was not lowered to 65 until 1925. Another welcome reform of equal importance was the National Insurance Act – Health and Unemployment (1911), which introduced sickness and unemployment benefits paid for by contributions from both employers and employees.

The shocking extent of poverty in the richest country in the world should not lead us into the mistaken assumption that all working-class people lived at this dismal level. By 1901 most working-class families were not desperately poor. Neither the tradesmen and artisans nor the semi-skilled workers with regular jobs had any feelings of brotherhood with the unskilled and casual workers. 'He's only a tap-room man' was a common saying, for even some of the pubs were segregated. He in his turn looked down on the street sellers of coal, lamp oil, tripe, crumpets and muffins, and fruit and vegetables. The lowest of the low were the sellers of fire-wood, rag-and-bone families, bookies' runners, idlers, part-time beggars and petty thieves. Well over half of the working classes were above the poverty line at any one time and many were reasonably well-off. They ate well and since the mid nineteenth century standards of personal cleanliness had improved considerably. Studio photographs show them dressed in their best clothes, the men with hats, waistcoats and watch-chains and the women in elaborate long dresses, but other old photographs of street scenes and local events which caught people in their everyday attire reveal that most were clothed adequately, if rather drably and uniformly. The working classes were immediately distinguished by their clothes. Their children often wore hand-me-downs but the majority did not go barefoot and clothed in rags like the young ragamuffins who were photographed in urban courts and yards or outside rural hovels. Most working-class people could afford a set of new clothes and shoes when the occasion demanded them, even if their weekday clothes were made to last and were often patched and shiny and sometimes second-hand. New clothes for Whitsun-tide were the ambition of every respectable working-class family that took part in the annual Sunday school processions, particularly in the north of England. Mass-produced clothes and footwear sold through multiple chain stores such as Hepworth's and Freeman Hardy Willis, which opened in the 1870s and 1880s, found a ready working-class market, concerned not just with price but with fashion.

Most of us have working-class ancestors, for that section of society formed about 75–80 per cent of the population of England and Wales in 1901. They were the ones who were separated from the rest of society by earning their living with dirty hands and faces. The middle classes formed a much smaller proportion of the population than now, however widely we define them. In 1909 about 280,000 householders in England and Wales had an income of £700 a year or more. Another 800,000 householders who paid tax on incomes at a lower level also thought of themselves as middle class, though their standard of living was far below that of the occupants of the wealthier suburbs, who had made their money in commerce and industry or the leading professions. The middle classes were not at all a well-defined group. They ranged from the wealthy families in the more salubrious suburbs and the 'principal inhabitants' who were listed in Victorian directories at the beginning of each village entry to minor professional people and the better-off shopkeepers and small businessmen. The great changes in British society that came with the growth of managerial and

professional positions and the decline of manual labour lay a long way
ahead.

The census office found the middle classes difficult to classify and so
could not count them accurately. One method that was introduced in the
1904 report was a 'standard of comfort' indicator based on the number of
female servants. The report showed that between 1891 and 1901 the
number of barristers and solicitors, most of whom lived and worked in
London, rose 5.1 per cent to 20,998; physicians, surgeons and general
practitioners increased by 19.2 per cent to 22,698; dentists and their assistants now numbered 5,309 and veterinary surgeons 2,941 (a lower figure
than usual because many had joined the war in South Africa). The more
successful painters and musicians were able to afford a middle-class life-
style and 16,379 men and women pursued literary and scientific careers.
Another 530,685 men and 59,914 women were employed in commerce, a
considerable increase since 1891, but many in this category were not
middle class. The 1904 report commented in particular on the remarkable
development of banks and building societies with branches in surrounding
villages.

Aspirants to lower middle-class status included managers, commercial
travellers and head clerks. The number of clerks in business and government, especially local government, quadrupled between 1861 and 1891,
from 91,000 to 370,000, but did not include many women. Literacy, accuracy, neatness and, above all, respectability were essential requirements,
yet most clerks earned scarcely as much as many skilled workers. London
suburbs such as Holloway or Hammersmith were much favoured by the
better-off clerks who desired a respectable life-style in a modest, semi-
detached villa. This was the world of *The Diary of a Nobody* (1892),
George and Weedon Grossmith's gentle satire of the tastes and preten-
sions of Charles Pooter, a City clerk, who lived at The Laurels, Brickfield
Terrace, Holloway – 'a nice six-roomed residence, not counting basement,
with a front breakfast parlour' – who thought it a great compliment to be
asked to take the plate round at church services and whose heart 'beat like
that of a schoolboy's' when he received an invitation to a trade reception
and ball at the Mansion House.

The middle classes followed the fashions of the wealthiest sections of
society, though in a more restrained way, for the conspicuous consumption
of the rich set them apart from the rest. Male servants, especially footmen,
were a particular status symbol in the West End. Wealthy ladies paid exor-
bitant prices for their elaborate long dresses, decorated with lace trimmings, and for their furs and enormous feathered hats, but the men had
become more restrained in the way they dressed, having abandoned morning coats and top hats in favour of suits and bowlers except for the most
formal occasions. The old aristocratic 'season' was still maintained in
London, though Siegfried Sassoon found it consisted of 'Ascot, Lord's, a

few dances and theatres, dull dinner-parties, one or two visits to the Opera – that was about all'. The top residential areas of the West End – Belgravia, Mayfair, the better parts of South Kensington, and around Bayswater – retained a decidedly upper-class character. During the second half of the nineteenth century the large town houses facing Hyde Park in Bayswater were the homes of many men with lucrative positions at the Colonial Office. West and east London were worlds apart.

Urban and Rural Settlements

By 1901 the population of England and Wales had reached 32,527,843, an increase of 3,525,318 or 12.17 per cent since the last census in 1891. During the one hundred years that had passed since the first census the population of England and Wales had nearly quadrupled, from 8,892,536 in 1801. This staggering increase during the nineteenth century would have been even greater had not hundreds of thousands of families emigrated overseas, to the United States of America, Canada, Australia, New Zealand, South Africa and other far-flung parts of the world.

By 1901 nearly 40 British towns had more than 100,000 people, and between them they accounted for well over a third of the population of England and Wales.

Victoria's reign had been marked also by industrial growth, imperial expansion, and a huge shift of the population from the countryside to the towns. By 1901 Britain was the most urbanised nation in the world. Less than one-quarter of the population of England and Wales lived in rural districts and only seven per cent of the workforce were employed in agriculture. The great ports and the manufacturing and mining districts now dominated the national economy. The 1851 census had been the first to report that more English and Welsh people lived in towns than in the countryside, though the urban category included many small towns with little more than 2,000 inhabitants. At that time, few towns were large by later standards. The dramatic growth of the urban population came in the second half of the nineteenth century. By 1901 nearly 40 British towns had more than 100,000 people, and between them they accounted for well over a third of the population of England and Wales. The huge numbers of extra people were mostly housed in these rapidly-growing towns. In 1831 just over 1 million inhabitants of Great Britain (or less than one-tenth of the total population) had lived in large towns outside London. By 1901 that number had grown to nearly 9 million, or about a quarter of the British people. During the same period, London increased its share of the total population of the nation from 11.5 per cent to 17.8 per cent. The capital had always overshadowed other towns, but now it was gobbling up its neighbours at an unprecedented rate and outpacing the provincial cities.

Victorian London sprawled miles beyond the old limits of the medieval walled city and its early suburbs. London had expanded from the 8.5 square miles depicted on Rocque's 1746 map to more than 120 square miles in 1901. By the end of the nineteenth century the population of the

administrative county of London had reached a total figure of over 4 mil
lion people. Greater London, a collective term for those new suburbs that
lay beyond the old county boundary, grew from 414,000 inhabitants in
1861 to 2,045,000 at the turn of the century. London had reached a size
and complexity that was unparalleled at that time. It had become characterised by miles upon miles of Victorian terraced and semi-detached housing in suburbs that extended in all directions and which were often
markedly different from their neighbours. The centre reflected London's
role as an imperial capital, but it was never dominated by royalty or the
aristocracy. Rather, the capital city was essentially a commercial centre,
where great fortunes could be made a mile or two from the most appalling
slums.

By 1901 12 English provincial towns or cities had populations of over
200,000: Liverpool, Manchester, Birmingham, Leeds, Sheffield, Bristol,
Bradford, Kingston-upon-Hull, Nottingham, Salford, Newcastle-upon-
Tyne and Leicester. The aggregate rise of the population in the top
75 towns between 1891 and 1901 was 14 per cent, compared with the
12.2 per cent growth of the entire population of England and Wales. The
highest rates of growth occurred in the metropolitan suburbs of East
Ham (where the population nearly trebled in 10 years), Walthamstow,
Willesden, Hornsey, Leyton, Tottenham, West Ham and Croydon. The
Birmingham suburbs of Kings Norton, Northfield, Handsworth and
Smethwick also grew spectacularly in the last decade of the nineteenth
century, as did the dockside towns of Wallasey and West Hartlepool.

Population figures, however, do not always provide a clear picture of
what was actually happening in a district. The 1904 report on the previous
census noted that the falling off in the rate of increase, or even an actual
decline, in the population of a great town was not necessarily an indication
of a corresponding decline in its prosperity. For example, space might have
been required for business premises to such an extent that dwelling
houses were acquired for the purpose, and consequently the inhabitants
had to seek residences in suburbs outside the administrative boundaries of
the town. That had certainly happened in central London, parts of which
experienced population decline while the surrounding suburbs mushroomed. In the 'outer ring' the population increased by 45.5 per cent
between 1891 and 1901, having already risen by 50.7, 50.0 and 50.1 per
cent in the three previous decades. The overflow of the metropolitan population now extended even beyond 'Greater London', which had grown by
nearly 1 million since 1891.

The great industrial centres of the north and the midlands grew spectacularly during the second half of the nineteenth century. The population
of Bradford, for example, rose from about 13,000 in 1801 to 104,000 in
1851 and to 211,000 in 1901. The migrants who flocked to the Victorian
towns came mostly from the traditional catchment areas up to 30 miles

away, but poor farm labourers from the south of England headed north in droves in search of higher wages and better housing. The Industrial Revolution reversed the traditional drift from north to south, an ancient pattern which was re-established during the twentieth century. By the end of Victoria's reign Liverpool was challenging London as England's chief port. Much of the country's wealth was created in specialised industrial districts: Lancashire cotton, West Riding wool and worsteds, Sheffield steel, Birmingham metalware, Tyneside shipbuilding, East Midlands hosiery, South Wales coal and iron. Although most of the great Victorian towns had already had a long history as market and industrial centres, during the late nineteenth century they acquired a completely new character and a national importance. City status was granted to Manchester (1853), Liverpool (1880), Newcastle (1882), Birmingham (1889), Leeds and Sheffield (1893), and Bradford, Hull and Nottingham (1897). By the end of the century the great shift of the national population was almost complete. After the First World War, population growth slowed dramatically and cities stopped growing at such an intense rate.

Our image of Victorian England and Wales is first and foremost one of burgeoning industrial towns in an era of rapid change. The image is certainly correct, yet we must be careful not to overlook the traditional elements that survived, not just in the countryside but in the towns themselves. London remained a horse-drawn society. Most of the industrial towns of the north and the midlands were ancient market centres whose central streets retained their medieval shapes and names. Far from disappearing, this market role expanded to feed and clothe the growing population. Birmingham, for example, developed one of the largest retail markets in Victorian England, with space for 600 stalls every day of the week. All the largest towns rebuilt their market halls and corn exchanges to cater for the increased demand. Meanwhile, small market towns remained profoundly characteristic of the Victorian age. Many grew at a modest pace, still fulfilling their traditional functions, while others practically stood still and some, such as Petworth (Sussex), declined in size and lost their market. Towns such as Beverley, which served a large hinterland, had corn mills, tanneries, breweries, malthouses, brickmaking and agricultural engineering industries, inns and a variety of professional services on offer, as well as numerous skilled craftsmen such as tailors, dressmakers, glovers, shoemakers, saddlers, blacksmiths, wheelwrights and ironmongers, but by the 1880s or 1890s the great annual livestock fairs were a thing of the past. When Joseph Morris wrote his *Little Guide to the North Riding of Yorkshire* in 1911 he found Bedale 'a very small, very sleepy old market town', Easingwold 'a quiet old town, with a number of respectable houses', Hawes 'a rough little mountain town, with houses that confront one another at every sort of angle', and Northallerton 'a dull old town, consisting chiefly of one long, broad street, with cobbled pavements, and a

number of old-fashioned houses'. Most country towns were of no more than local importance, but on market day, when stalls were set up and sheep and cattle were sold in the central streets, they gave a sense of bustle and pleasure, as well as business, to the people who had come in from the surrounding farms and villages.

In the countryside, even up to the edges of the industrial towns, an older way of life was preserved. The carrier's cart was still the chief means of riding to market for those who had no horse. It has been estimated that in 1900 Britain had 3.5 million horses, of which 2 million were directly employed in agriculture. In East Anglia and many other parts of England the men in charge of the horses were the most respected workers on a farm. Agricultural labourers, clad in their corduroys and leather gaiters, still worked with hand tools, as indeed did numerous craftsmen both in the towns and the countryside. The 'industrial' category in the various census reports included blacksmiths, wheelwrights, cabinet makers, and other traditional craftsmen who worked in workshops rather than factories. George Sturt (alias Bourne) conveyed the skill and pride of such craftsmen in *The Wheelwright's Shop* (1923), and in his earlier publications, such as *The Bettesworth Book* (1901), he gave a sympathetic portrait of the farm labourer as a skilled worker far removed from the caricature of Hodge, the dull, sluggish oaf. Many parts of England and Wales had no industries beyond the traditional ones that provided tools and machinery for farmers and serviced the produce of their farms, and even the counties that had seen the most rapid industrial changes still contained rural enclaves that seemed undisturbed by the frenzied activities of their neighbours. Country villagers within a few miles of the busiest towns continued to follow their old, slower rhythms. The third edition of the Ordnance Survey maps, based on surveys made during the 1880s, shows that even the largest provincial cities, such as Birmingham or Sheffield, were still enclosed within ancient landscapes of small settlements dispersed among fields and woods. The suburbs had not yet spread far into the countryside.

A concern to preserve the physical surroundings of deferential societies was particularly marked where the squires of landed estates deliberately rebuilt their estate villages in traditional vernacular styles. The number of inhabitants in these villages was kept low to exclude the poor, and fell further as people left to seek more lucrative work in the towns. Almost all the farming villages of England and Wales reached their highest level of population sometime between 1831 and 1871, before declining to much lower levels by the end of the century. They were totally different in character from the populous industrial villages that owed no allegiance to a squire, that were built in idiosyncratic styles of whatever materials that came to hand, which were often untidy and formless, where chapels attracted larger congregations than the parish church, and where the pubs were the noisy centres of social life.

On the narrow band of magnesian limestone that separates the old and the concealed coalfields of south Yorkshire stand a group of estate villages that still seem a world apart from the surrounding towns and pit villages. How much stronger was the contrast before the roads were given a firm surface and journeys were reduced from hours to minutes. A sign on a village green once read: 'The Earl of Halifax invites you to rest awhile and enjoy Hickleton.' In the 1840s his ancestor, Sir Francis Wood, had rebuilt the village in the vernacular style of the Elizabethan and Stuart age, using local stone and pantile roofs. Hickleton has no pub and no chapel. The parish church was extensively restored in the 1870s and 1880s by the second Viscount Halifax, the lay leader of the Anglo-Catholic Unity Movement. Such was the viscount's influence on the neighbouring gentry that all the surrounding parish churches became (and remain) High Church, though none matched Hickleton in the number and quality of its statues, religious paintings, Bodley screen, choir stalls and gilded reredos. Hickleton Hall stands aloof, almost remote from the village, in spacious grounds enclosed by a forbidding wall. It now houses a Sue Ryder home for disabled people.

On census night in 1901 Charles, Viscount Halifax was at home with his family, his chaplain, butler, valet, under butler, footman, page boy and 16 domestic servants, many of whom had been born far from Hickleton. His steward came from Gloucestershire, his farm bailiff from Doncaster, his head gardener from north Yorkshire, his gamekeeper from Manchester and his coachmen from Gloucestershire and London. The vicar had been born in Whitehaven; only the estate valuer had been born and bred in the village. Clearly the squire could call on staff from far and wide. The estate workers and their wives who rented the cottages in the village street were

Almost all the farming villages of England and Wales reached their highest level of population sometime between 1831 and 1871, before declining to much lower levels by the end of the century.

mostly from Yorkshire, but altogether only 5 of the 27 heads of household had been born in Hickleton and only 4 others came from adjoining parishes. Two miles up the road, the estate village of Hooton Pagnell had a more characteristic pattern; half of the 42 male heads of household had been born within 4 miles of the village and only 9 had come from beyond Yorkshire (including the vicar from Devon and the doctor from Aberdeen).

The nearby villages, particularly Hooton Pagnell, Sprotborough, Cusworth and Brodsworth, had also been rebuilt in traditional styles by their squires during the reign of Victoria. The vicar of Sprotborough praised the comfort of the new cottages and thought that 'the poor now enjoy houses not to be excelled by the poor of any parish around'. There is no doubt that the farmworkers and craftsmen who were tenants of estate cottages such as these lived in superior accommodation to those who lived beyond the reach of a squire. Yet some labourers preferred inferior housing, job insecurity and a long walk to work to the deferential life-style of the estate village, where a man had to doff his cap and his children were taught to curtsy whenever a member of 'the family' passed by.

A few miles to the north of Hickleton stands Brodsworth Hall, a remarkable house of the 1860s in the Italian style, now restored by English Heritage. A small village stretches along the valley below the hall and the medieval parish church of St Michael. Brodsworth had belonged to the Archbishop of York and the Earl of Kinnoul before it was purchased by Peter Thellusson, an immensely wealthy City of London merchant and speculator of French-Swiss extraction. Charles Sabine Augustus Thellusson, born in Florence in 1822, was the heir to his great-grandfather's fortune. In 1861–62 he built an Italianate house designed by Casentini of Lucca, which used the most up-to-date technology and was surrounded by formal gardens. Charles died in 1885 and was succeeded by the last of his four sons, a man who combined the role of squire of Brodsworth with the more glamorous world of international yachting. He lived in a cosmopolitan world that was beyond the imagination of his tenants.

The squires of these estate villages were far from being remote country gentry with limited horizons. William Aldam of Frickley Hall (1814–90), for instance, was a successful businessman who invested in canals and railways. So when it became profitable to sink deep mines under the magnesian limestone in the early years of the twentieth century the squires were more than willing to benefit from the royalties that they could earn. But the names of the new collieries – Frickley, Brodsworth Main and Hickleton Main – were deceptive because the squires took care to preserve their own environment and to insist that the mines were sunk beyond their parish boundaries and that new pit villages should be built out of sight from their halls. The Frickley miners were housed in South Kirkby and South Elmsall, the Hickleton men in Thurnscoe and

Brodsworth Hall
The Italianate Victorian house of the Thellusson family, now owned by English Heritage. The miners of Brodsworth Main Colliery were housed in a model village at Woodlands, out of sight of the hall.

Goldthorpe, while the estate villages continued in their old, sedate manner. In 1905–8 Brodsworth Main pit was sunk to the famous Barnsley seam, but no coal miners settled in Brodsworth. The colliery owners built a new model village, further east in the next parish, to the designs of Percy Houfton, a Chesterfield architect who had recently completed another model village for the colliers of Creswell (Derbyshire). In 1907 the new village was built immediately north of the grounds of 'Woodlands' house, between the Roman road from Doncaster and its successor, the Great North Road. The plan of the estate and the original miners' houses are well preserved. Woodlands was perhaps the most ambitious mining village ever built in Britain. It had a very low density of six houses per acre. The houses were set amid large greens, none had fewer than three bedrooms, and all had baths and hot water. Two Methodist meeting houses were built straight away and the church of All Saints was opened in 1913. Facilities for various clubs and societies were provided from the start, with a full-time social worker employed to run them. This successful scheme was followed in 1920 by a development known as Woodlands East and in the late 1920s by another estate to the north, neither of which were as spacious as the original village. Woodlands became a prototype for the council estates that were built after the First World War, a planned community that was completely different from the terraced houses of the normal pit village at that time.

Far more typical was the village built by the owners of the colliery at Denaby Main, a few miles further south, where houses were built to a density of 46 per acre. Sunk in 1864, well away from other settlements, the colliery was in commercial production with about 250 colliers by 1868; it experienced its first major industrial dispute between March and September

1869. The company's village was extended in 1893 when Cadeby Main colliery was opened on the other side of the River Don. By 1901 the village of Denaby Main was virtually complete, with houses for the families of about 2,500 employees at the two collieries. It was laid out to a simple plan in two blocks close to the mines, spoil heaps, railway line and sidings. Between the two residential areas stood the schools, the Anglican and Roman Catholic churches, shops, an hotel, a cricket pitch and a football ground. On three sides of the village lay extensive allotment gardens. These were the only green areas; trees and shrubs were noticeably absent. The villas of the managerial staff were the only distinctive houses. Every street was a straight, parallel row of red brick, two-up, two-down houses with no baths and with communal yards containing stand pipes and brick-built, outside earth lavatories at the back. Some minor improvements were made in a second phase of building, when almost all the houses that were erected between 1890 and 1905 were given a horizontal, decorative brick band in their walls and a triangular tile decoration along the roof ridge. By the early 1900s the houses were lit by gas instead of by candles and paraffin lamps. The original miners came from far afield – especially from Derbyshire, Nottinghamshire, Staffordshire, Ireland and Durham – but they soon formed themselves into an organised body. The owners were determined, risk-taking entrepreneurs with experience in west Yorkshire, men of very different outlook from the paternalist owners of Brodsworth Main colliery. The two sides came into regular, bitter conflict, which erupted into major strikes and the eviction of strikers from the company's houses. Over 200 miners lost their lives in explosions in the two pits.

So new, sprawling colliery towns existed alongside pretty estate villages and industrial districts spread deep into the countryside. In an age before the motor car and the radio English and Welsh people still lived in intensely local worlds, whose general character and living standards varied considerably one from another. Everywhere, people felt that they belonged to a local society that was distinguished from its neighbours by its environment, the nature of the work, its buildings, its religious allegiances, its leisure patterns, its speech and its kinship networks. This strength of feeling was not diminished by the great industrial and demographic changes that had transformed the nation during Victoria's reign, but was actually strengthened by it. The nineteenth century was the period when people became proud of being Yorkshiremen, Lancashiremen, Brummies or Geordies.

In Wales, the contrast between the old and the new can be focused on the decline of the Welsh language. In 1901 half the population of Wales and Monmouthshire over the age of three (or 928,222 people) spoke only English, another 648,919 spoke both English and Welsh, and 280,905 people spoke only Welsh. Welsh speakers formed a mere 13 per cent of the inhabitants of Monmouthshire, but the proportion rose to 50 per cent in south Wales and to 71.5 per cent in north Wales (where 30 per cent spoke Welsh only). The figures for south Wales were, of course, affected by the two populous towns of Cardiff and Swansea, which had attracted large numbers of migrants from England and elsewhere. The counties that lay furthest from the English border and which were essentially rural in character were the places where Welsh was (and is) most likely to be heard. In Merionethshire 93.7 per cent of the inhabitants spoke Welsh, in Cardiganshire 93 per cent, in Anglesey 91.7, in Carmarthenshire 90.3 per cent, and in Caernarvonshire 89.5. More than half the population of Merionethshire and Cardiganshire spoke Welsh only, and in Anglesey and Caernarvonshire the proportions were a little under half. The effects of compulsory schooling could already be seen in the spread of the use of English among the young. Although the number of Welsh speakers remained little changed by 1911, population growth meant that the proportion of the population who spoke Welsh was declining. The decline was particularly noticeable in the industrial south-east, which was closer to England and subject to much immigration. During the nineteenth century population growth had transformed Wales from a rural country of only 587,000 inhabitants to a nation of 2,012,900 people, most of whom worked in industry. The coal boom of 1901–11 enabled the population to rise by another 20 per cent.

During the late nineteenth century English dialects also began to lose some of their distinctive character. The Revd J. C. Atkinson, the scholar-parson of the North York Moors parish of Danby, wrote in his *Forty Years in a Moorland Parish* (1890): 'There is a singular amount of old and unchanged custom, habit, feeling, among us,' but the one change that stood out was 'the decay of the old pure Yorkshire speech. Time was when I heard it all round me, and from the mouths of all my old parishioners'. He blamed its decline on the school teachers and school inspectors. But language is continually changing and dialects remained rich and varied into the second half of the twentieth century. Accents, of course, can still betray a person's geographical origins.

Britain was the most powerful and advanced nation in the world, but even in most of the industrial towns the old could be found alongside the new. Towards the end of the nineteenth century, the values of the older world that had been championed by John Ruskin, William Morris and Leslie Stephen seemed increasingly attractive to writers, painters and musicians. The favoured style for public buildings was English Baroque, domestic buildings were designed according to the principles of the Arts and Crafts movement, the distinctively English music of Delius, Elgar and Vaughan Williams reflected the renewed interest in folk song, and London writers, escaping for the weekend to the Sussex Downs, turned consciously to the past and imagined a rural England that was stable, harmonious and morally superior to life in the towns. The railway allowed

Edward VII's Coronation
The state coach and guards
proceed through the Canadian
Arch and past the Home Office
on the way to the coronation
service at Westminster Abbey
on 9 August 1902.

Londoners to reach Brighton every hour, on the hour, and in the hour, and cycling and walking clubs were formed by people of modest means who wished to explore the countryside at the weekends. George Gissing wrote from Eastbourne in 1887, 'You come upon old, old hamlets, warm, peaceful, sheltered with old trees. Each has its little Norman church, generally built of flints, and with churchyards that make one always think of Gray's Elegy … never have I seen such quaintness and old-world beauty.' This supposedly idyllic rural world, where village greens were surrounded by thatched cottages with roses framing the doors, was entirely mythical, of course. The reality of life in the countryside was very different; 'Merrie England' simply did not exist except in the minds of town dwellers. Yet the myth dominated much of English culture right up to the Second World War. A small group of counties in the south were imagined to represent 'real England', a place of virtue, beauty and harmony. England had never been like that and was now the most urbanised country in the world, yet at its best this yearning for an older, more secure world led to rewarding intellectual enquiries into England's past, to the foundation of antiquarian societies, the Folk Lore Society, the English Folk Dance Society, the National Trust, the Victoria History of the Counties of England, a respect for traditions and old buildings, and the achievement of Joseph Wright's six-volume *English Dialect Dictionary*, which celebrated the diversity of provincial life.

The image of Britain as an old nation that was now great and powerful was on full display at the coronation of King Edward VII and Queen Alexandra, which finally took place on 9 August 1902. Every race in the British Empire was represented at the event. Eight grey horses drew the antique golden coach through enormous, cheering crowds to Westminster Abbey. The guns of the Tower fired a resounding salute and church bells pealed throughout the land. Elgar's 'Coronation Ode' and a choral setting of 'Pomp and Circumstance Number One' roused the congregation to shout their support, when after an hour's service the Archbishop of Canterbury brought the crown down from the altar and placed it on the king's head. Edward was proclaimed 'By the Grace of God, of the United Kingdom of Great Britain and Ireland, and of the British Dominions Beyond the Seas, King, Defender of the Faith, Emperor of India'.

CHAPTER TWO

FAMILY LIFE: BIRTHS, MARRIAGES AND DEATHS

TRACING OUR Victorian and Edwardian ancestors is not usually a difficult task, for family relationships then were far more enduring than they are for many people at the beginning of the twenty-first century. Neither divorce nor desertion were common, most households comprised parents, children and sometimes other close kin, and both in the towns and the countryside relations lived close by. The young D. H. Lawrence, for instance, had 18 cousins living within two miles of his home at Eastwood on the Nottinghamshire-Derbyshire boundary. If an ancestor cannot be found in one particular place, he or she usually turns up in a neighbouring town or village. Of course, we all find exceptions to this rule and each of us can tell of ancestors who remain elusive, but on the whole people stayed close to their roots unless they were driven to seek a better life in an industrial town, the capital city or overseas.

The records that we are able to search improved in quality and rose in quantity from the early years of Victoria's reign. The indexes of the civil registration of births, marriages and deaths begin in 1837 and census enumerators' books are available every 10 years from 1841 to 1901. By the later nineteenth century the accuracy and completeness of the data in these two sets of records had improved a great deal. They enable us to speak with confidence about fundamental matters such as the ages at which couples married, the number of children they had and how long they might have expected to live. The official report on the 1901 census, which was published three years later, has much to say about these vital events in family life and how national trends over the previous half century could be observed through comparisons with earlier census returns.

Of course, the national records that are available are not perfect. Census enumerators' books, for example, do not always give accurate information about ages. It is common to find that people have apparently not aged ten years from one census to the next. Women were worse at recording true ages, but the elderly seem to have had a fair idea of exactly how old they were. Extreme inconsistencies, however, are rare and demographic studies have found that, on average, recorded ages are reasonably accurate when checked against other sources, such as civil registration records. From 1866 ages are recorded in death certificates and from 1871 marriage certificates normally give what purport to be accurate ages instead of noting, as they had often done in the past, that a person was either a 'minor' or 'of full age'. In 1901 nearly all the minors and about 79 out of 80 of the adults who married stated their ages in the marriage register. During the last three decades of the nineteenth century we therefore have more reliable information for analysis than ever before.

Marriage

The 1901 census counted 5,317,520 married couples in England and Wales. Although the national population had risen substantially over the previous 30 years, this was a smaller number of marriages than that recorded in 1871. The reason, of course, was that people were not marrying at quite so young an age as their parents had. The rather high age at marriage that had been normal in the Tudor and Stuart period had fallen noticeably during the eighteenth and early nineteenth centuries. Earlier marriages had meant more children and so a huge rise of population had occurred. Large families had been usual for much of the Victorian era, but during the closing decades of the nineteenth century the picture began to change.

The median age at marriage for spinsters in England and Wales in 1881 was 23.2. By 1891 it had risen to 23.7, by 1901 to 24.0, and by 1911 to 24.5. This upward trend may not seem to matter a lot when we look at our great grandparents by themselves, but across the nation it represented a significant shift and helps to explain why the rapid increase in the population in the nineteenth century was not maintained in the twentieth century. At the same time, marriage became less frequent. The proportion of English women who never married rose to nearly 14 per cent by 1901 and to 16 per cent by 1911, a significant section of the marriageable population. Yet real incomes were rising for most of this period. In earlier times a higher standard of living had encouraged couples to marry at a younger age, but now people were deliberately choosing to have fewer children or not to marry at all in order to enjoy a more comfortable way of life.

On the whole, men have traditionally married at an older age than their spouses, but during the late nineteenth century the disparity between the ages of husbands and wives was reduced. After 1871 the proportion of married persons who were aged under 25 to the total number of married couples decreased steadily. At the ages of 20–25 only about one-sixth of the men and little more than one-quarter of the women were married; at 35–45 more than four-fifths of the men and about three-quarters of the women were married; at 45–55 the proportion of married men was slightly higher, but the proportion of married women was distinctly lower, and nearly one-sixth of the women were widows. At 65–75 nearly two-thirds of

The 1901 census counted 5,317,520 married couples in England and Wales.

the men were married, but the widows outnumbered both the married women and spinsters taken together; at 75–85 nearly half of the men and more than seven-tenths of the women were widowed. In nearly all age-groups the highest proportions of married persons of both sexes were reached in the census returns of either 1871 or 1881. Working-class women who did not marry were expected to fend for themselves, but spinsters were a problem for middle-class families that disapproved of women working and even more of their 'marrying beneath them' in the social order.

For many young people, their terms of service as domestic or farm servants prevented their marrying young. Domestic servants brought to the marriage market the money they had saved and the skills they had acquired as competent household managers. Upon marriage, farm servants stopped living on their employer's farm and moved into a cottage as day labourers or on to a small farm of their own. In *The Agricultural Community in South-West Wales at the Turn of the Twentieth Century* (1971) David Jenkins shows how marriage was connected to securing a farm. In the south Cardiganshire parish of Troedyraur children did not normally marry while they were living in the parental house. As it was extremely rare for parents to retire in order to allow a son to succeed, a man could not marry until a vacant farm became available or his parents died. Each child had a share in the patrimony, but the common practice was for the youngest son to inherit the tenancy of the family farm. Marriages took place either in February (before sowing) or in the autumn, when Michaelmas tenancies fell in and farm work was slack.

Different farming systems had other rhythms. On the North York Moors, for example, most weddings took place in July, August or September, after the hay or corn harvests. In *Forty Years in a Moorland Parish* (1890) the Revd J. C. Atkinson, the long-serving minister of Danby, regretted that old wedding customs such as horse races, the firing of guns and spiced bride-ales were by then mere survivals, but he approved of the lessening of 'exuberant festivity' that degenerated into drunkenness. The long lists of wedding presents that guests brought to help the new couple set up home were faithfully reported in the local newspaper.

Nearly all weddings were solemnised in a church or chapel. Since 1837, local registrars were empowered to conduct the marriage ceremony, but in practice registry office weddings remained rare until modern times. The Victorian aristocracy and gentry led the way in providing big weddings, with the bride dressed in white, followed down the aisle by a retinue of bridesmaids, a large and prolonged reception and formal departure on honeymoon, but it was not until the later years of the queen's reign that the better-off working-class families could afford more modest versions. When my grandfather married his housekeeper in 1900, they got up, milked the cows, walked two or three miles to church, then walked back,

A Wedding Group in 1894
Thomas Henry Johnson, his bride, Harriet Eliza Wallis, and five bridesmaids pose for the camera at Great Barrets Farm, Leigh, near Tonbridge, Kent.

got changed and started work again. The event was not captured on camera. Old photographs show that the present fashion for men to wear top hats and morning coats was not usual in Victorian weddings. Receptions were mostly held at the bride's home, which explains why wedding photographs were often taken in back gardens, sometimes with ladders leaning against the wall and the corrugated iron roofs of outbuildings framing the background. The careful arrangement of wedding groups against the black background of a studio or a wall of the parish church came later.

For most of the nineteenth century, the upper and middle classes were determined to marry only with their social equals. The Married Women's Property Acts of 1870 and 1882 gave women control over their own earnings and then over their own property, and the 1891 case of *Jackson v Jackson* established that a husband could not legally detain his wife in his house against her will, but for most middle-class women the stuffy, restricted life portrayed in E. M. Forster's novels was only too real. One barrier that had been broken down by 1900, however, was that couples were marrying across the religious divide of church and chapel; only the older dissenting sects stood firm. Within the working classes, marriages crossed the boundaries of social subdivisions, though miners' sons tended to marry miners' daughters, largely because of the isolated nature of their communities. Only the girls who became domestic servants sometimes got the opportunity to marry upwards into the lower middle class. Many of us find that our ancestors were working class on all sides of the family.

Family Size

The rising age at marriage meant that by 1901 families were smaller than they had been in the first half of the nineteenth century. On average, six children were born to each family in early Victorian times, but one of these would die in infancy and another before maturity. By the close of Victoria's reign the new pattern was well established. From the 1870s both the crude birth rate and the fertility rate had begun their prolonged decline and by 1901 they had dropped about 25 per cent from their peaks. Delayed marriages and rising celibacy accounted for about half the drop in fertility between 1871 and 1911; the other half can be explained only by birth control. The fall in fertility was the deliberate choice of married couples across the land, but how this was achieved is not clear, for such matters were not talked about openly. Rubber sheaths were used as contraceptives from the 1870s, and by the 1890s several firms were supplying the market, but oral history suggests that at this time sheaths were not much used by the working classes, who relied instead on withdrawal, abstinence and the unlikelihood of conception during breast feeding.

In general, in the earlier part of the twentieth century, the higher the social class, the smaller was the family size. The 1911 census was the first to record fertility by social and occupational classes. By then, the average number of children in a middle-class family had fallen to 2.8 and in an aristocratic one to 2.5. Middle-class life-styles were becoming more costly and ambitious, with more money spent on having servants and on the education of children. Working-class families were significantly larger than these, despite having fallen in size over the past generation, but they varied considerably in size across the land. The father's occupation had a surprising influence on the number of children that a married couple were likely to have. By 1911 textile workers had 3.19 children on average, unskilled workers 3.92, farm labourers 3.99 and miners 4.33. The relatively low size of families in the textile districts can be explained by the employment opportunities that were available to women, who returned to work as soon as they could, while the miners often lived in separate communities and so were less affected by outside trends. Place rather than occupation may have been the determining factor, with the general practice of a neighbourhood influencing people of all occupations. Farmworkers were another group that were slow to limit their family size. In 1911 the fertility of farmworkers was 12 per cent higher than that of farmers, 14 per cent higher than the average family and about 45 per cent more than upper- and middle-class families. As children in the countryside tended to live longer than those bred in towns, large families remained a significant cause of rural poverty.

Meanwhile, despite the later age of marriage, the general illegitimacy ratio, as a percentage of all live births, fell from 6 per cent in the mid nineteenth century to 4 per cent in 1900, and the proportion of brides who were pregnant when they married fell from about 40 per cent in the early nineteenth century to under 20 per cent in the early twentieth century. Contraception probably explains some of these trends, but restraint seems to have been the major factor. The social pressure to avoid unwanted pregnancies was greater than it had been a couple of generations earlier. Even in the poorest urban districts unmarried mothers were now thought to have lowered the social standing of their families. Illegitimacy rates were higher in the countryside, where attitudes were less disapproving.

The continuous noise of children at play must have been a common experience up and down the land. The early twentieth century was the heyday of girls' and infants' singing games in the streets. Victorian writers often commented on the youthfulness of their society and spoke of Britain as an old country whose population was paradoxically younger than most. The presence of so many children – seen in old photographs of town streets and country lanes, dressed like miniature adults – helps to explain why Victorian and Edwardian Britain was an authoritarian society where corporal punishment was used to enforce obedience and to act as a deterrent, both at home and at school. As most working-class families had very little space in their cramped quarters and their resources were barely sufficient for their needs, discipline was essential in a well-managed home. Children spent a lot of their time on household chores, sharing tasks until they were old enough to go out to work at 12 or 13. But this does not mean that they were not loved and well looked after. Oral accounts insist that most children were cherished and that smaller families meant that more attention could be given to individual children. Recollections of childhood agree that the respectable majority of households were regulated and disciplined and that badly-behaved children came only from the poorest and most disreputable families, where parents took little care of their offspring. The National Society for the Prevention of Cruelty to Children, which was founded in 1883, was soon investigating over 10,000 cases a year in homes such as these, yet it could deal with only the fringe of the problem. The Children's Act (1908) gave some legal protection against the worst abuses.

Birth certificates show that babies were normally born at home rather than in hospital. Unofficial midwives who were well known in the locality helped with deliveries as a neighbourly service free of charge. The Midwives Act (1902) sought to suppress them on the grounds that they were sometimes dirty and often ignorant. The first section of the Act was enforced in 1905, but unofficial midwives were allowed to register their names and to continue without qualifications up to 1910. Babies were not often photographed at this time, for this involved a trip to the studio. Even baptisms do not feature large in family collections of old photographs. Many of the names that were chosen for children are still popular ones, but the generation born in the late-nineteenth and early-twentieth centuries has its share of names that show no sign of coming back into fashion; names such as Leonard, Lionel, Percy and Walter or Doris, Hilda, Ida and Mabel. It had become common in Victorian times for both men and women to be known by two names, such as Albert Edward (after the prince) and John Thomas, or Mary Ann and Elizabeth Jane. My father was known as George Arthur all his life, but someone called William Henry often ended up as Harry and a James Edward might have been known as Ted. The pet forms of women's names are not always easy to follow. Millie for Emily, Bessie for Elizabeth, Jinny for Jane, Sally for Sarah, Nancy for Ann are plausible, but Peggy for Margaret and Polly for Mary are difficult to work out unless we know they have come via Meg and Molly.

Infant and Child Mortality

In present-day England and Wales only one or two per cent of children die before they reach the age of five. In the early years of Victoria's reign infant and child mortality had been as high as 25–28 per cent. The risk of death was particularly high in a child's first year, whatever the social class of the parents. The mortality rate had fallen in the 1870s, but this welcome trend was reversed from the mid 1880s to reach a peak of 163 deaths per 1,000 live births in 1899, before it fell sharply to 151 in 1901 and 95 in 1912 and then continuously downwards during the twentieth century. Even so, as late as 1921 it was still about 11–13 per cent. In large, industrial towns and colliery districts, infant mortality rates remained much higher than the national average. In Sheffield, for example, it reached 202 per 1,000 in 1901. Between 1901 and 1905, in England and Wales as a whole, the infant mortality rate was 138 deaths per 1,000 births, but the rates were much higher in Lancashire (163), Durham (157), the East Riding of Yorkshire (152), Warwickshire (152), Staffordshire (151) and Leicestershire (144) and significantly lower in rural Wiltshire (91), Hertfordshire (92), Dorset (92), Westmorland (97) and Surrey (105). Children had the lowest chance of reaching their first birthday in places such as the Lancashire cotton towns, where mothers soon gave up breast feeding to return to work and where parental physique was worsened by heavy or prolonged labour. High infant mortality rates were often associated with high illegitimacy, low literacy and excessive drinking. The deaths in 1901 of 1,550 infants who were suffocated in the same bed as their mothers prompted much gossip as to whether these 'accidents' were due to ignorance, chance or deliberate action.

The most frequently mentioned causes of infant deaths were gastro-intestinal disorders, leading to diarrhoea and dysentery. These disorders were largely the result of overcrowding, dirt and poor sanitation; they came from contaminated water and from food and drink infected by flies.

Horse dung attracted flies in the town streets, while in the countryside cesspools and open drains invited disaster. Summers were dry and hot in the latter part of the nineteenth century and the flies seemed to be everywhere. Inadequate nursing contributed to the number of deaths. At a meeting of the Royal Statistical Society in 1893, with Charles Booth, its President, in the chair, Dr Hugh Jones claimed that, 'Half the deaths of infants are attributable to bad feeding. This bad feeding depends upon ignorance.' He thought that the lower infant mortality rates in the countryside were not because of fresh air but the result of the better training of young girls who were familiar with caring for children from their earliest days. Mortality rates improved in the twentieth century because of a higher standard of living and better nutrition, public health reforms, some control of infectious diseases and effective medicine. Though many towns were slow to acquire a decent water supply – North Shields, for example, did not get one until 1897 – and many small settlements continued to rely on wells or springs well into the twentieth century, by 1914 polluted drinking water was rarely a problem. National death rates for the under-fifteens peaked at about 1,500 per million in 1870 and declined to about 1,000 per million by the end of the century.

The stark expectation that most families would experience the death of a child helps to explain why sentimental Victorian novels were so popular and why, for instance, the character of Little Nell in Dickens' *The Old Curiosity Shop* (1841) could be portrayed in such a cloying manner. Past generations were preoccupied with death because it struck in unpredictable ways and was a constant threat at all stages of life, but particularly in infancy. The necessity of being prepared for death was a recurrent theme in religious books and magazines, which featured death-bed scenes and emphasised the promised happiness of the hereafter.

The modern world is nowhere more different from the Victorian one than in the expectation that children will survive infancy. Diphtheria, scarlet fever and measles, the three most dreaded diseases, were likely to strike at any time of the year, but children were most prone to sickness in winter and spring and risked dying of secondary pneumonia. Autumn deaths were often caused by diarrhoeal infections caught in the summer months. School log books are full of references to coughs, colds, sore throats, bronchitis, influenza, whooping cough, mumps, chicken pox, skin disease, outbreaks of diphtheria, scarlet fever and measles and rare cases of smallpox. Illness was ever-present and every few years large numbers of schoolchildren succumbed to epidemics.

The battle against infectious diseases in the second half of the nineteenth century was fought by local authorities. A major victory was achieved over smallpox. In 1853 the vaccination of children had been made compulsory, but no provision for the enforcement of the law was made until 1867. Four years later, all poor law unions were required to

The modern world is nowhere more different from the Victorian one than in the expectation that children will survive infancy.

Mourning a Loved One
Frank Burdekin's family dress in black to mourn his death at the Chatsworth estate village of Edensor in 1901.

appoint vaccination officers. Smallpox epidemics nevertheless continued to occur, with national outbreaks in 1870–73 and 1902–5 and local ones such as that in Middlesbrough in 1897–98, which infected 1,411 people and caused 198 deaths. Child diseases that can now be controlled, such as measles, were often fatal in the nineteenth and early-twentieth centuries. Measles was one of the most infectious diseases, endemic in London and other large towns and industrial districts, and liable to break out in epidemics in the countryside. It first became prominent in England as a killer of children in the late-eighteenth and early-nineteenth centuries, replacing smallpox as the major threat. In the middle of the nineteenth century scarlet fever caused 10,000 deaths per annum, especially among children from the ages of one to five, of all social classes. Between 1868 and 1870 it swept through the towns of England and Wales, but it became one of the first infectious diseases to be brought under control, so by the end of the century the number of deaths had been reduced to about a fifth of what they had been. Whooping cough was also one of the great killers of nineteenth-century children. It struck all classes of society, especially infants; two out of every three of its victims were less than two years old.

Diphtheria first made a major impact in the epidemic of 1858–65 and its nature was not understood until the London epidemic of 1888–95 was observed to follow a random pattern, suggesting infection. Diphtheria was widely epidemic in English and Welsh towns during the late 1880s, but a serum treatment was introduced successfully in 1894.

Tuberculosis (or consumption as it was still commonly known) remained a scourge for both children and adults, claiming 75,000 British deaths per annum in the early twentieth century, a third of them cutting down people in the prime of life. Consumption was widely feared, with just cause, by all levels of society, though it was most widespread in London and industrial districts. In 1900 it was still the leading killer after heart disease. The most common form of the disease was respiratory (pulmonary TB or phthisis), but the bacillus could also infect bones and joints or lead to scrofula, lupus or meningitis. Those who fell victim to this cruelly debilitating disease faced a lingering death. Isolation hospitals modelled on German sanitaria began to offer effective treatment in the Edwardian era. Meanwhile, water-borne diseases, such as cholera and dysentery, which had once been a major concern of public health authorities, had become a thing of the past and a general improvement in personal cleanliness, from regular bathing and clean underwear, led to the disappearance of typhus, which was spread by body lice. The number of London children found to be flea-bitten dropped steadily from 30 per cent in 1908 to under 4 per cent in the 1920s and the picture was much the same in other cities.

Britain was the richest country in the world, but large numbers of its children were still liable to succumb to rickets. Lack of vitamin D caused defective bone growth, but as middle-class children were affected as well as those from poorer classes it was not simply a matter of deficient diet. An insufficient amount of sunlight in the polluted atmosphere of large towns and manufacturing and mining districts seems to have been the major cause of rickets. Some progress was made from the 1870s, but rickets remained one of the most common disorders in our cities up to the 1920s. Robert Roberts remembered many of his fellow schoolchildren in an Edwardian slum in Salford who suffered from rickets, bow legs and open sores that remained untreated.

Great advances in medical knowledge were made between 1870 and 1910, but old, mistaken ideas of the causes of disease and the remedies that could be applied survived at a popular level, for a visit from a doctor was an expense that most working-class families could not afford. Many families treated themselves with patent medicines or with folk remedies, such as sticking brown paper or red flannel on chests to drive away a cold or cough, or applying celandine to weak eyes. The *London*

An advertisement for the beneficial effects of Abbey's Effervescent Salt, 1901.

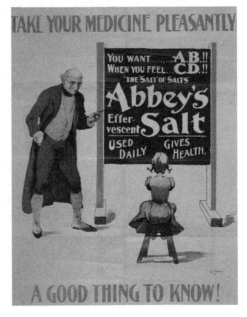

Illustrated News for 1901 contained regular advertisements for Carter's Little Liver Pills which, it was claimed, would absolutely cure biliousness, sick headaches, torpid liver, furred tongue, indigestion, constipation, dizziness and sallow skin, or Beecham's Pills for all bilious and nervous disorders, sick headaches, constipation, wind and pains in the stomach, impaired digestion, disordered liver, and female ailments. Sales of Beecham's Pills exceeded six million boxes per annum. Dr De Jongh's Light-Brown Cod Liver Oil, 'unrivalled in consumption and bronchial affections', and Clarke's Blood Mixture, 'the world-famous blood purifier and restorer', offered further relief. The newly-literate products of compulsory education were an easy target for advertisers in newspapers, for they lacked the knowledge to judge the worth of the offered remedies. In the later Victorian period liberal doses of Godfrey's Cordial, Atkinson's Infants' Preservative or Street's Infants' Quietness were given to crying babies to make them sleep. The condensed milk that became widely available from the 1890s was safe but of a low nutritional value. It seems likely that about 80–90 per cent of babies were breast fed, if only because this was the cheapest and easiest method available. Social investigators repeatedly showed that children from poorer families were shorter, lighter and less healthy than those from better-off homes and that those parents who were least able to afford large families were the most likely to have them. Ignorance and lack of means contributed to the ill health of the poor. Toothbrushes were hardly used and so teeth decayed, ill-fitting footwear caused chilblains, and defective eyesight or hearing went uncorrected. School meals and medical inspections, introduced from the 1890s by the most progressive local authorities and throughout the country in Edward VII's reign, made a huge difference to the health of working-class children. All too often, their mothers suffered from rotting teeth, varicose veins and faded complexions.

An inadequate diet left children prone to disease. Although rising real wages meant more purchasing power, large numbers of working-class families still had to make do with one good meal a day and frequent cups of tea accompanying bread spread with jam or dripping. Typical wage rates at that time included 7d. an hour for bricklayers' labourers and 10¼d. an hour for skilled craftsmen such as carpenters. A 'wage census' published by the government in 1906 showed that over a quarter of adult workmen received less than 20 shillings a week in wages and that nearly two-thirds earned less than 25 shillings. Although diets were more varied by 1901, bread and potatoes were still the basic foods. Other vegetables and fresh fruit were rarely seen on the tables of many working-class families in the towns, nor was much fresh milk available, for at 2d. a pint it was relatively expensive and had to be supplemented by tins of condensed milk made from evaporated skimmed milk which lacked vitamins A and D. The father was often the only member of the family who occasionally ate relishes or other treats. Cockles and mussels could be bought from buckets or push-carts hawked around the streets, but at the time only the lowest social classes bought their dinners from one of the new fish-and-chip shops. By 1900 most of the blatant practices by which food was adulterated had been stamped out by local government officers, but in that year 13 per cent of coffee and 9.9 per cent of milk were still found to be below standard. Publicans still watered down their beer or added salt on the pretext of providing flavour but in reality stimulating thirst. In the cottages of the countryside, vegetables were grown in gardens or allotments, but meat was scarce. In the south Cardiganshire parish of Troedyraur, for instance, a cottager very rarely had fresh meat except when he had killed the pig he had been fattening for months. Salt bacon was the basis of the broth that was the main meal of the day for farmworkers during the greater part of the year. In *Lark Rise to Candleford*, her memoir of the hamlet of Juniper Hill (Oxfordshire) in the 1880s, Flora Thompson recalled how the family pig was as much a topic of conversation as the weather and that visitors were taken to see the animal. Many English cottagers kept no pig, but those who did saw them as an investment that helped to pay off debts and which added much needed variety to the normal plain diet.

By the end of the nineteenth century most children were dressed reasonably tidily for their school photographs, but were often seen in ill-fitting, threadbare cast-offs when photographed elsewhere. In later life their rough footwear often caused corns, callouses and bunions that affected the way they walked. In the worst slums up to a quarter of a class of children might arrive barefooted at school. Little girls wore dresses made of drab cloth and stuff, a print pinafore, dark stockings and stout boots, which were blacked weekly. The boys' jackets and trousers were often made out of their father's threadbare hand-me-downs, with plenty of leeway until they grew into them. Their footwear was either heavy, nailed boots or clogs. Outdoors, they usually wore a cap and, in winter time, a woollen scarf. Country boys put on their leather gaiters in bad weather. Adults wore far more clothes than we do. Working-class women photographed standing by their doors were well-padded and clad in dresses and aprons that almost touched the ground. They rarely ventured far without a shawl. Their men folk kept their waistcoats on while they worked and usually their caps as well.

Old Age and Death

At the beginning of Edward VII's reign anyone could spot whether a man belonged to the upper or the working classes by his physical appearance, his dress and his manner of speaking. The average Englishman was only 5ft. 7in. tall and it was exceptional to find someone who was a 'six-footer'. The tallest and heaviest people were generally those who belonged to the

The expectation of life in
middle-class Hampstead was
50 at birth, but in working-class
Southwark only 36.

well-fed, wealthier classes. By 1901 upper-class people could expect to live
for nearly 60 years, double the average life expectancy of the very poor,
who were no better off in this respect than their Tudor and Stuart fore-
bears had been. The expectation of life in middle-class Hampstead was 50
at birth, but in working-class Southwark only 36. In Manchester, as in
many other cities, the general death rates for the most prosperous wards
were half those of the poorest. The inhabitants of central Birmingham
were four times more likely to get tuberculosis than those who lived in the
wealthy suburb of Edgbaston. In the middle-class suburbs 4 out of 100
infants would die; in the worst slums 1 in every 3 would not live beyond
their first year.

Some people lived to a ripe old age, but there were far fewer of them
than at the present time. The proportion of elderly people in the population remained static in the later nineteenth century, but rose steadily in the
first half of the twentieth century and increased dramatically during the
second half. In both 1871 and 1901 those aged from 60 to 64 accounted
for only 2.7 per cent of the population, whereas in 1931 they amounted to
4.1 per cent. Those aged between 65 and 74 amounted to 3.4, 3.3 and 5.4
per cent, respectively, and those aged over 74 to 1.4, 1.4 and 2.0 per cent.
Altogether, the over-sixties formed 7.5 per cent of the population in 1871,
7.4 in 1901 and 11.5 in 1931. The really impressive changes were yet to
come. By 1991 men over 60 formed 18.7 per cent of the male population
of the United Kingdom and women over 60 formed 25.8 per cent of the
females.

The demographic profile of England and Wales began to change from
the 1870s as fewer children were born and young and middle-aged adults
began to live longer. Mortality rates fell significantly from 21.8 per 1,000 in
1868 to 18.1 in 1888 and down to 14.8 in 1908. The Edwardian population
was not as youthful as the early-Victorian one had been. Life expectancy
was higher in the countryside than it was in the towns, even among the
farm labourers. As yet, we know little about health and mortality in rural
nineteenth-century England and Wales, for historians have concentrated
on the experience of townspeople, but we are well aware that, although
farmworkers lived longer than townsmen, in later life they commonly suffered ill health and pain from rheumatism, leg ulcers and bronchitis.
These illnesses were brought on by regular exposure to wet and difficult
working conditions and to the damp and draughty state of many of their
cottages. When they fell ill, membership of a friendly society might help
for a while, but usually they had to treat themselves as best they could or
else endure the indignity of the workhouse infirmary.

In Victorian times working-class people usually tried to work as long as
they were able, simply out of necessity. It is rare to find a nineteenth-
century death certificate which states that a man was retired, even when he
had been forced to give up work because of ill health. In the 1890s 29 per

cent of people aged over 64 were paupers, with 21 per cent on outdoor relief and 8 per cent living in the workhouse. Children could be brought to court if they failed to support their parents. Charles Booth had found that in London 5 per cent of old people were wholly dependent on their relations and that another 25 per cent were partly dependent on them, but over half the aged had earnings or private means to support themselves.

Institutions

The various census returns provide numerous insights into the life of institutions such as workhouses, hospitals and prisons and tell us a little about the sort of person who lived in a lodging-house. By far the worst of these lodgings were the horrific East End 'doss houses' that charged 4d. a night for those who could find only casual work in the docks. William Booth, the Salvation Army general, witnessed at the dock gates the 'terrible scene of men, 600 of them, waiting the chance of a job, but less than 20 of them get engaged ... No sooner is the foreman seen, than there is a wild rush to the spot and a sharp mad fight to "catch his eye"'.

The punishment of criminals gradually became less severe from the 1870s and by the turn of the century the proportion of serious offenders who were sent to prison had almost halved. The treadmill was abolished in 1902, young offenders might be put on probation from 1907 and flogging ceased in 1917. In 1902 about 170,000 people were sent to prison, including 52,000 females. The overwhelming majority of them were from the labouring poor and over 40,000 were sentenced to hard labour in default of the payment of a fine. In 1908 over 27,000 people were imprisoned for begging and 'sleeping out'. Some people were sent to prison over and over again. When, in 1905, the *Salford Reporter* noted the death of 60-year-old Susan Wilson from 'general exhaustion and decay brought on by excessive intemperance' it claimed that she had made 174 appearances before the magistrates for drunkenness and wilful damage and therefore had spent much of her life in Strangeways Prison, where she was always 'a woman of good behaviour'. Although the East End of London and some of the poorer districts of the industrial towns had their notorious criminal gangs, the level of crime was much lower than it is today. In 1906 only 59,079 indictable offences were recorded in the whole of England and Wales; that is less than two crimes per policeman.

The 1901 census recorded 39,184 patients in hospitals, excluding workhouses and other poor law institutions, in roughly equal numbers of males and females. The proportion of hospital accommodation varied considerably in different parts of England and was exceptionally large in London. By 1900 Sheffield was typical of many of the new cities in having two hospitals that had grown out of workhouses, an infirmary built by public subscription, a women's hospital donated by a private benefactor, a civic

Dinner in the Workhouse
This celebrated illustration of the regimented nature of an evening meal in a workhouse accompanied an article on the St Marylebone workhouse in George Sims, *Living London* (1901).

hospital, a children's hospital and an asylum for the mentally ill. The 1901 census for England and Wales listed 90,658 people in lunatic asylums, whose buildings are characteristically major Victorian monuments of considerable architectural merit, standing in their own grounds beyond the towns, each with accommodation for about 300 inmates.

Away from the larger towns and cities, infirmaries attached to workhouses often provided the only medical treatment that was available to the worse-off. A welcome innovation was the employment of trained nurses to care for the sick, such as those trained in the Shoreditch Infirmary school from 1889. A local poor law inspector reporting on the inadequacies of nursing in the workhouses of East Anglia in the 1890s remarked that 'Not infrequently a single paid nurse was in charge of 30 or 40 patients, and this meant that almost everything for the sick had to be done by pauper inmates'; however, 'Guardians were beginning to recognise the fact that nursing is a skilled business, and that it is worth while to pay for its being done properly'. Whereas only half of the 41 nurses attached to Norfolk workhouses in 1891 were properly trained, five years later two-thirds of the 145 nurses had received adequate training.

Sickness and death cost families dearly, though by 1901 half the adult male population was covered by health insurance schemes that were operated by burial clubs and friendly societies. Lloyd-George's National Health Insurance Act, which came into effect in 1912, was as important to working-class people as were his old age pensions. Nevertheless, we should recognise that before then the poor law system had enabled many families to survive and that poor relief was often accepted without shame, as it was considered a right. In 1891 an estimated 30 per cent of all country men and women aged 65 and over received some form of poor relief. The workhouse was the final resort, when old people were incapable of looking after themselves. Practice varied across the country. On 1 January 1899 south Wales had, on average, only 3.9 paupers per 1,000 population in its workhouses and 25.9 per 1,000 on outdoor relief. North Wales had 4 per 1,000 and 33.4 per 1,000, respectively. The Welsh made strenuous efforts to keep people out of their workhouses and had a lower indoor pauper rate than any English county. Shropshire and Sussex with 8 workhouse inmates per 1,000 and Berkshire and Gloucestershire with 8.2 were the lowest in England. The 1901 census revealed that the total number of pauper inmates, including those in workhouse infirmaries and schools, in the whole of England and Wales was 208,650 (120,285 males and 88,365 females), a proportion of one to every 131 males and one to every 190 females. Males outnumbered females in workhouses throughout the land and at all stages of life.

Seebohm Rowntree reported that on 1 January 1901 York had 492 people in its workhouse and that 1,049 others received outdoor relief. The position was only marginally better in summertime, for on 1 July 1901 the workhouse had 443 inmates and another 1,060 Yorkers received outdoor relief. The inmates on 1 January comprised 62 able-bodied people (split exactly in half into males and females), 256 old and infirm (144 males and 112 females), 68 imbeciles, 20 epileptics, 21 women in the lying-in ward, 70 children and 141 infants under the age of two. York was typical in having far fewer poor people in the workhouse than those who were usually relieved at home. Local officers knew the men and women who were claiming relief and judged their cases accordingly. The twentieth-century welfare system grew out of the practices of the poor law, for, in effect, poor relief served the role of a pension, albeit one that was given as charity. The escalating costs of providing for the poor was a strong argument of those who advocated the introduction of state pensions.

The basic system remained in place until 1929, when provision for the poor was transferred to county and county borough councils. Late in Victoria's reign a new enlightened approach softened the harsh, Dickensian image of the workhouse. From 1885 old couples in workhouses were officially allowed to stay together, in the early 1890s guardians provided newspapers and books, then tobacco and snuff, and in 1895 the Local Government Board recommended that older inmates should be allowed to wear individual clothing rather than pauper uniforms. In some northern towns, however, able-bodied workers still wore a large letter P on the seats of their trousers in Edwardian times. On the other hand, when the Salford Workhouse Committee were told in 1906 that up to 60 tramps queued up to two hours each day to gain admittance to the Tramp Ward, they voted to allow them to wait in a shed inside the walls to protect them from the weather, but also to stop them being an eyesore to passers-by. The rough diet of the workhouse – broth, bacon and dumplings – was good enough by the meagre standards of the Edwardian poor, though as old people had no false teeth and few natural ones they often had difficulty eating it. Despite these improvements, poor people did all they could to avoid the workhouse. When Bettesworth, George Sturt's gardener, was removed there in old age, he was widely regarded amongst his friends and acquaintances as 'finished'.

Burials

The rich and the poor had different funeral customs and attitudes to death. The ostentatious funerals that we associate with the Victorians, with everything and everybody draped in black, were those of the upper and middle classes. The cult of mourning was at its extreme upon and after the death of Prince Albert and was spread by the influence of the royal family and the wealthier sections of society. Its excesses led to a reaction in favour of simpler and more dignified ceremonies by the later nineteenth century. We need to distinguish between public ceremonies and the great majority of funerals, which were conducted modestly, often in accordance with the wishes of the deceased. The elaborate graves and memorials in church-yards and public cemeteries were more a feature of the early and middle years of Victoria's reign than the later ones. Cremation became legal in 1884, after a debate that had started in 1870s, but this practice was slow to gain acceptance. Even after the Cremation Act of 1902, London had only 105 cremations in the next five years and by 1908 only about 800 people had been cremated in the whole of Britain.

Burials were costly, except for the very poor whose simple funerals were paid for by the poor law unions. A decent funeral was thought necessary to preserve a family's standing in a community; a pauper burial was considered the ultimate disgrace. In the nineteenth and early twentieth centuries the working classes made small weekly payments to burial clubs (often a local friendly society or a national body such as the Ancient Order of Foresters). When someone died, the family's first step was to find a 'layer-out', a good neighbour, who would wash and dress the body. For many years one of my grandmothers fulfilled this role in her local commu-nity. Then an undertaker was sent for, to place the body in an open coffin for all to view and pay their respects, whilst ordinary family life carried on in the other rooms. A vigil was commonly held on the night before burial, but this was a restrained affair to which only a small group of close friends and relations were invited. Festivities did not begin until after the funeral service, when a meal was provided for all who had come. Ham and cakes were such the normal fare that to say a person had been 'buried with ham' became a common, jocular phrase. However, even on the North York

Moors, where old customs lasted longer than in most other places, these meals had been reduced in size by the end of the century. In 1890 the Revd J. C. Atkinson observed that in his parish of Danby 'great assemblages and colossal providings are now mainly things of the past'.

Households and Kinship

Old people lived independently as long as they were able, but near to their children, if possible. In Victorian and Edwardian England and Wales families usually found their kin close by, in neighbouring streets or the next village. The old usually moved into their married children's households only when they were too infirm to fend for themselves. In York Rowntree found that nearly half the old people shared a household with their children or grandchildren, but these descendants were generally unmarried; they were either children who had never left the parental home or older grandchildren who had moved in because their own homes had become too crowded. The long-standing practice, which goes back to the middle ages, whereby old people kept their own homes as long as possible still prevailed. In York one in four old people took in paid lodgers. Of course, many old people who were not able to manage by themselves had no families to look after them. By the age of 70, one in every five Edwardians was a pauper, and at the age of 75 one in every three. Nearly a tenth of old people ended their days in a workhouse.

In 1901 the average household size was 4.6 people, more or less the same as it had been for centuries, but thereafter, it fell dramatically. By 1985 the average household size was only 2.6.

Census returns show that most households were composed of husband, wife and unmarried children only, but the printed reports have little to say about households and families. In 1901 the average household size was 4.6 people, more or less the same as it had been for centuries, but thereafter, with the decline in fertility and the reduction in the number of domestic servants (from 14 per cent of households in 1861 to 1 per cent in 1951) it fell dramatically. By 1985 the average household size was only 2.6. Individual census returns can provide a picture only at certain points in time; they fail to capture movement in the intervening years. Family history research and oral accounts of the past help to fill the gaps. Barry Reay has shown, for example, that in nineteenth-century Blean (Kent) at least as many households went through an extended phase as experienced only the simple family structure, and that for some groups of rural workers the complex household was more common than that of just parents and children.

If we look at the changing households in a small settlement through all the census returns from 1841 to 1901, we find how misleading average figures can be. The Pennine hamlet of Catshaw, where I lived as a boy, provides a suitable example of the various permutations and changes. The Goldthorpes, who live in the old farmhouse and its extension, are the sixth and seventh generations of the family to live in the hamlet and to earn their living as small farmers and millers. In 1861 Charles and Rhoda Goldthorpe had 10 children living in their farmhouse; 10 years later the household had changed to parents, five children and a granddaughter. The four cottages which face down the valley of the River Don, across the lane from the farmhouse, were each occupied by the families of farm labourers or workers of similar status. Three of the cottages were only one-up and one-down, with a scullery at the back, so it is no surprise to find that they were normally the homes of small families. Most tenancies changed hands from time to time but the Kenworthys lived in the first cottage throughout the century.

In 1841 the old farm house at the top of the lane at Catshaw Cross was the home of Jonathan and Amelia Woodhouse and their five children. Ten years later, Jonathan was described as a farmer of 13 acres who also worked as a labourer on neighbouring farms. He and his wife lived with their two youngest boys and two grandchildren. In 1861 Jonathan and Amelia, their son Joseph (who then worked at the Goldthorpe's mill, but who was employed on the roads 10 years later) and a new granddaughter, Martha Bottomley, were living there. They were all still in the same house in 1871, but Amelia died before the next census, when Jonathan was an 85-year old widower, living with his bachelor son, Joseph (now a plate layer on the railways) and his granddaughter, Martha, a 30-year-old domestic servant. In 1891, five years after the death of Jonathan at 90 years of age, Martha was recorded as Joseph's housekeeper. The Woodhouses had lived in the old farm house at Catshaw Cross at each enumeration between 1841 and 1891, but they were no longer there in 1901.

In 1861 a new cottage at Catshaw Cross was the home of Vincent Smith, a 'field waller and agricultural labourer'; his wife, Tamar; their daughter Annis, who worked as a washer woman; their son, Benjamin, a collier; three younger children and two grandsons. Ten years later, Vincent was working on the roads and he and Tamar were living with their two youngest daughters and six grandchildren, three of whom had 'Bastards' written across their names in the census return. They were succeeded by John and Harriett Higgins, their three young children and a step-daughter. John was a coal miner, as were his two lodgers. By 1901 other members of the Higgins family had succeeded them; the men worked in the coal mines, the girls in the local umbrella factory.

The census returns tell us a great deal about the nineteenth-century inhabitants of Catshaw. In the first place, they reveal how families were prepared to look after grandchildren, step-children and other relatives if the need arose. In 1861 the hamlet contained 10 children under the age of 10 years and 12 more under the age of 20. Only 4 of the 45 people who lived at Catshaw in 1861 had been born outside the parish of Penistone and none of these had travelled more than 12 miles. Thirty-six of the inhabitants had been born in that part of Penistone parish which was

known as Thurlstone township, many of them at Catshaw itself. They
formed a very local society, with limited horizons. Some of the cottagers
who lived at Catshaw during the reign of Queen Victoria were there for
most of their adult lives. The 1901 census recorded a group of working-
class families of local origin. Most of the men, women and children had
been born in Penistone parish and nobody came from more than 15 miles
away.

Surprisingly, historians know more about kinship, neighbourhood and
community in the seventeenth century than they do about the nineteenth.
Elizabeth Roberts has written that 'It is almost impossible to define precisely who were or who were not regarded as family by working-class
people' in Victorian and Edwardian times. Mothers and daughters, in particular, kept in regular touch, but the composition of households does not
provide a good measure of the support that families could call upon in
times of trouble. Friends as well as relations were there to help, but the
working-class neighbourhood is even harder to define than the kinship
network. Oral history is our chief guide. Accounts agree that the higher
standard of living of working-class families and reduced family sizes in the
later part of the nineteenth century led to more companionable family
relationships. They also insist that male and female responsibilities within
families remained clear and separate. The mother was more often than not
the driving force, with many roles to play. She emerges from oral history as
someone who was not dispirited or defeated by poverty. When almost
everybody in the same neighbourhood shared the same low standard of
living, a hard life had to be endured as cheerfully as possible. Robert
Roberts's account of his childhood in Edwardian Salford, *The Classic Slum*

(1971), concludes that, 'In spite of abounding poverty it would be wrong to assume that the district lay slumped in despair. Much banter and good-natured teasing was to be heard. People laughed easily, whistled, sang on high days and jigged in the street – the great recreation room.' He went on to say that, 'Despite poverty and appalling surroundings, people brought up their children to be decent, kindly and honourable.' The home was the focus of love and everyone's interests, so much so that 'Home, sweet home', first heard in the 1870s, had almost become a second national anthem.

Life was experienced by most people at a distinctly local level. Robert Roberts recalled that, 'In our community, as in every other of its kind, each street had the usual social rating; one side or one end might be classed higher … End houses often had special status. Each family and individual had a tacit ranking.' In Troedyraur, David Jenkins found that talk of relatives and of relationships was pervasive, not only about the speaker's own kinsmen but about other people's as well. Conversations were full of references to the relationships of people and speakers expected that their listeners would know the main facts about their neighbours' kin connections. How kinsmen regarded each other and how a person's behaviour would affect his relatives were common topics of conversation. But although knowledge of kin was widespread, some individuals had no interest in such matters. South Cardiganshire families were still closely associated with the farms that they occupied, even if they held them for only a short period. People were commonly known by their Christian names or surnames with the names of their farms attached, or simply by the names of the farms. When a family moved to another farm because of changing circumstances, landlords usually accepted their recommendation that one of their kin should take their place. The same custom has been observed in different parts of rural England.

The closeness of family life was not always beneficial, of course. Not everyone got on with his or her relations and Robert Roberts remembered that as a child before the First World War, 'I hardly knew a weekend free from the sight of brawling adults and inter-family disputes.' Yet those involved in disorderly behaviour came from a comparatively small section of the community and respectability could be found even in the slums. The strength of family feeling is immediately obvious when we open our treasured albums of old photographs, which depict our ancestors dressed in their best or sometimes in curious studio costumes, staring solemnly ahead, their heads held firmly in place by a wire frame hidden from sight. As Arnold Bennett wrote in *The Old Wives' Tale* (1908): 'Nothing will sharpen the memory, evoke the past, raise the dead, rejuvenate the ageing, and cause both sighs and smiles, like a collection of photographs gathered together during long years of life.'

$\mathscr{M}$IGRANTS AND NATIVES

BY 1901 THE POPULATION of England and Wales had reached 32,527,843, an increase of 3,525,318 or 12.17 per cent since the previous census. The nineteenth century had seen an astonishing growth in the number of people living in mainland Britain. England and Wales now supported almost four times as many inhabitants as they had a hundred years earlier. Most of this increased population had been absorbed in the burgeoning industrial towns and cities. By 1901 75 urban districts each contained over 50,000 inhabitants. London (the administrative county) had 4,536,541, Liverpool 684,958, Manchester 543,872, Birmingham 522,204, Leeds 428,968, Sheffield 380,793 and Bristol 328,545. But these figures take no account of the spread of urban conurbations beyond their borders. Over 6.5 million people thought of themselves as Londoners, including the inhabitants of such places as West Ham, East Ham, Walthamstow and Leyton (all of which still lay in Essex) or Willesden, Tottenham and Hornsey (which were included within Middlesex). The population of England had become predominantly urban, while Wales had experienced a massive shift of population to the coal mines, iron works and docklands of the south.

This spectacular rate of growth was uneven across the country. The highest rates of increase in the 22 counties whose population had risen over 10 per cent since 1891 were mostly in those around London (Middlesex, Essex, Surrey, Kent and Hertfordshire) and in the manufacturing and coal-mining districts (Lancashire, Yorkshire, Glamorganshire, Northumberland, Durham, Monmouthshire, and to some extent Staffordshire, Derbyshire, Leicestershire and Nottinghamshire). But 10 of the counties that were agricultural in character had lost population during the last decade – Huntingdonshire (-7.04 per cent), Rutland (-5.59), Montgomeryshire (-5.08), Cardiganshire (-4.26), Westmorland (-2.73), Oxfordshire (-1.70), Herefordshire (-1.62), Flintshire (-0.71), Merionethshire (-0.55) and Brecknockshire (-0.17) – and others were only just holding their own. The population of most of these counties had fallen in previous decades too, except during the summer months when migrants came to help with the harvest. Elsewhere, the evidence of the decline of the rural population of a county was masked by the growth of a neighbouring large town, such as Hull in the East Riding of Yorkshire or Grimsby in Lincolnshire, which distorted a county's figures.

Growing numbers of immigrants were recorded in the 1901 census, yet slightly more people (0.2 per cent) left England and Wales during Victoria's reign than entered the two countries. Between 1815 and 1930 nearly 60 million Europeans migrated overseas, over 10 million of them from the British Isles, in the most massive shift of population that the world has ever known. The United States of America was by far the most important destination for these migrants, but many preferred the British dominions and colonies or South America. People of every occupation and social class tried their luck overseas. Many returned in later life, sometimes as failures, but usually because they had always intended to. By the later nineteenth century the typical emigrants were young single adults, with males outnumbering females by about two to one. The majority travelled steerage on crowded steamships from Liverpool. The Atlantic crossing must have been an arduous and sometimes frightening one, yet businessmen did it regularly in search of orders. During his lifetime, George Wolstenholme, the Sheffield cutlery manufacturer, made 30 journeys across the Atlantic, so important was the American market for his Bowie knives and other wares. The barriers to long-distance movement were not as formidable as we might suppose.

Between 1815 and 1930 nearly 60 million Europeans migrated overseas, over 10 million of them from the British Isles, in the most massive shift of population that the world has ever known.

Immigration

The official report on the 1901 census noted that the number of English emigrants had fallen in the previous decade by about half a million, while at the same time Jewish immigrants from the Russian Empire had risen considerably, so that the numbers of emigrants had exceeded immigrants by only 68,330. Of the 32,527,843 people enumerated in England and Wales in 1901, 31,269,203 had been born there. Those born elsewhere comprised 426,565 from Ireland, 316,838 from Scotland, 35,763 from islands in the British seas, 136,092 from British colonies and India, 3,946 on ships at sea, and 339,436 from foreign countries. In other words, 99 per cent of the people resident in England and Wales at the end of Victoria's reign had been born within the limits of the British Empire. Those born in foreign countries amounted to 10.4 per 1,000 of the population, an increase of 45 per cent since 1891. They included 227,301 who had been born in Europe, 1,245 in Asia, 462 in Africa, and 18,311 in America. If we eliminate those who were born to British parents, the number of foreigners falls to 247,758, or 7.6 per 1,000 people. More than half of these (135,377) were enumerated in London, with a further 20,542 in the four surrounding counties of Surrey, Kent, Middlesex and Essex. Lancashire had 28,603 foreign-born inhabitants, Yorkshire 17,019, Durham and

Chinese Graves
A Chineseman in traditional dress, with his hair in the customary pigtail, tends a grave in an East London cemetery in 1901.

Northumberland 9,455, and Glamorganshire 6,517. In all, 88 per cent of the foreigners lived in these 10 counties, almost exclusively in or near London, the industrial towns and seaports.

In late-Victorian and Edwardian times Britain was the world's major economic power, drawing labour and capital from less-developed nations. The tramp ships that moved from port to port throughout the British Empire, picking up whatever cargo was available, employed men from the colonies to stoke their furnaces and boilers. Indians, Chinese, Malays, West Indians, West Africans, Arabs and Somalis were prepared to do these insecure but heavy jobs, which involved long and often unpredictable periods away from home, and which nobody else wanted to do. Their world was immortalised in the novels of Joseph Conrad. Some of the seamen who worked for the East India Company and other shipping firms settled in the East End of London or other dockland districts, such as Cardiff, where Butetown's multiracial character earned it the nickname of Tiger Bay. By the 1880s a Chinese quarter had been created in Limehouse, centred on just two streets in London's East End. By 1902 it had grown enough for a journalist to coin the nickname 'China Town'. Work on ships or in the docks was all that was available there until 1901, when the first Chinese laundry was opened. Within 30 years Britain had over 800 such laundries.

Many more immigrants came from the continent of Europe. In 1901 the population of England and Wales included 49,133 Germans, 20,467 French and 20,332 Italians. The major textile centres, especially Manchester and Bradford, had long attracted German businessmen, and since the introduction of compulsory military service in Germany in 1871, young men had emigrated and set themselves up as pork butchers in English towns. The French were also well established, but the number of Italians had doubled since 1891. They were found especially in London, where a part of Clerkenwell was dubbed 'Little Italy', but also in other large cities such as Manchester. Paul di Felice's study of Ancoats, Manchester's 'Little Italy', shows how the community grew from 600 in 1891 to 2000 by the First World War. They came from rural Liguria in north-west Italy or from Caserta, south-west of Rome, to live in an industrial district of poor housing, inadequate sanitation and cramped living conditions. Oral history has revealed the importance of family and kinship ties and the role of the *padroni* who provided accommodation in lodging houses and employment by hiring out barrel organs, then ice-cream carts, on a daily basis. These memories are confirmed by the 1881 and 1891 census returns which show the *padroni* owning lodging houses and lodgers working as ice-cream vendors or organ grinders. By 1901 most of the Italian community lived in their own houses and worked at other jobs, but they never forgot the exploitation of their fellow-countrymen. The oral tradition also recalled the importance of the casual, but skilled work of terrazzo floor laying, a trade that was never mentioned in the census returns.

The importance of family and neighbourhood links and the role of the church in ensuring daily survival when immigrants first arrived are evident too among the Irish. The total number of Irish immigrants to England, Wales and Scotland may eventually have reached 1 million. They formed by far the largest group of immigrants in Victoria's reign, though by the end of the century their numbers were declining. In the wake of the famine, the 1861 census had recorded 601,634 Irish-born people in England and Wales, but by 1901 the number had fallen to 426,565 (or 13.1 per 1,000 of the total population) and by 1911 to 375,325. Of course, these figures take no account of the large, but unquantifiable number of children born to Irish parents after they had settled on the mainland. Very many families can now claim at least one Irish ancestor. The scale of emigration from Ireland to America and mainland Britain during the second half of the nineteenth century was such that by 1901 the population of Ireland had dropped to slightly under 4.5 million, about half the size it had reached in 1851.

The favoured destinations of Irish immigrants were London, Liverpool and Glasgow. They formed an insignificant element of the population in the agricultural counties, except perhaps at harvest time. In 1901 nearly two-fifths (163,569) of those born in Ireland were enumerated in Lancashire and Cheshire. Most of the rest were found in London (60,211) and its surrounding four counties (33,850), Yorkshire (39,145), Northumberland, Durham and Cumberland (38,480) and Hampshire (13,430, many of whom were soldiers or sailors). These 12 counties accounted for 82 per cent of the Irish born. Liverpool (45,673), the first stop across the

Irish Sea, was second only to London as the most popular destination. In 1901 8,624 Irish-born inhabitants were enumerated in the Scotland Parliamentary Division of Liverpool alone. Irish quarters such as this were often sub-divided into neighbourhoods where the inhabitants came from the same parts of Ireland. The other popular destinations were within easy travelling distance of Liverpool: Manchester and Salford had 28,194 inhabitants who had been born in Ireland, Leeds 6,443, Bootle 5,857 and Birkenhead 5,306.

The 1881 census returns for York illustrate the way in which migrants still stuck together many years after they had arrived. Proceeding along Walmgate, in the poor north-eastern part of the city, the enumerator turned from number 114 into a yard called Johnson's Buildings, then after number 116 he entered Turner's Yard. The 17 households in these two yards contained 76 people. Fourteen of the heads of household had been born in Ireland and the other three possessed distinctive Irish surnames: Antony Garvy, aged 50, born in Knaresborough; James Kelly, aged 29, born in Manchester; and Edward Boyne, aged 25, born in York. As the sons and daughters in these yards had commonly been born in York, up to 25 years previously, it is clear that most of these Irish families had been in the city for some time. Only one child (aged nine) had been born in Ireland. If we look at all 76 people in these two yards, we find that 27 of them had been born in Ireland, including 11 in Mayo, 4 in Galway, and 1 each in Donegal, Roscommon and Sligo; the rest gave just 'Ireland' as their place of birth. Most, if not all, had emigrated from a group of counties, centred on Mayo, in western central Ireland. Thirty-five of the younger ones had been born in York, 9 in other parts of Yorkshire and 4 elsewhere. The most surprising piece of information to come from this small sample is that 23 of the 32 men worked as agricultural labourers, a job that must have involved a long walk to work beyond the city walls. Another man was an agricultural drainer, 4 were general labourers, 2 were hawkers, 1 was a tinner and the other gave no occupation. The few recorded female occupations included 2 servants, a housekeeper, a charwoman, a hawker, and a labourer in the fields. This last was Kate Conlin, a 29-year-old married woman with a daughter, who had been born in Mayo. Twenty years later, Seebohm Rowntree commented on York's Irish population: 'Of those who remain, many find work as general labourers, while some of the women pick up more or less precarious livelihoods by working in the fields outside the city, often tramping out for miles in the early morning to their work. On summer evenings it is a common sight to see the women in the Irish quarter sitting on the kerbstone outside their cottages, smoking clay pipes.'

The London Irishmen worked in the docks, as porters at Covent Garden and at other semi-skilled and unskilled trades. Elsewhere, they found employment as labourers in heavy industry or as hawkers. The

The 1881 census returns for York illustrate the way in which migrants still stuck together many years after they had arrived.

women sought domestic or laundry work or jobs in the Lancashire cotton mills. Irish families inhabited the worst slums of Victorian England. The rat-infested Irish ghetto by the London docks was notorious even by East End standards. The immigrants faced a hostile reception, for not only were they poor and unskilled, they had a reputation for drunkenness and fighting and at first were widely regarded as inferior colonials who were members of the Roman Catholic church. By the end of the nineteenth century, however, even the poorest Irish had become generally accepted as part of the wider working class. Instead, popular indignation had turned against the immigrant Russian Jews.

The number of Scottish-born immigrants to England and Wales had increased steadily from census to census and by 1901 had reached 316,838. Their distribution followed closely that of the Irish, though naturally more were found in the Border counties. London and its four surrounding counties contained 93,191 people who had been born in Scotland; Northumberland, Cumberland and Durham 68,908; Lancashire and Cheshire 66,165; Yorkshire 24,094 and Hampshire 9,973. These 12 counties accounted for 83 per cent of the Scots. Like the Irish, they were not attracted to the agricultural counties, for work was not on offer there. Apart from London, they headed for Liverpool (16,998), Manchester and Salford (10,508) and the four northern towns of Newcastle-upon-Tyne, Gateshead, Sunderland and South Shields (nearly 24,000).

Britain was widely seen not only as a land of economic opportunity but also as a liberal place that welcomed refugees. That policy came under increasing strain in the last two decades of the nineteenth century when thousands of poor Jews fled the Russian Empire under the threat of Tsar Alexander III's pogroms. Small groups of Sephardic and Ashkenazic Jews had long been settled in a few English towns, but now they were heavily outnumbered by the refugees who came mainly from Russia and Poland, but also from other western parts of the Russian Empire, stretching from the Black Sea to the Baltic. The 1901 census enumerated 61,789 natives of Russia and 21,055 from Russian Poland who had settled in the East End of London, Manchester, Leeds and other large cities. By 1911 London had 68,420 Russian Jews, Manchester had about 30,000 and Leeds some 20,000. Like all groups of immigrants, they lived together in well-defined quarters. The Leylands district of Leeds was already 85 per cent Jewish by the late 1880s. Only a narrow range of jobs was available to the first generation of settlers, usually in the clothing trade, cabinet making, boot making and the retailing of cheap goods. A lot of them spent many years in 'sweated workshops' run by the more enterprising of their fellow immigrants, some of whom rose from humble beginnings to prosperity. Famously, Marks & Spencer trace their origins to

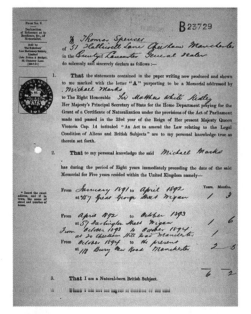

The Home Office record of Michael Marks' declaration of residence, 1896. Thomas Spencer, his business partner, supported his claim that he had lived at various addresses in Lancashire over the past six years.

Russian Jewish Immigrants
A temporary shelter for poor Jews in the East End of London, provided by their fellow immigrants. These men were probably recent arrivals.

the Penny Bazaar that Michael Marks established in the covered market at Leeds in 1884. In Manchester, the community leaders became merchants, manufacturers and professional men who played an important role in the development of the city and university, but the poor Jews had to work in the needle trade, especially in the Cheetham Hill district to the north of the city centre. In London, it became the ambition of every aspiring Jew to get out of the East End to live in Golders Green.

The report on the 1901 census noted that the most popular occupations for male foreigners were those of tailor, clothier, sailor, waiter, cabinet maker, upholsterer, furniture dealer, French polisher, boot, shoe and slipper maker, commercial or business clerk, domestic or indoor servant, maker of or dealer in bread, biscuits, cake, jam preserves, etc., costermonger, hawker, street seller, hairdresser, wigmaker, musician, music master, worker in theatre, cook (not domestic), butcher, meat salesman and slaughterer. The most popular occupations for female foreigners were domestic indoor servant, tailoress, clothier, teacher, milliner, dressmaker, staymaker, shirtmaker and machinist.

In 1901 the East End of London, especially the borough of Stepney, was home to 53,537 Russian Jews. Natives of Russia and Russian Poland had formed 42 per cent of foreigners in Stepney in 1881, but this proportion rose steeply to 68 per cent in 1891 and to 77 per cent in 1901. Of the 28,999 male European foreigners who lived in the borough, 24,363 had found employment; of this number 9,152, or nearly two-fifths, were tailors and clothiers, 2,806 were boot and shoe makers, 1,378 were cabinet makers, 761 were makers of hats and caps, 709 were sailors, 669 were engaged in tobacco manufacture, and 633 were costermongers or hawkers. The proportion of all foreigners to the total population in London reached 30 per 1,000, the highest in the country at county level, but within London, in the borough of Stepney, the proportion rose from 57 per 1,000 in 1881 to 113 in 1891 and 182 in 1901. The proportion of foreigners to the native population was also high in five other metropolitan boroughs. In Holborn (where over one-third of the foreigners were Italians) it reached 96 per 1,000, in the City of Westminster 65 per 1,000, in St Marylebone 42, in Bethnal Green 36 and in St Pancras 35. In the large provincial towns foreigners numbered 22 per 1,000 in Manchester, 21 in Tynemouth, between 13 and 18 per 1,000 in Cardiff, South Shields, Leeds, Grimsby, Kingston-upon-Hull, Liverpool and Bournemouth, and a little above 10 per 1,000 in Hornsey, Swansea and Willesden. The proportion of foreigners to the general population therefore exceeded 10 per 1,000 in only 12 provincial towns and 6 metropolitan boroughs.

By 1901 the population of the borough of Stepney had reached 298,600. A third of these inhabitants were living in overcrowded conditions. In one part – the civil parish of St George in the East – the figure rose to 45 per cent. Whereas the average number of persons per acre for the whole of London was 61, in the borough of Stepney it was 169, while in three of its constituent parishes – St George in the East, Mile End New Town and Spitalfields – it rose to 201, 308 and 328, respectively. The *Report of the Royal Commission on Alien Immigration*, a body appointed in March 1902, primarily to 'inquire into the character and extent of the evils which are attributed to the unrestricted immigration of Aliens, especially in the Metropolis', concluded 'that the greatest evils produced by the presence of the Alien Immigrants here are the overcrowding caused by them in certain districts of London, and the consequent displacement of the native population'. The problem was confined to the East End of London and certain parts of the larger provincial towns. The strong tendency of alien immigrants to settle in certain localities is shown by the fact that 48 per cent of the total foreign population in England and Wales were resident in six metropolitan boroughs and in the three cities of Manchester, Liverpool and Leeds.

The findings of the 1904 report on the 1901 census informed the political debate on the desirability of restricting immigration. It was widely agreed that, for the first time, controls must be imposed. In 1905 the Conservative government passed the Aliens Act, which restricted entry into the country of Jews from the Russian Empire. The Conservatives were supported by both the Liberals and by Trades Unionists, who feared job losses and who were appalled by the sweated labour that the immigrants had to endure.

Mobility and Stability

The bulk of the population led local lives and never met a foreign immigrant. Although they could now move quickly and cheaply by train to other parts of the country, most people remained within the same districts that their ancestors had occupied over the centuries. The great majority of

Although they could now move quickly and cheaply by train to other parts of the country, most people remained within the same districts that their ancestors had occupied over the centuries.

English and Welsh people never visited London. Neither of my grand-
fathers ever ventured beyond Yorkshire and Lancashire and my father got
to London only once. Personal mobility was, as yet, unaffected by the
invention of the motor car. In *Mobility and Migration in Britain since the
Eighteenth Century* (1998) Colin Pooley and Jean Turnbull have analysed
the movements that were recorded in the family histories of 1,388 amateur
historians. They found that, altogether, 16,091 individuals born between
1750 and 1930 made 73,864 moves to new homes, but the great majority
did not travel far. People were prepared to move frequently, but on the
whole they travelled only short distances within the neighbourhood that
they had known well since they were children. The immigrants who
boosted the populations of Victorian towns and cities were drawn mainly
from the surrounding areas. Only London attracted people from far and
wide. This ancient pattern of movement changed little over time, despite
improvements in communications and growing affluence. Pooley and
Turnbull have calculated that mean average migration distances were
around 22 miles until about 1880, but that they then increased steadily to
around 35 miles in the first part of the twentieth century. All over Britain
the trends were essentially similar. The authors conclude that long-
distance moves, in all periods of time, were of minor importance when we
consider the population at large.

We have already noted the local origins of the population of Ridgmont
(Bedfordshire) in late-Victorian times. Most of the inhabitants of the
Chatsworth Park estate village of Edensor had the same characteristics.
Fourteen of the 27 male heads of household in 1881 had been born in
Edensor itself and 7 others came from nearby Derbyshire villages. The
female population had similar origins: 12 had been born in Edensor,
another 19 came from Derbyshire villages and 18 came from further
afield, though none of the latter shared the same birthplace. The core
population was local in origin, but plenty of individuals had come from
afar to work on important jobs on the estate.

The Shropshire parish of Myddle is celebrated for the remarkable history that was written in 1701–2 by one of its inhabitants, Richard Gough.
It is clear from Gough's account, and from a study of the parish register
and other local records, that he and his neighbours felt a strong sense of
identity with their parish but that they moved within the wider 'country' of
north Shropshire, bounded by the market towns of Shrewsbury, Ellesmere
and Wem. Two hundred years later, the 1901 census returns reveal exactly
the same picture. Thirty-five of the 135 male heads of household had been
born in Myddle parish and another 76 had been born in neighbouring
parts of north Shropshire. In other words, 82.2 per cent of male householders came from the local parishes that Gough had known so well. Only
one man had crossed the Severn from south Shropshire and very few
had come from beyond the adjoining counties. The parishes of north

Shropshire still formed a remarkably cohesive local society at the end of the Victorian era.

The distribution patterns of surnames recorded in the civil registration death certificates of the 1840s and the census returns of 1881 show that the centuries-old tendency for families to remain close to their origins was not overturned by the industrial and population upheavals of the Victorian age. Every county in England still had its collection of distinctive surnames, which were rarely found beyond its borders, and most of these names, especially those that were of single-family origin, were concentrated in particular parts of their native counties. Generally speaking, their bearers had not moved far from the homes of their ancestors, unless they had plucked up their roots to try their fortunes in London or across the oceans.

A small sample of rare surnames, taken from the civil registration death registers for England and Wales in 1901, shows that family names were beginning to spread further afield but that the highest numbers were still found in or near the districts where they were formed back in the middle ages. Whereas over three-quarters of the Rounds had lived in the modern county of the West Midlands in 1842–46 and half had been registered in Dudley alone, in 1901 only 31 of the 69 deaths occurred in the West Midlands and only 10 were recorded in Dudley; a further 22 had moved to the industrial parts of Yorkshire and Lancashire and the rest were scattered thinly elsewhere. The Earps, however, another family with a single ancestor, were still found chiefly in the Black Country or not many miles away. Some of the Eardleys and Wedgwoods had moved away from their original homes in north Staffordshire, but most had remained within the registration districts of Wolstanton, Newcastle-under-Lyme and Stoke-on-Trent, close to the hamlets from which these names were derived. The Shaftoes and Harbottles of Northumberland and the Arscotts, Guppys and Luscombes of Devon shared the same tendency to remain in their native districts. Twenty-five of the 33 Luscombes who died in 1901 were registered in Devon, for example. Meanwhile, surnames such as Argent, Aylett, Death and Nice were still associated with Essex and Suffolk, though London had proved irresistible to some. The distribution patterns of these and many other family names were not radically different at the end of Victoria's reign from what they had been at the beginning.

The residential persistence of core families such as the bearers of these surnames helps to explain why local societies retained their own customs and their distinctive ways of speaking. Even today, a person's speech often places him or her in a particular district, though now it is simply a matter of accent and not of a local dialect that is incomprehensible to outsiders. Commonwealth immigrants have learned to speak like their neighbours, just as newcomers have always done. People used to refer to the neighbourhood to which they felt that they belonged as their 'country'. This old usage was still familiar to Victorian novelists such as George Eliot and Thomas Hardy, and it survives in the name of the Black Country and in district names such as Hallamshire and the Potteries. The local societies that made up the numerous 'countries' of England and Wales were intensely localised in their outlook and connections. This was as true of the urban world of Arnold Bennett's 'Five Towns' as it was of Hardy's 'Wessex' or the neighbourhood of Eastwood (Nottinghamshire) in D. H. Lawrence's first novel, *The White Peacock* (1911). Old attachments to particular places and to wider districts remained strong.

This feeling of belonging to a local society was found in the poorest urban districts as much as in the older communities of the countryside. In his memoir of *The Classic Slum* Robert Roberts described his particular part of Salford as 'our village'. During the first quarter of the twentieth century 'the population of our village remained generally immobile: the constant shifts of near-by country folk into industrial towns had almost ceased', but even so the population was still growing. He thought that people stayed put because they had to work, their kin were all around them, they had a certain social standing in their community which might be lost if they moved away, and they feared change. The urban working classes were not very mobile before electric trams provided transport that cost half as much as the old horse trams and were over twice as fast. At the turn of the century cheap travel became available for the first time. One could go three-quarters of a mile for ¼d. and more than two miles for 1d. The electric trams broke down the old ingrained parochialism. Previously, urban women had rarely moved beyond their immediate district, but now

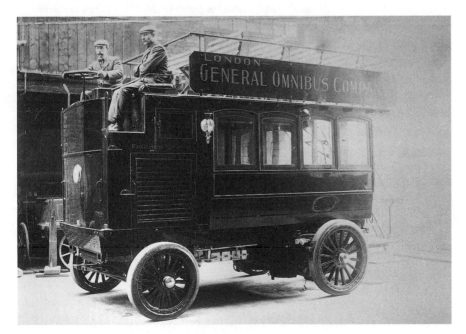

A London General Omnibus
One of the improved methods of public transport that drove the horse-drawn omnibuses out of business. Transport improvements in the late Victorian and Edwardian period allowed people to live further away from their place of work.

*M*anchester spent £1.5 million on 140 miles of track and 400 tramcars, and by 1903 the city's horse-drawn trams had disappeared.

they could get to municipal parks or the city centre. Manchester spent £1.5 million on 140 miles of track and 400 tramcars, and by 1903 the city's horse-drawn trams had disappeared.

Some of the working-class suburbs of London had become stable communities by the middle of Victoria's reign. The recorded birthplaces of the inhabitants of 101–139 Gossett Street (which we shall return to later) show that by 1881 Bethnal Green was a settled local society. Not only had most of the children been born locally, but so had their parents. Foreign surnames were strikingly absent. The men had been born in Bethnal Green (15), City of London (4), Spitalfields (3), Shoreditch, Mile End New Town, Pentonville and Lambeth, together with four immigrants from Warwick, Cambridge, Norwich and Blakeney. The women had been born in Bethnal Green (17), City of London (3), Spitalfields (2), Shoreditch, St Luke's, Kensington, Greenwich, Lambeth and Bishopsgate, with only three from beyond London: from Plaistow (Essex), Norwich and Somerset. The inhabitants of Gossett Street had moved no further during their lifetimes than had the average families in the English and Welsh countryside.

The male heads of household in numbers 74 to 134 Provost Street, a short distance away, had been born overwhelmingly in Shoreditch (12) or in neighbouring parts of north or north-east London: Clerkenwell (4), St Luke's (4), Islington (3), St Pancras (3), City (2), Blackfriars (2), Holborn, Stoke Newington, Bethnal Green, St Giles, Whitechapel and Finsbury. Another four had been born in Southwark, Peckham, Chelsea and Staines, and four more had been born further afield. The other men (not including sons) were just as local in origin: Shoreditch (3), St Luke's (3), Hoxton, St Pancras, Bloomsbury, and two hotel workers who had been born in Chelsea and Nottingham. Strong evidence of the local origins of most of the adult women (excluding daughters) is provided by their birthplaces: Shoreditch (12), St Luke's (10), Bethnal Green (2), Clerkenwell (2), St Pancras (2), Cripplegate (2), Holborn, St George East, St Andrew's, City, Westminster, Islington, Tottenham Court Road, Holloway, Paddington, Blackwall and Lambeth (2). In all, 42 women had been born in London and 10 had started life beyond the metropolis. The people in Provost Street formed a very settled 'local' society.

Charles Booth was well aware of the stability of some of London's working-class communities. He observed that,

> In many districts the people are always on the move; they shift from one part of it to another like 'fish in a river' … On the whole, however, the people usually do not go far, and often cling from generation to generation to one vicinity, almost as if the set of streets which lie there were an isolated country village.

But not all of London's suburbs were like this. In 1881 Gillespie Terrace formed a part of Upper Holloway that was a new settlement which had attracted families from far and wide. Only 9 of the 20 male heads of house-holds in the terrace and in the adjoining part of Gillespie Road had been born in London; two in Islington, and the rest in Holloway, Marylebone, St Pancras, Hoxton, Kensington, Paddington and Norwood. The other 11 came from Bristol, Brixham, Torquay, Llandaff, Mornington and Sandford in the west, Horsmonden (Kent), Buntingford and Baldock (Hertford-shire), and further north from Stamford and from Weir (Durham). Eight other men (not including sons and nephews) had been born in Islington, Colchester, Cambridge, Bedford, Oxford, Bristol (2) and Torquay. Eigh-teen of the 30 birthplaces of females other than daughters were in London: Islington (5), St Luke's (3), Marylebone (2), Hackney (2), and St Pancras, Newington, Clerkenwell, Fulham, Chelsea and Norwood. The rest came from Binchley, Farnsham and Hartford (Kent), Nine Elms and Esher (Surrey), Chelmsford, Bedford, Brighton, Somerset (2), Hereford-shire and Edinburgh. On the whole, the women had travelled shorter dis-tances than the men.

New industrial communities in other parts of the country were also attracting outsiders. In 1801 Middlesbrough contained just 4 houses and 25 inhabitants, but by 1901 its population had soared to 91,302. Migrants had travelled long distances to find employment in the iron and steel works. The 1871 census revealed that nearly half of the town's population had been born outside Yorkshire, including 3,622 Irish, 1,531 Welsh, 1,169 from the West Midlands and about 600 who were born overseas. By contrast, Sheffield and other old industrial centres continued to draw upon their traditional catchment areas for most of their workforce, though they too were now attracting immigrants from more distant parts of the country. Across the Pennines, the new chemical industries on Mersey-side created towns such as Widnes and St Helens that were largely popu-lated by immigrants, whereas the cotton towns of central and eastern Lancashire were inhabited mostly by people whose surnames betrayed their local origins.

Miners were traditionally the most mobile group of workers, men who were prepared to move right across the country, though by the end of the nineteenth century most mining families had usually settled once large collieries mining deep seams offered regular employment. New pits beyond the old 'exposed' coalfields had to bring in outsiders at first. Between 1891 and 1894, for example, the Bolsover Colliery Company built a model village for its workers, complete with allotments, a co-operative piggery, a village green, schools, institute, a Methodist chapel, orphanage, co-operative stores and space for cricket, bowls, tennis and football. New Bolsover was a self-contained community set apart from the old town, down the slope below the castle.

The 1901 census enumerators' books provide a vivid picture of this new community. The first houses to be recorded were those of the colliery

View in Corporation Road, Middlesbrough.

Middlesbrough in 1903
A view along Corporation Road of a town whose population had grown from 25 inhabitants in 1801 to 91,302 in 1901. Immigrants flocked to this new Teesside settlement from far afield in search of employment in the iron and steel works.

company's secretary and cashier, the school master, the mechanical engineer, a teacher and her housekeeper, the colliery book keeper (who also acted as the local preacher), the colliery clerk, the under manager, and the farm bailiff. A few other clerks, the co-operative stores manager, the butcher, saddler, carpenter, joiner, two blacksmiths, two horse keepers, drayman, gardener and two labourers lived in the village, but nearly every other head of household worked down the mine or at the pit head. They included 6 deputies, a foreman, 7 men who worked and maintained the stationary engines, a plate layer, 2 lamp men and 78 miners, 8 of whom were 'contractors' in charge of small teams of hewers and 'stallmen'. If we add the 71 sons and boarders to the 119 heads of households, we see how New Bolsover was totally dependent on the colliery. One hundred men worked at the coal face, 22 boys were pony drivers, and another 37 worked on haulage and servicing the mine.

Where had all these people come from? The recorded birthplaces of both men and women show that on the whole they had not travelled far. The great majority had been born within 15 miles of Bolsover, in the towns, villages and hamlets of the Derbyshire, Nottinghamshire and south Yorkshire coalfields. Fifty-three of the male householders had been born in Derbyshire, 31 just over the border in Nottinghamshire and 10 in south Yorkshire. Another 6 had moved from Staffordshire and 3 from Leicestershire, both mining districts, and the rest had come in ones and twos from further afield. The birthplaces of the wives followed the same pattern. Seventy-nine per cent of the men and 87 per cent of the women had been born in Derbyshire, Nottinghamshire and south Yorkshire, within easy travelling distance of New Bolsover. The places where their children had been born show that these families had been prepared to move around the coalfields in search of work, but this movement was hardly different in scale from that of farm workers and other labouring groups. The coalfield was their 'country'.

As coal production soared, foreign competition and exhausted seams brought about a catastrophic decline in the mining of copper, tin and lead and the migration of workers to other parts of the country or to a new life overseas. For example, between 1861 and 1911 Wensleydale lost 5,769 people through out-migration and Swaledale lost 5,541. More than one-third of these losses occurred during the single decade, 1881–91, when the fortunes of the lead industry reached a new low point. Reeth school lost over half the children on its register in 1882 and by 1891 over a quarter of all houses in Swaledale and 10 per cent of those in Wensleydale stood empty. A few Dales people migrated overseas, but most settled in the nearest industrial towns. Christine Hallas has used the 1871 census returns to identify 36 people born in Wensleydale or Swaledale who were living in two streets just across the Pennines in Burnley. Nearby Brierfield was another favoured destination, from as early as the 1820s, for it was an accessible coal mining and textile district that offered familiar employment for more than one member of a family. The experience of these migrants demonstrates the importance of locality links, the significance of letters home, reports in the local press, and the influence of family and friends who had gone before. The Dales migrants formed several groups from different levels of society, who left for different reasons and went their separate ways. The number of Dales people living in Brierfield increased from 62 to 248 between 1851 and 1871. They were a recognisable group who formed a substantial section of the membership of Brooklands Chapel, Burnley. But by 1891 their numbers had declined to 88, and there is no knowing where they went. The support of kin and friends had been vitally important only in the short term. More people left the Dales in the 1890s when younger sons of farmers settled near Liverpool as cow keepers. They were part of a general drift of the rural population to the towns.

The Wakefields: a Lincolnshire Family

Wakefield, a medieval market town and centre of a huge lordship in the West Riding of Yorkshire, is the source of the surname of many different families who migrated far and wide in the middle ages. Several households of Wakefields were well-established in Lincolnshire by the seventeenth century. Two hundred years later, one family were publicans and farmers in the little village of Oasby in the parish of Heydour on the fertile soils that overlie the oolitic limestone belt, half-way between Grantham and Sleaford. Many of Lincolnshire's fine medieval churches, whose distinctive and elegant spires soar high above the villages, are built of oolite from the famous quarries at Ancaster, five miles to the north of Oasby. The houses in Heydour parish were constructed with stones obtained from local quarries. This is a quiet part of England, with gentle scenery and small settlements whose Viking place-names end in -by and -thorpe, a mixed farming district untouched by industry.

During the eighteenth century Lincolnshire had been a prosperous county for both farmers and labourers. The farmers were mostly tenants-at-will of the great landlords, but their rents were low and farms continued in the same families for generations. The Earl of Yarborough boasted that he did not get tenants in Lincolnshire, he bred them. The absolute size of the labour force grew until the mid-nineteenth century, but the squires and farmers of 'closed' villages deliberately controlled population levels to keep down the poor-rates. Twenty-six Lincolnshire 'closed' villages declined in population between 1801 and 1851, but at the same time 21 market towns and 158 'open' rural parishes doubled in size. After the parliamentary enclosure of open-fields and commons and the transformation of the landscape with neat hawthorn hedges, labourers lost their cows and their common rights to become an agricultural proletariat. Many were faced with the extra expense and fatigue of having to walk long distances to and from work on the large farms in the 'closed' villages. The rise in the county's population figures from 1851 to 1901 masks the shrinking of many rural settlements as the agricultural depression hit the region hard. From the 1870s the rural population was in decline virtually everywhere in the East Midlands. Small owners survived in the fens and marshes, but with the spread of new fodder crops, especially turnips and artificial grasses, sheep farming in the uplands was hit hard and many small farmers were driven out of business when corn prices fell because of American competition. Migration beyond the county's boundaries to Sheffield, Nottingham or London, facilitated by the railways, became increasingly common during the second half of the nineteenth century.

Oasby and Heydour lie in the midst of a group of small parishes that stretch from Grantham to Sleaford, the two market towns on either side of the limestone belt. This distinctive neighbourhood, or 'country', extends from the River Witham and the Great North Road in the west towards the Roman Car Dyke in the former fen to the east. The Roman Ermine Street heads northwards along the limestone from Bourne towards Lincoln, just to the west of Oasby. Until 1917 much of the land in and around Heydour parish was owned by the Houblons of Culverthorpe Hall, the descendants of a famous family of bankers of French extraction. Sir John Houblon (1652–1712), who is portrayed on the £50 note with his house in Threadneedle Street, was the first governor of the Bank of England in 1694, Lord Mayor of the City of London in 1695, and Lord of the Admiralty, 1694–99. His brother, Sir James, was deputy governor of the bank and MP for the City, 1698–1700. The combined population of Aunsby parish, Culverthorpe chapelry and Heydour parish (including the hamlets of Oasby and Aisby), within the district dominated by the Houblons, rose steadily from 253 in 1801 to a peak of 516 in 1851, then just as steadily it declined to 316 in 1901. The quiet, unspoiled appearance of the local countryside is largely the result of outward migration in the second half of the nineteenth century as people sought employment elsewhere.

How did the Wakefield family fare at this time? The first member to settle in Oasby was Thomas Wakefield (1805–73), who had been born in Sleaford. His wife, Mary Fisher (c. 1808–89), came from Ropsley, a few miles south of Oasby, where the Fishers were and still are a well-established local farming family. Their eldest sons, George and Thomas, were born at Aunsby in 1833 and 1835 and their two girls, Mary Ann and Fanny, were born at Culverthorpe in 1838 and 1840, but the next boy, John, was born at Oasby, in 1843. In the 1851 census return for Oasby, Thomas was described as a publican and farmer; also listed were his wife, his daughters Mary Ann (13) and Fanny (11), and his sons, John (8), William (2) and Fisher (8 months), together with a female servant, aged 20, and two male agricultural servants, aged 30 and 11. George (17) and Thomas

(15) were not at home, but were presumably farm servants in nearby villages. George eventually moved to London to work as a coachman and groom, so he must have learned to work with horses as a boy. Thomas was back with his parents, working as a butcher in 1861; upon his marriage he lived in a thatched cottage three doors away, where he was eventually succeeded by his bachelor son, another Thomas. The pub was named the *Red Lion* in White's *Lincolnshire Directory* in 1856, but by 1881 it bore its present name of *The Houblon Arms* in deference to the squire.

A sample of households in the 1881 census returns for Oasby, Heydour and Aisby reveals that nearly all the 32 male heads were born locally: 6 in Oasby, 5 in Aisby, 2 each in Aunsby, Braceby and Culverthorpe, 9 in other villages between, in, or just beyond Sleaford and Grantham, and 2 from a little further south. This identification with the neighbourhood or 'country' on the limestone belt between the two market towns is made all the more remarkable by the contrast with the figures of authority who had been brought into the district by the Houblons. The other four heads of households were a farm bailiff from Nottinghamshire and the vicar, curate and organist who came from Middlesex, Yorkshire and Essex, respectively.

The same pattern is observable when we look at the birthplaces of the women, ranging from widows to servants, but excluding daughters. The geographical distribution was slightly wider, but was concentrated in the same neighbourhood. The pattern for male farm servants was similar, for in both cases the great majority were born in the Grantham-Sleaford neighbourhood. Four came from scattered places to the south and five from further north, but even they had not ventured far. Hardly anyone came from west of the Great North Road or from the fen edge to the east. Lincoln, Newark, Bourne and Stamford were focal points for different 'countries', not for the parishioners of Heydour. The Victorian population was overwhelmingly local in origin.

The vicar's family were a race apart. At the vicarage in Heydour the census enumerator listed Gordon Deedes (66), vicar, born Willingale (Essex), widower; his daughters, Agnes (36) and Isabella (31), his son, Arthur (Oxford undergraduate; 20), all of whom had been born in Willingale; a cook from Westminster, a parlour maid from the Isle of Wight, and a gardener from Hertfordshire; only the housemaid (aged 21) was born locally, at Pinchbeck. Next door, perhaps brought there by the vicar, lived William Craxford (31), a blind organist, born in Aldgate, London, with his wife Rose (32), born at Umballa, East Indies, and their five children, aged five months to six years, all born in Heydour. The curate came from Kildwick (Yorkshire).

The occupations of the other 29 male heads of households included a farmer of 300 acres, a farmer of 70 acres and the Wakefields; the farm bailiff, a butcher and grazier, a tailor, boot maker, joiner, carpenter, stone quarry man, blacksmith, and carrier; 15 agricultural labourers and 2

A sample of households in the 1881 census returns for Oasby, Heydour and Aisby reveals that nearly all the 32 male heads were born locally…

cottagers. The other males (excluding sons) who were recorded in the census comprised 13 farm servants, 6 agricultural labourers, a general labourer, a shepherd, a gardener, a journeyman blacksmith, and 3 annuitants. A large part of the local population were farmworkers with no land of their own, except their gardens. The women and older girls (excluding daughters) included 7 domestic or general servants, 2 housemaids, a parlour maid, a dairy maid, a housekeeper, a 'help', a charwoman, a laundress, a nurse, a schoolmistress, 3 annuitants, a boarder, an 87-year-old 'visitor' on parish relief, and Mary Wakefield, 'farmer and innkeeper'.

A family gravestone just inside Heydour churchyard records the deaths of Thomas Wakefield (68) and Mary (82), their daughter, Mary Ann (21) and their fourth son, William, 'Who Died on Board the Steamship Morocco, April 22nd 1877, Aged 28 years, Interred in the Cemetery Gibraltar', an unlikely ending for a Lincolnshire publican and farmer's boy. The other son, John, disappeared from local records. Perhaps he followed his brother George to London, for a J.M. Wakefield witnessed the marriage of George's son there in 1902. The youngest son, Fisher, stayed at home and inherited the pub and farm. In 1881 *The Houblon Arms* was tenanted by his mother, Mary, aged 73; Fisher was a 30-year-old 'farmer's son' farming 60 acres. With them lived two male farm servants (aged 66 and 13), two male agricultural labourers described as lodgers (58 and 53), and a female general servant (32). Different circumstances produced different household structures. By 1891 Mary had died and Fisher was married with two young children; living with them were his wife's widowed mother (80), a male farm servant (26) and a female general servant (18).

The sale of a large part of the Culverthorpe estate (2,170 acres) belonging to Major H.L. Archer Houblon in 1917 included:

> The Village Inn known as The Houblon Arms situate in Oasby, together with the Buildings, Stockyard, Garden and Paddock, 1a.0r.38p. Tenant Mr Fisher Wakefield. Vacant possession 7 April 1919. £650. The House is Stone Built and Tiled, and contains Bar, Private Sitting Room, Cellar, Old Bar, Tap Room, Scullery, and Six Bedrooms, Wash House, Coal House, etc. The Buildings are quite a useful and convenient lot comprising Trap House, Cow House for Three, Two-stall Stable, Two Loose Boxes, Two-bay Wagon Hovel, Cart House, Stable for Three, Chaff House, Barn, Granary, Calf House, and Crewyard with Tiled Shelter and Piggeries.

The photograph in the sale catalogue shows that the inn has not been altered greatly since that time, though it now has a new roof and the windows have been replaced in similar style. The interior retains much of the original appearance. Fisher Wakefield is remembered as a well-to-do farmer, who eventually retired to Paddock Cottage in Oasby, where his granddaughter, Nora, lives with her husband. Fisher and Mary Ann's gravestone stands behind Heydour's fine medieval church on the opposite side of the churchyard to that of his parents.

Thomas and Mary Wakefield's eldest son, George (1833–1904), had left home to work as a farm servant by 1851. Somehow he must have heard that a country lad who could work farm horses might earn a living as a coachman for a rich family in west London. Getting there would have been easy, for the Great Northern Railway had a station at Grantham on its main line to King's Cross. He was described as 'coachman' when he married Thurza Evans at Marylebone parish church in the summer of 1871. The births of their daughters (both named after their mother, for the first one died as an infant) were registered at St George, Hanover Square and in 1877 the family were living at 23 Brooks Mews. This house has been altered almost out of recognition, but enough survives to suggest that they lived above the coach house and stable. A mew was originally a cage for hawks, but after the Royal Mews at Charing Cross had been converted into stabling for horses and housing for coaches the name changed its meaning. As grand new houses were built in London's West End, nearby mews were erected in much the same way as later rows of garages were provided for the motor cars that replaced the horse-drawn coaches and carriages.

By the time their son, William, was born in 1879, George and Thurza had moved to 3 McLeods Mews, South Kensington. The first few cottages have been demolished but most of the row still curves along the narrow lane to the rear of Emperor Gate. The traditional coachman's home was a simple, two-up, two-down building, one room deep, with a flat roof so that it did not block the light entering the rear of the five-storied houses of the wealthy West Enders. The former coach houses and stables have been converted into garages and extra living space and 'Mews' has become a chic word much favoured by estate agents, but in Victorian times such streets would have had a workaday appearance. McLeods Mews was first recorded in 1873, only a few years before the 1881 census return. George was away from home on census night (and was not recorded elsewhere), but the enumerator wrote his name before he crossed it out and began the entry with Thurza. McLeods Mews, Osten Mews and Pennant Mews stood at the rear of Cornwall Gardens and other large houses to the north of Cromwell Road, the homes of Members of Parliament, magistrates, barristers and people 'of independent means'. Thirteen of the 52 cottages in these mews were uninhabited, perhaps because this new district was not yet fully settled or because census night was on 3 April, too soon for the London 'season'. Thirty-two heads of household were coachmen, one was a groom, one an ostler, and another a livery stable keeper. The most colourful character in Osten Mews was Georgina Caunter, a 37-year-old woman, born by St Paul's Cathedral, who described her occupation as 'horse training for riding (hunts)' and who lived with her young daughter, a nurse, and two grooms. The other three cottages were occupied by the families of a house painter and a pianoforte porter, and by an old man who

The Wakefield Family
Wedding of William
Wakefield and Jenny Bull,
1902. Next to William is his
father, George Wakefield, who
moved from Lincolnshire to
become a coachman in
London. William's elder sister,
Thurza, stands behind him.

lived next door to his son. The mews must have echoed to a babble of
dialects, for the coachmen came from many different parts of the country:
Berkshire, Buckinghamshire, Derbyshire, Devon, Essex, Gloucestershire,
Hampshire, Herefordshire, Hertfordshire, Kent, Lincolnshire, Norfolk,
Nottinghamshire, Oxfordshire, Shropshire, Somerset, Surrey, Sussex,
Scotland, Wales and various parts of London. George Wakefield was the
only one from Lincolnshire.

   The Wakefields proved difficult to trace in London, for they moved
several times, but a clue was provided by William's wedding photograph in
1902, which included his father but not his mother. Working backwards in
the civil registration indexes at the Family Records Centre, I discovered
that Thurza had died at St George's Hospital in 1895 from the shock of
extensive burns at a fire in her home (since demolished) at 53 Blantyre
Street, Chelsea. The coroner's inquest failed to establish the cause of the
fire. I then found the Wakefields were living at the same address four
years earlier, at the time of the 1891 census. This provided the vital clue
that George had been born at Aunsby, Lincolnshire. In 1901 he and his
daughter were still living in Blantyre Street, but the following year George
moved to his son's new home in Balham, near Tooting Common. There, he
died in 1904, aged 70, a 'coachman (domestic)'. The cause of death was
given as 'Gangrene of foot. Paralysis and Exhaustion'. Was this caused
by diabetes, we wonder? William worked as a builder and decorator all
his life and as far as we know never visited his ancestors' home in
Lincolnshire.

CHAPTER FOUR

VICTORIAN AND EDWARDIAN HOUSES

Country Houses and Fashionable Suburbs

THE VICTORIAN AND EDWARDIAN aristocracy had a stock of very old properties, ranging from medieval castles and Tudor manor houses to country mansions built in a Baroque or Palladian style, to which they retreated when the London 'season' and foreign holidays came to an end. The Duke of Rutland returned to Belvoir Castle, which, like the castles at Alnwick, Arundel and Windsor, had been 'restored' on the grandest scale, or to the genuine medieval and sixteenth-century architecture of Haddon Hall, while Earl Fitzwilliam had the choice of his vast Palladian mansion at Wentworth Woodhouse, the updated Rockingham Castle or smaller properties elsewhere when his family tired of their town house in Grosvenor Square. Many more new country houses had been built in the second and third quarters of the nineteenth century, often with new money from industry and commerce, but this burst of activity peaked in the 1870s before the agricultural depression and death duties bit deep into landed fortunes. Few aristocrats were able to build country mansions on the scale of their Georgian and Victorian predecessors after 1900, but the Edwardian years were notable for the number of smaller country houses that were designed for the more prosperous of the middle classes.

Few aristocrats were able to build country mansions on the scale of their Georgian and Victorian predecessors after 1900...

The nineteenth century had seen a great revival of ancient styles, ranging from the Gothic that was favoured by church builders to Tudor or Elizabethan houses that incorporated tall chimneys, mullioned windows, timbered gables and huge fireplaces. Victorian country houses were extraordinarily varied in appearance, for architectural fashions changed quickly and both clients and designers were deliberately eclectic in their choice of styles. Simple labels cannot be applied with conviction. The enormous Eaton Hall (Cheshire) that Alfred Waterhouse remodelled for the Duke of Westminster in the 1870s used a free mixture of Gothic forms in its arches, windows, steeply-pitched roofs and great clock tower. It had a passing resemblance to the new town hall that Waterhouse had just completed in Manchester. The house and grounds were run by 50 indoor servants and 40 gardeners. The Duke of Westminster, who died in 1899, was very conscious of the duties that he believed went with his position as

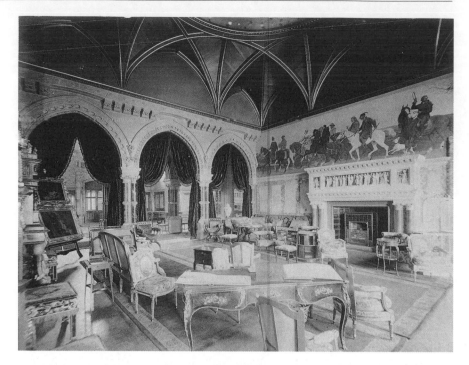

a great landlord. He devoted much of his time and spent a large part of his vast income on charitable causes, his park was always kept open to the public and during his lifetime he built 48 farmhouses, 360 cottages, 8 schools, 7 village halls and 3 churches for his tenants.

Eaton Hall came at the end of an era, for by the 1870s Gothic was going out of fashion as the favoured style of country house building. Instead, an 'Old English' style using traditional vernacular forms such as half timbering, tall Tudor chimneys, casement windows with small leaded panes, sturdy beams and decorative plasterwork was combined with the new technology that had become available: electric and gas lighting; central heating radiators filled with steam, hot air or hot water; lifts for goods and luggage; and plumbing systems that provided hot and cold water in wash basins and baths, and water closets that could be flushed. Appropriately enough, this new technology was used at Cragside, the country house built for the wealthy Tyneside industrialist, Lord Armstrong, between 1869 and 1884, to the designs of Norman Shaw, the most gifted of the architects who used the new Arts and Crafts style. Cragside had electric lights, telephones, a hydraulic passenger lift, a hydraulically-turned spit in the kitchen, a laboratory and a telescope. Its famous grounds, carved from the surrounding moorlands, were provided with lakes and bridges and planted with millions of trees and rhododendrons. This 'palace of a modern magician' was visited by a succession of notables, ranging from the Prince and Princess of Wales, the Shah of Persia, the Crown Prince of Afghanistan and the King of Spain to various Japanese and Chinese war-lords. Norman Shaw's Bryanston House, near Blandford Forum (1889–94), Philip Webb's house at Standen, near East Grinstead (1892–94), and Edwin Lutyens's Deanery Gardens at Sonning (Berkshire), which he designed in 1901 for Edward Hudson, the owner of *Country House* magazine, were other beacons for the attractive, comfortable, irregularly picturesque homes that were designed by the leading Arts and Crafts architects. This quintessentially English movement, together with the 'Queen Anne revival' of a classical style of architecture in the 1880s and 1890s and a passion for English Baroque in public buildings, replaced Gothic and gave the English little time for Art Nouveau.

Middle-class businessmen too built houses in the countryside, once railways had provided easy access from the cities where they worked. In the Peak District they erected solid stone houses like Losehill Hall and Thornbridge Hall, set in spacious grounds, and in south-east England they clad their brick and timber buildings with hung tiles. Some owners cherished their privacy and hid their homes away down long private drives; others chose to display their wealth on prominent hillsides. Surviving examples have mostly been converted into country hotels, nursing homes, educational buildings or prestigious company headquarters.

Most middle-class families, however, built their villas in the suburbs. When our largest Victorian towns became commercial and entertainment centres, the middle classes stopped living over their offices and shops and moved away from the smoke and the slums. They walked to work or rode on horse-drawn omnibuses or the railways from suburbs that were no more than two or three miles distant from the city centres. Late-Victorian and Edwardian Ordnance Survey maps show that, before the widespread use of the motor car, towns and cities had not spread far into the countryside. Before the arrival of cheap mass transport in the 1890s, the largest English towns had become socially segregated, with the working-classes living close to their places of work and the middle classes residing in leafy suburbs far from the smoke, dirt and noise. The wealthy went in for Italianate or mock-Tudor villas set back in large gardens and half-hidden by imported trees, flowering shrubs and Virginia creepers, but most villas were plain, commodious houses, decorated only with barge-boards and repetitive ornamental surrounds to door lintels. The individual architectural qualities of each house mattered less than the quality of the design of the whole estate. The most successful, such as Roundhay (Leeds) and Edgerton (Huddersfield), allowed for individual privacy within a picturesque whole.

Only the wealthiest families bought their own homes; most were content to pay rent to the speculative builders who had put up a few houses or had chanced their arm with a new estate. A residential district that was deliberately aimed at the lower middle class has survived relatively untouched at Muswell Hill in north London. Movement out of central

Muswell Hill
View of the Grand Avenue about 1905. Muswell Hill was a new north London suburb for business and professional families.

London had been facilitated by rising real wages, shorter working hours and the lower fares charged by overhead and underground railways and horse-drawn omnibuses and trams. At the end of the nineteenth century London still had nearly a quarter of a million horses pulling road vehicles of all kinds; some 80,000 pulled omnibuses and trams. The omnibus stand that was erected at Muswell Hill in 1902 is still a prominent central feature, now used as a bus park and traffic roundabout. The transformation of the small rural village beyond the northern limit of Greater London into a middle-class residential suburb began in 1897, when James Edmondson, a developer whose firm had already built extensively in north London, began to build a middle-class suburb with central 'shopping parades' and residential 'avenues' of substantial terraced houses. The Collins family and other builders soon added more houses in an Arts and Crafts Free Style that combined classical forms with details from the vernacular tradition. The mellow brick houses were given stone dressings, ornate pargetting, bay windows, porches, little balconies, small-paned upper windows, and decorative wooden features picked out in white paint. Much thought was given to the appearance of street corners, where the buildings were turned and sometimes given turrets. The spacious rooms of the houses were often as attractive as the exteriors. Muswell Hill's appealing mixture of town and country was enhanced in 1900 when the adjoining Alexandra Park and other nearby rural amenities such as the woods on the southern side of the new settlement were acquired for public use. Muswell Hill was a 'respectable' place with five churches, where sedate behaviour was expected. Although some of the inhabitants earned a living by providing local services, the new suburb was essentially a residential district for people with good jobs in central London. Manual workers were conspicuously absent.

The 1901 census enumerators' books record the varied occupations of the business and professional people who had recently moved into their new homes and the names of the domestic servants that they employed. Some of the new inhabitants of Muswell Hill were 'living on their own means' and a few had retired, but most of the men must have travelled to the City every working day. They included barristers, solicitors, accountants, auctioneers, surveyors, company secretaries, brokers and underwriters, numerous clerks who worked in banking, commerce, insurance or the law, a great variety of merchants, agents or wholesalers who sold cotton, silk, cutlery, cigars, colonial produce, paper, leather or corn seed, and a few manufacturers who specialised in lamps, mantles, horse hair and patent medicines. Their neighbours included clergymen, doctors, engineers, architects, photographers, journalists, publishers, builders and shopkeepers. This was indeed a very respectable suburb.

Working-Class Urban Housing

Although the housing conditions endured by the majority of Queen Victoria's subjects seem deplorable to us, they undoubtedly improved during the course of her long reign. The Public Health Acts and the determined application of local by-laws made a great deal of difference to sanitation and building construction, while smaller families and rising wages towards the end of the century meant increased space and more money to spend on comforts. Statistical information that was gathered every 10 years by the census officials proves that during the reign of Victoria overcrowding gradually became a less serious problem, though it remained bad enough at the end of the century. At the census taken in 1901 the number of inhabited houses in England and Wales amounted to 6,260,852, an increase of 809,355, or 14.87 per cent, over the previous 10 years. Not since the 1830s had the rate of building increased so quickly. A further 448,932 houses were returned as uninhabited on census night (a rise of 20.6 per cent since 1891) and another 61,909 as under construction. The 1901 census was the first to record whether uninhabited houses were in fact normally occupied. It turned out that only 189,137, or 42.1 per cent, were used as homes, for many of the 'uninhabited' houses in towns were simply 'lock up' shops. Only in the countryside could the rise in 'unoccupied' houses be explained by a temporary lack of inhabitants caused by migration.

Defining a house was not as straightforward a task as it might appear. The 1904 report noted that 'the satisfactory definition of what constitutes a house has … baffled successive generations of census authorities, and the census returns have from time to time abundantly proved that overseers and enumerators have not always been one-minded in their interpretation of such definitions as have been devised for their guidance'. The report

At the census taken in 1901 the number of inhabited houses in England and Wales amounted to 6,260,852, an increase of 809,355, or 14.87 per cent, over the previous 10 years.

lamented that, 'Unfortunately, there is no trustworthy record of the size and capacity of houses at different periods.' The available statistics were of sufficient quality, however, to show that during the nineteenth century the number of persons to a house had fallen and the size of houses had increased. Housing standards had certainly improved, even if they left much to be desired. The average number of persons to a house in 1901 was 5.4 in urban districts and 4.6 in the countryside. The numbers differed widely from town to town; from as low as 4.12 in Rochdale, 4.21 in Halifax, 4.25 in Huddersfield, 4.34 in Great Yarmouth, 4.36 in Bradford and 4.39 in Stockport to 7.93 in London, 8.01 in Gateshead, 8.03 in Newcastle-upon-Tyne, 8.12 in South Shields and 8.83 in Devonport. Theoretically, these figures might indicate much smaller houses in Rochdale than in Devonport rather than overcrowding, but the statistics for tenements suggest that overcrowding was indeed still a major problem in some industrial cities and towns.

The recorded number of tenements, or separate occupations (as distinct from houses), in the whole of England and Wales in 1901 was 7,036,868, giving an average of 4.62 persons per tenement or family, against 4.73 in 1891. The proportion of tenements with five or more rooms rose from 47.7 in 1891 to 53.2 in 1901, while the percentage of each class of smaller tenements had declined. One-roomed tenements accounted for 251,667, or 3.6 per cent of all houses, with 507,763 occupants, but the number of one-roomed tenements had dropped by over 35,000 since 1891. All these figures suggest less crowding in the smaller tenements than in earlier times, though the problem was still very real. After examining the data for London, the report concluded that 'from whatever point of view these statistics are regarded it is evident that the London population was unquestionably better housed in 1901 than in 1891, although in many parts of the metropolis obvious overcrowding calls for further action by local sanitary authorities'. In 1911 about 30 per cent of Southwark's population, for example, still lived in one- or two-roomed tenements.

A large proportion of the houses that were inhabited in 1901 can still be viewed on walks through the old working-class districts of our largest towns and cities. Considerable differences in the quality of construction and finish are immediately apparent. By the later years of the nineteenth century new housing was expected to conform to national standards, but many families still lived in old, inferior houses, in grimy terraced rows and courtyard slums. Their two-up, two-down cottages with back yards and narrow alleys had a bleak utilitarian appearance. Although the English enjoyed the highest standard of living in the world at that time, their houses were generally small, and in London 2,000 people slept on the streets each night.

The homes of our ancestors can often be located from the census returns, civil registration records and large-scale Ordnance Survey maps,

Although the English enjoyed the highest standard of living in the world at that time, their houses were generally small, and in London 2,000 people slept on the streets each night.

Children in a Slum Street
A photograph taken in 1905 by James Ramsay MacDonald. The children crowd in the doorway to try to prevent eviction. The house next door may have been boarded up for the same purpose.

especially after the fashion for numbering houses by street spread during the later nineteenth century. It is common, however, to find inconsistencies between one census return and the next where houses were renumbered. I have found the Alan Godfrey versions of the 1893 edition of the 25-inch map of Shoreditch and the 1914 map of Bethnal Green useful in locating some of my wife's ancestors. By then it had long been obvious that London was a class-divided city. Much of the East End was still Dickensian in its squalor. Dickens had placed his fictional thug, Bill Sikes, amid the poverty, dirt, drunkenness and violence of Bethnal Green. On opening the 1893 map of Shoreditch one is struck immediately by the dense crowding of the houses, factories and workshops and the lack of open spaces. Shoreditch had no parks before the Second World War, so the only spaces that were open to the public were the churchyards. The houses had been built mainly in the first half of the nineteenth century for better-off workers such as City clerks, but they had moved out of Shoreditch and their places had been taken by poorer workers and thousands of Irish and other foreign immigrants, who often lived two or more families to a house. Crowded houses meant that people went out for their leisure to the abundant public houses, which provided light, warmth, company and food, as well as drink.

The first serious attempts at improving sanitary and housing conditions had been made in the 1860s, and towards the end of the century the new London County Council cleared the worst slums, notably the one marked by a large blank space on the 1893 O.S. map off Shoreditch High Street. This blank space was the site of the notorious 'Nicholl', which Arthur Morrison gave the fictional name of the 'Jago' in his novel, *A Child of the Jago* (1896): 'A square of 250 yards or less – that was all there was of the Jago. But in that square the human population swarmed in thousands.' The London County Council had demolished this slum and were about to build the Boundary Street estate on the site, but no alternative housing had been provided for the displaced slum-dwellers, so they crowded into other poor houses in the district. Cheap lodging houses and the workhouses remained full, and spectacular drinking bouts, resulting in weekly visits to the pawnbroker or moneylender, were still all too evident, but by the closing years of the nineteenth century Charles Booth thought that the quality of life in Bethnal Green had improved. In general the old roughness was disappearing and the district had a reputation for much lively good humour. Unemployment was low and the area did not have the notorious criminal associations of neighbouring Hoxton. Old photographs of the main streets show large buildings with awnings, under which produce was offered for sale, and swarms of people on the crowded pavements.

The 1893 O. S. map of Shoreditch allows us to plot the streets where members of the Bull family lived. In 1881 James Bull was enumerated as a 32-year-old meat salesman at 368 Bethnal Green Road, where he lived with his cook, Mary Ann Morris, an unmarried servant, aged 50. In a Post Office directory of 1894 James was named as a butcher at the same address. This part of Bethnal Green Road was entirely occupied by shops. The occupations of James Bull and his neighbours, from number 374 down to 356, were described in both the 1881 census and the 1894 directory. By 1894 the greengrocer's shop had become a fishmonger's, the cheesemonger's a grocer's, the eating house an ironmonger's, and the grocer's a boot maker's, but the tripe dresser, baker, oilman, coffee house keeper, and butcher still plied their trades at the same premises.

Henry Bull II (1859–1935) was recorded in the 1881 census as a 21-year-old pork butcher, who lived with his step-father and mother, Thomas and Elizabeth Crump, at 121 Gossett Street, Bethnal Green. The following year, Henry was married with a baby daughter and living in a terraced house in nearby Nelson Street. In 1881 Thomas Crump was a 70-year-old ivory turner and both he and his wife were said to have been born in Bethnal Green. The census enumerators' books of that year reveal a great deal of information about his neighbours from 101 to 139 Gossett Street. Nearly all the various households consisted of parents and children only; just two lodgers and one nephew were recorded. Seven buildings were shared by two households each, and number 115 was divided into three (although it housed only eight people in all, one of them living alone).

The 1881 census enumerators' books provide a great deal of information about the Bulls' neighbours. Sixteen of the 33 buildings from 74 to 134 Provost Street were divided between two households and five more were shared by three families. Of course, the enumerators' books give no indication of the size of the buildings, some of which may have been spacious before they were sub-divided. The stability of the population suggests that overcrowding was nowhere near as bad as it was soon to become in Stepney. Most households in Provost Street consisted of just parents and children. Lodgers were recorded in only 8 of the 59 households, and in-laws hardly at all.

Seebohm Rowntree's survey of York, published in 1901, observed that almost all the inhabitants of the city lived in separate houses or cottages. Practically all these homes were two-storeyed brick dwellings that had neither cellars nor attics. The best were the comfortable houses of the well-to-do artisans in the newer parts of York. These provided accommodation for 1,466 families, or 12 per cent of the workers, in streets up to 35 feet wide. They usually had five rooms and a scullery. Their frontages (which were sometimes adorned with a bow window) ranged from 15 to 17 feet, set behind a little railed-in front garden of about 10 or 12 square yards. Each house had an entrance passage, from which the stairs reared up. A sitting room was positioned in the front, with a kitchen or living room to the rear, leading to the scullery and pantry, and a water closet stood in the small cemented yard at the back. The sitting room, which was used chiefly on Sundays or for receiving visitors, often contained a piano and had a decorated mantelpiece over the fire. Families in such houses spent most of their time in the rear room, where food was cooked in pans placed on a large open grate over a coal fire and bread was baked in the adjacent oven. Floors were covered with linoleum and a large home-made hearth rug. The scullery had a water tap and sink and a 'copper' for washing. Each of these houses had three bedrooms, two with fireplaces, but few had a bathroom. A tin bath in front of the fire had to suffice.

Much more common were the more utilitarian houses occupied by 7,145 families, or 62 per cent of York's working class who earned moderate but regular wages. These houses were, for the most part, four-roomed, set in narrower streets, and dull and dreary in appearance. Many were jerry-built. They lacked the bow windows and front gardens of the homes of the better-off artisans and were on a smaller scale. Many had just two bedrooms and the great majority had an average frontage of only 12ft. 6in. The street door opened straight into the living room, which combined the roles of parlour and kitchen, with an open range and oven around the fire. The tiles or boards that formed the floor were covered with linoleum. A table, two or three chairs, a wooden easy chair, and perhaps a couch

sufficed for furniture, and the walls were papered and decorated with
coloured almanacs and pictures. A door at the rear led to a small scullery, 9
feet by 12, where the sink and copper were fixed. Some houses had a small
pantry in the back yard, near the privy midden. Rents ranged from 6s.6d. a
week down to 4 shillings.

The worst houses of all were found in the poorer districts, which
accommodated 2,949 families or 26 per cent of York's working class.
Although some houses were only slightly inferior to those described above,
many were slum dwellings with only two or three rooms. Set in narrow
streets, their outside walls were dingy in appearance and devoid of architectural relief. Most of these houses had been built before the Public
Health Acts or local by-laws had imposed improved standards. Some stood
in narrow alleys paved with cobbles, others in confined yards with little
sunlight or air, and the back-to-back was a common type of building.
Inside, Rowntree's assistants found a few houses that were kept clean and
tidy, but most were dark, dirty, damp and overcrowded. Broken and dirty
windows were stuffed with rags or pasted over with brown paper, and the
general appearance of dilapidation was made worse by apathy and care-
lessness. In the back yards, where one tap often supplied a large number
of houses, many ashpits overflowed and the shared earth closets were
inadequate and insanitary, while offensive smells permeated the air from
nearby slaughter houses. These were the homes of the struggling poor,
who paid rents as low as 2 shillings a week, rising to 4s.6d. for the better
properties.

York's stock of working-class housing was typical of that found in most
English and Welsh towns. In 1911 Lady Florence Bell, whose team of
social workers had visited over a thousand homes, wrote that most houses
in Middlesbrough had a kitchen or living room that opened straight from
the street, a parlour or bedroom behind, with a little scullery at the back,
and two bedrooms above. She judged these houses to have sufficient space
for parents and 2 or 3 children but that they were woefully inadequate for
the families of 10 or 12 children who were sometimes found there. Most
building was speculative and cheap and even the newest houses were
packed together. On the eve of the First World War, Birmingham had
more than 40,000 back-to-backs, over 40,000 houses without any drainage
or water tap, and nearly 60,000 without a separate lavatory. In parts of
Tyneside houses were notoriously overcrowded. Each town still had its
dreadful slums, but our appalled reaction to them must not blind us to the
fact that the great majority of working-class people were housed adequately by the standards of the time. Respectable working-class families
certainly did not think of themselves as belonging to the same rank of society as the slum dwellers. Although children often slept two, three or more
to a bed, the better working-class houses had a table and chairs in the
living room-cum-kitchen, a wall dresser and some prints, and an open fire

*On the eve of the First World
War, Birmingham had more
than 40,000 back-to-backs, over
40,000 houses without any
drainage or water tap, and
nearly 60,000 without a
separate lavatory.*

and oven range. The parlour contained a sofa, piano, wall engravings, stuffed birds, a mantelpiece with china ornaments framing the clock, lace curtains, and perhaps a potted plant in the window. The pegged rugs made from old garments added cheerful colour when they were newly made. On the walls were printed mottoes, such as 'Bless this House' and 'Home is Best' and even in the worst districts many families struggled to keep their houses clean. Friday night was the time for scouring and personal hygiene, and Saturday morning for scrubbing and colouring the doorstep and cleaning the pavement in front of the house. Women could be seen sitting on upstairs window sills with their backs to the street cleaning the outside of their windows. They spent much of their time washing clothes, scrubbing wood and stones and 'black-leading' their fireplaces.

An advertisement for Bray's gas burners. At the end of Victoria's reign gas lighting was replacing paraffin lamps in urban homes.

The construction of the canals and railways had enabled mass-produced, machine-made bricks of regular size to be moved quickly and cheaply from the large brickfields, such as those in Bedfordshire or Accrington, and roofing slates to be taken from the Welsh quarries to distant parts of Britain. Rows upon rows of terraced houses, built of standard bricks and usually roofed with Welsh blue slates, looked far less attractive than older houses built with local roofing materials and hand-made bricks, whose imperfections added to their beauty, but they were economical. Even middle-class owners who faced the fronts of their houses with stone or stucco often used standard bricks at the sides and rear. The monotonous appearance of brick terraces was often broken by small builders who erected a short row of houses in a style different from neighbouring buildings, sometimes with a different alignment or a lower roof level.

Technology brought other benefits to some. Street lamps powered by electricity were first used in the 1860s and 1870s, then in 1880 Cragside became the first house in the world to be lit by hydro-electric power, using the light bulbs patented by a Newcastle man, Joseph Swan. The first municipal power station was built at Bradford in 1889. Soon, electric lighting became normal in public places such as theatres, but it did not become widely used at home or at work until the 1930s. The greatest advance in domestic technology in the late nineteenth century was the rapid spread of gas cooking and lighting. The slot meters which were widely installed from the 1890s onwards made all the difference. Gas lights replaced sooty paraffin lamps, and gas cookers took over from open fires. Another major improvement was the supply of piped water, though it still had to be heated in pans on the fire or in a fixed container in the kitchen or scullery known as a set pot or copper, which had a coal fire underneath. Friday was bath night in a tin bath in front of the fire, and Monday was the appointed wash day. Most families have handed-down memories of how the washing and boiling of clothes, followed by mangling, drying and ironing were tiring and tedious jobs for the women and girls, made worse by the fashion for white pinafores and thick underclothes. A survey by Manchester City Council in 1918 found that washing for a family of five took 9 hours 20 minutes a week. It was particularly unpleasant in wet weather, when clothes had to be hung to dry on a 'winter hedge' in front of the fire or from clothes lines strung across the ceiling.

By 1914 most houses, except those in remote parts of the countryside, had their own supply of piped water and the majority of dwellings in the larger English towns had their own water closets. In 1911 water closets had been installed in the majority of houses in 85 of the 95 English towns that had a population of over 50,000; in 62 of these towns, over 90 per cent of the houses had water closets. Only in the north-eastern towns of Darlington, Gateshead, South Shields and Stockton did the majority of houses still have privies in the back yard. The rate of conversion had accelerated in recent years; between 1907 and 1911 9,785 privies had been demolished in Sheffield, 7,758 in Bradford and 6,894 in Oldham. The northern towns were beginning to catch up with those further south.

For most working-class families, the best way of finding better housing was to move further out of the city centre and away from the old industrial districts. Cheap and regular transport services, especially those provided by electric trams at the end of the century, enabled men to live beyond the shadow of their place of work. Some London suburbs had provided superior housing for the better-off workers from much earlier in Victoria's reign. An Ordnance Survey map of Highbury and Islington in 1871 shows terraced housing already covering most of the area. By the time that another map was published in 1894 the few remaining spaces had been mostly filled in. The now overcrowded borough of Islington was no longer the genteel suburb that it had once been. Its population had risen enormously from 37,316 in 1831 to 335,238 in 1901, so that Islington then had more people than any other borough in the south of England and more people than either Belfast, Edinburgh or Newcastle-upon-Tyne. By that time, most of the middle classes and many of the better-off artisans had moved further north in search of more desirable accommodation. In the middle years of the century a mixed prison and the construction of the Great Northern Railway line to King's Cross and its massive goods yard had altered the tone of the district adversely. Many families moved only a short distance further out to Upper Holloway, a part of Islington which had been developed from the 1820s, when the first villas and cottages had been built. From the 1870s rows of respectable terraced houses, suitable for artisans and aspiring clerks of the type satirised in *The Diary of a*

Nobody covered most of the available building land there, and the old villas were either redeveloped or put to other uses. By the end of Victoria's reign the area to the north of the railway line had become the local shopping district. Upper Holloway had three tramways and one horse bus depot, but few large industrial sites other than the factory that had been built like a Venetian palace for Stephen's Ink in Gillespie Road in 1892.

In 1881 James Joseph Wilkinson (1848–1934) and his family lived near this factory. He had been born at 1 Hope Street, Holloway, the son of James John Wilkinson, hatter, and Sarah (née Gostick). Both he and his wife lived not far away with her parents at 14 Dorset Street, off Liverpool Road, at the time of their wedding in 1870, when James was a painter. Dorset Street is not marked on the 1894 O.S. map, so it had either been demolished, incorporated into a longer street, or re-named. This is a common problem when trying to locate the home of a Victorian ancestor. By 1881 James and his wife, their five children, and his mother Sarah, lived half-a-mile further north at 11 Gillespie Terrace, the next to last house in the row, but this cannot be located precisely on the 1894 O.S. map either, as it marks only Gillespie Road.

The 1881 census for Gillespie Terrace and a small part of Gillespie Road, as far as the Board School, shows that the houses were often divided between different families. The Wilkinsons shared number 11 with a carpenter, his wife and baby son. Going along the row, numbers 10, 8, 5 and 4 were also each divided into two, and numbers 2, 3 and 6 were each divided into three. Number 7 was not officially divided, but the household consisted of husband, wife, son and two daughters, together with two unmarried lodgers and a married lodger, his wife and baby son. No wonder the census enumerators sometimes got confused as to what exactly a house was. Number 5 was not divided either, but the household consisted of husband and wife, three sons, three daughters, a lodger and a visitor. In this small sample another four females and three males were described as either boarders or lodgers. The typical household was nevertheless that of husband, wife and unmarried children. The only other kin were three nephews and a grandson. By 1925 James Joseph Wilkinson and his family had moved to nearby Conewood Street, near the entrance to the Arsenal football ground. In the will that he made that year, he referred to 'my late trade of house decorator' but described himself as a retired master builder. In an age when so many new buildings were going up, a man could earn a reasonable and regular living in the building trades.

Urban houses in the late nineteenth and early twentieth centuries were largely the creation of speculative builders, many of whom erected only a few at a time, offering different types of house plan to suit the purses of potential customers. H. J. Dyos's classic study of Victorian Camberwell showed how the history of every part of what appeared to be an unintelligible mixture of house types, rows and streets could be fitted together in an intricate pattern of development. Most English and Welsh people rented their houses; working class owner-occupation was common only in a few places, such as the prosperous Lancashire cotton towns. In early twentieth-century Oldham, for instance, nearly a third of the town's 33,000 houses were owned by 'artisan proprietors'. Working-class families in the towns and villages of south Wales were also noted for owning their own homes. By the First World War 46,000 south Wales miners (almost 20 per cent of the workforce) were said to do so. This was an attractive choice by then, for house rents everywhere were rising to meet the cost of improvements.

In the late nineteenth century building societies, especially those of northern towns which have since become household names, such as the Halifax or the Bradford & Bingley, financed large, speculative housing projects. The old system of providing loans to small investors so that they could build their own houses was abandoned in favour of a new policy which enabled the purchase of ready-built houses. Meanwhile, employers continued to build houses for their workers to rent. By 1900 coal owners had replaced mill owners as the principal providers, for mills stood in areas that were already built up, whereas mines were often isolated and new housing was needed to attract a large workforce. The terraced house of either the 'through' or the 'back-to-back' variety remained the usual form of cheap accommodation. The better-quality and well-ventilated 'through' house plans had become standardised to a large degree. The usual type of 'through' on which the Bradford Equitable Building Society gave loans in 1898 included a living-room, a scullery, two to four bedrooms, a cellar, a water closet and an ash-hole. 'Throughs' were built in both rural and urban areas, as densely as possible, wherever land was available, but the number of new 'back-to-backs' declined. By-laws increasingly prohibited their construction, but in Leeds and elsewhere they continued to be built in the early twentieth century. By the 1890s 'back-to-backs' were invariably provided with a basement or cellar, a living room and scullery on the ground floor, two bedrooms on the first floor, and more often than not a third bedroom in the attic. Local by-laws gradually improved the arrangement of back yards and the condition of conveniences, though dreadful slums still disfigured the industrial towns.

The later nineteenth century saw real improvements in the stock of working-class housing. Model by-laws issued by the Local Government Board in 1877 were widely adopted. They recommended that streets over 100 feet in length should be at least 36 feet wide, that each house should have an open space of at least 150 square feet at the rear, and that windows should have an area of at least one-tenth of the floor space. The house styles and street layouts of working-class districts in English towns and cities were largely determined by the rigorous application of such by-laws in the 40 years before the First World War. In Newcastle, for

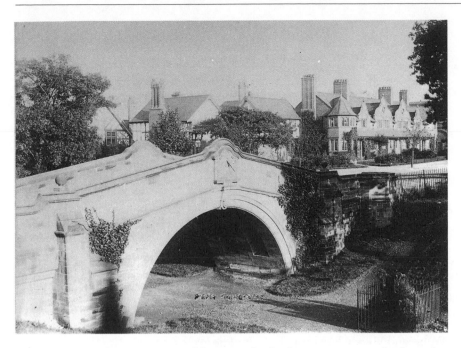

Port Sunlight
The attractive village that William Hesketh Lever built for his workers, featuring Arts and Crafts elements such as Tudor chimneys, Dutch gables, mullioned windows and timber-framed gables.

example, high density terraced housing built about 1900 stretched up the slopes from the riverside industrial belt to the west of the city centre. The drawback was that such estates were unduly monotonous in the rigidity of their street patterns and in the internal layouts of gloomy houses whose frontages were only one room wide. The garden-city movement was soon to react positively to all this.

A small number of model housing schemes provided superior accommodation for lucky workers. Their importance rests on their contribution to national concerns over housing, health and social welfare and their influence on later council housing. Philanthropic owners, motivated by paternalism, evangelicism and altruism, had built workers' villages such as Saltaire and Akroydon in the West Riding much earlier in the nineteenth century to match the rural estate villages of the aristocracy and landed gentry. Other employers took up the challenge in a new way late in Victoria's reign by giving their villages an 'ancient' character. Great attention was paid to the design of rural-type cottages laid out in a spacious setting. In 1888 William Hesketh Lever (later Lord Leverhulme) bought 56 acres of land on which to build a factory and workers' houses in a village he named Port Sunlight. By 1900, 400 houses, with three or four bedrooms, bathrooms and outside water closets, had been completed. The houses were varied in design, including timber-frames and gables, and they were set in small groups among trees and gardens, and provided with allotments and recreation grounds. Port Sunlight set new standards, which a few other enlightened owners soon began to emulate.

An equally famous venture was that begun by the Cadbury family, who in 1878 moved their chocolate business from the centre of industrial Birmingham to the countryside to the south, in the valley of Bournbrook. In 1895 George Cadbury bought 120 acres adjoining the factory to develop the Bournville Estate as a model village. Lord Leverhulme had relished his paternalistic role at Port Sunlight, but the Quaker Cadburys (like the Rowntrees at York and the Clarks at Street) were more restrained in their approach. George Cadbury decided to build for a mixed community, where the proportion of Cadbury workers was less than half. The finest houses, however, were reserved for his key workers. Bournville was centred on The Green, a reconstruction of a traditional village centre, surrounded by public buildings, including a church, a Friends' Meeting House and a school, but not a pub. The houses were made to look like old cottages, distinguished from each other by the varied use of simple elements such as bay windows and porches. Some were given thatched roofs.

A third model village was built shortly afterwards at New Earswick, north of York, close to Rowntree's chocolate factory. The factory owners chose Raymond Unwin's designs, which enabled working-class families to benefit from many of the ideas that Arts and Crafts architects such as Webb and Voysey had brought to middle-class housing. New Earswick was an industrial garden suburb that resembled a rustic village. The houses were constructed in vernacular style, with steeply-pitched tiled roofs combined with a simple, often whitewashed exterior and fairly large windows. A wide frontage allowed a better organisation of living rooms to take advantage of sunlight, and each house had a utility room.

These three schemes were the immediate forerunners of the Garden City Movement, which took town planning in a new direction, and created an environment that was midway between town and country. Industrial buildings were placed on the perimeter of the town and the whole was surrounded by a 'green belt'. The publication of Ebenezer Howard's, *A Peaceful Path to Real Reform* (1898), led to the formation of the Garden City Association in 1899 and four years later to the first scheme at Letchworth (designed by Barry Parker and Raymond Unwin), followed shortly by Welwyn Garden City and Hampstead Garden Suburb. Emphasis was placed on the provision of low-density housing (including three-bedroomed 'cottages' for the working class) in a pleasant environment, with curving streets instead of a grid pattern.

A few local authorities, such as Liverpool in 1869, had obtained local powers to build houses for rent by working-class tenants, but it was the Housing of the Working Classes Act (1890) which authorised local councils to buy and demolish slum property and to replace it with houses built by public subsidies. Shoreditch Boundary Street estate, designed in 1900 by the Architects' Department of London County Council to replace the 'Nicholl', was inspired by Arts and Crafts principles. The first and best of several major slum clearance housing projects, it housed over 5,500 people in red and yellow brick blocks radiating from Arnold Circus. The Housing, Town Planning, Etc. Act (1909) was another important step forward which gave local authorities planning powers over land that they had earmarked for development. However, by 1914 even the most active authorities like London and Liverpool had managed to re-house less than two per cent of their populations. Over Britain as a whole, the 24,000 houses owned by local authorities in 1914 accounted for less than 0.5 per cent of the total housing stock. 'Council estates' were not built in significant numbers until after the First World War.

In 1901 the reality of life for most working-class families was very different from that dreamt of by the builders of model villages and garden suburbs. Improved housing for most families lay a long way ahead. Leeds City Council was one of many that had an appalling record of inaction on slum clearance. At the very bottom of the scale in 1901, the census for England and Wales enumerated 14,219 vagrants living in caravans, tents or in the open air, and in barns and sheds. This group contained four males to every female. Although it was not the hop-picking season, vagrants were far more numerous in Kent than in any other county. Nearly two out of every three were listed in the six counties of Kent, Surrey, Sussex, Essex, the West Riding of Yorkshire and Lancashire.

At the very bottom of the scale in 1901, the census for England and Wales enumerated 14,219 vagrants living in caravans, tents or in the open air, and in barns and sheds.

Rural Housing

The inhabitants of industrial villages were housed in much the same way as urban dwellers. On the whole, they fared better than farmworkers, though they had smoke and grime to put up with and sanitation facilities often remained poor. In the Black Country, for instance, the typical house was two-up and two-down, with neither an entrance hall nor a separate kitchen. In a small yard at the back stood a privy and ash pit and a workshop for making nails, chains, keys or locks. Other houses were built in short terraces with wells or pumps and communal bakehouses. In the West Riding weaving villages, houses and cottages were often arranged around courts and yards, as in the towns, or strung across steep hillsides in terraces that had one or two storeys more on the downward slope than to the rear. They were sturdily built with local stone, but the accommodation was cramped and the amenities were minimal.

The cottages of the Victorian rural poor were the frequent subject of official investigation and of vivid writers on the countryside such as Richard Jefferies and Francis Heath. All were agreed that standards of housing were generally deplorable, except where enlightened landlords had built superior cottages in their estate villages, and that the farmers of the agricultural counties of south-west England offered their labourers the lowest wages and the worst accommodation in the country. The Royal Commission of 1868–69 reported that in Devon some exceptionally good dwellings were found on a few estates, but that most labouring families were housed in overcrowded, two-roomed cottages. They deplored the general want of comfort, bad lighting arrangements and draughtiness caused by warped and badly-hung doors and ill-fitting casements. Canon Girdlestone, the incumbent of Halberton (Devon) who between 1866 and 1872 organised the migration of hundreds of poor labouring families to the better-paid, better-housed, industrial north, told the commissioner that many so-called cottages were ruinous hovels: 'In visiting the sick, I am often obliged to take great care that my legs do not go through the holes in the floor of the sleeping-room to the room below. ... Few cottages have more than two bedrooms; many have only one ... The rooms are small, low and badly ventilated; the drainage is bad ... the outhouses bad, and generally without doors.' The only things that he found satisfactory were the water supply and the gardens. The commissioner observed that the same picture was true in neighbouring counties and commented on the 'deficiency of cottage accommodation throughout the west of England'.

The Royal Commission on Housing (1885) reported that rural conditions varied considerably but that every part of England and Wales had tumble-down cottages with cramped rooms. In Cheshire, Lord Tollemache had recently built 300 excellent cottages, but in most parts of the country little progress had been made. The pretty estate villages that were built in local materials to a uniform style and in spacious surroundings were a credit to their landowners, but many farm labourers spurned the chance to live in relative comfort. The Royal Commission that reported in 1893 found that labourers often preferred to walk miles to work in order to live in villages where the cottages might be worse and rents higher, for they valued their independence and the society of their fellow countrymen. Even beyond the estate villages, however, the tenancy of a cottage was often tied to the job. Tied housing remained common in agriculture long after the practice had declined in industry. By 1900, for example, only about 15 per cent of coal miners lived in tied accommodation.

In 1892 the Royal Commission on Labour looked at cottage accommodation in parts of Berkshire, Buckinghamshire, Herefordshire, Oxfordshire and some other counties and concluded that, 'Cleanliness and tidiness are reasonable in most of the cottages, but it is often impossible to scrub the bedroom floor because the cracks in it let the water through into the sitting room ... The number of privies are being generally increased, though in each place instances occur where one privy is shared by three or four cottages, and in Truro it is a common thing to find a whole row of cottages without any privy accommodation at all.' Cottage furniture generally consisted of a table, a few simple chairs, perhaps a rough wooden dresser for pots and pans, and beds with mattresses stuffed with straw or with chicken feathers. In many districts adequate fuel was hard to find and cooking facilities were rudimentary.

Canon Girdlestone had commented that one of the greatest difficulties of an agricultural labourer's life was the absence of good water. In Dorset, for example, none of the cottages had piped water; instead, water had to be collected in rainfall tubs or taken from streams and ponds. At that time, only the more fortunate households had access to a well or a pump. In the years just after the First World War my mother lived in a farm labourer's cottage on the edge of the Pennines where all the water had to be carried from a distant well. Wash day was looked forward to with even less enthusiasm in such circumstances. Hot water could be obtained only by boiling in pans over an open fire. The dust and soot made by the fire and by paraffin lamps and candles made housework a lot harder. In some rural homes, cast iron ranges were installed, with two ovens on either side of the fire, but many families could not afford to fit them, so open hearths survived well into the twentieth century.

In *British Rural Life and Labour* (1911), Francis Heath looked back on his earlier tour of West Country villages in 1873 and reflected on the improvements that had been made. He remembered that in the past the counties of Devon, Dorset, Somerset and Wiltshire had 'bred a race of peasants notorious as being the worst paid and the worst housed, and the most generally wretched of all the classes engaged in the cultivation of the soil in Great Britain and Ireland and the islands of our seas'. Despite 'the beauty of the country itself, its great fertility, and the prominence and abounding displays of its harvests of all kinds', its farmworkers were paid the lowest wages in England. Entering a Somerset cottage in 1873, he had remarked, 'Unless we had seen it we could scarcely have believed that such a place could exist in England.' It was 21 feet long, 9 feet wide and 10 feet in height to the thatched roof, for it had no upper storey. The ground floor was divided into two equal compartments, each about 9 feet square, one a bedroom, the other a sitting room, with the ground paved irregularly with large stones, joined together with earth in the crevices. A 60-year-old widower had lived there for a quarter of a century; before his time it had housed a large family. A three-roomed cottage in a nearby village was the home of a family of 10. On return visits in 1880, Heath had seen many new cottages of better quality and by 1911 he was convinced that accommodation was generally a little less crowded and more sanitary than before. Overcrowding had been a disgraceful feature of so many rural villages 40 years previously, but he thought that standards had now risen, not because of more enlightened attitudes amongst the landowners but because the rural population had fallen so sharply. He was undoubtedly correct in this conclusion. The vast amount of evidence that had been collected about the poor state of rural housing conditions had led to very little improvement by the end of Victoria's reign, when descriptions of rural slums still

matched those of earlier decades. As late as 1917 the Royal Commission
on the Housing of the Population found lamentable housing conditions in
every part of the countryside.

Ashley Walk, New Forest

The field books of the 1910–11 valuation survey for the Board of Inland
Revenue (which are housed in the Public Record Office under IR 58) are
a rich source of evidence for both rural and urban buildings. The survey of
Ashley Walk, on the western edge of the New Forest, for instance, starts
with an 'old mud and thatch cottage containing two living rooms, three
bedrooms, with a garden and a wood and thatch shed' at Drybrook and
then lists several cottages at Godshill Wood. George Bryant had an old
mud and slate cottage, which consisted of a living room and pantry on the
ground floor and two bedrooms on the first floor; his piggeries were his
only outbuildings. Henry Bryant lived in another mud and thatch cottage
nearby, with two living rooms on the ground floor and two bedrooms
above; a pantry had been added in 1909, and a wood and thatch lean-to
provided other space. His neighbour, Albert Crook, had a brick and slate
cottage, which on the ground floor contained a kitchen and scullery, and
on the first floor three bedrooms. His outbuildings towards his orchard
consisted of a small brick and wood stable with a thatched roof, a cow pen
and dairy, piggeries, and a lean-to that served as a wood shed. The surveyor noted curtly 'bad settlement otherwise fair repairs'. Not far away,

Albert Wort lived in a brick and slate cottage with an orchard. Above his two living rooms and a pantry were three bedrooms; he also had a small lean-to, a shed and a piggery. The surveyor described Wort's property as 'new house in good condition'.

In the neighbouring hamlet of New Grounds, Godshill, Mrs Bessant's brick and slate cottage contained a living room, a back kitchen and two bedrooms, with a wood shed and a timber rain store. Samuel Bacon's house was made of mud and cement and roofed with thatch. A little sitting room and a wash house occupied the ground floor and two bedrooms (one of them very large) stood above; he also had a mud and thatched stable and a fuel house, cart house and pig sty. Henry Bacon's brick and slate cottage had two rooms on each of the two floors and a wood house constructed of timber and iron. His neighbour, J. Busly, lived in a mud and thatch cottage, with four rooms in fair condition, and he kept his fuel in a brick and tile turf house.

A similar range of domestic accommodation and some slightly larger properties were available not far away at Ogdens. George Busly had an old brick and thatch cottage with a living room and pantry on the ground floor and two bedrooms above; like many of the local cottagers, he had a piggery, a garden and about 24 fruit trees. William Lockyer had about nine acres attached to his 'old mud and thatch cottage and barn'. The ground floor contained a living room, dairy and scullery, and the first floor was occupied by two bedrooms; Lockyer also had a shed, a cart house, a stable and cow pens built of similar materials. Susan Loader's 'old mud and thatch cottage' consisted originally of two bedrooms above a living room and pantry, but in 1909 it had been extended by a concrete lean-to, which contained two living rooms. Her outbuildings included piggeries, cow pens, a mud and thatch stable, two stalls, and a store, all of which the surveyor considered 'very old and in poor repair', and her orchard contained about 80 fruit trees. Her neighbours, J. & H. Curtis, farmed nearly 15 acres and lived in a mud and thatch cottage whose front portion was cased in brick. Four bedrooms occupied the space above two living rooms, a dairy, a pantry and a scullery, and the outbuildings included two timber and slate stalls, cow pens, a cart shed and a barn; about 20 fruit trees grew in the orchard. Finally, George W. Dear, rented nearly 26 acres and lived in superior accommodation, partly built in brick and slate but much of it constructed of mud and roofed with thatch. The ground floor of his house consisted of two living rooms, a pantry and a dairy, and above were four bedrooms. A wash house, piggeries, a stable, a cow pen, two stalls and a cart shed with a loft formed the outbuildings, and about 30 fruit trees grew in the garden.

Many more examples could be quoted. At Godshill, for example, Mrs Susan Chalk's cottage was built of brick, mud and slate, the ground floor contained two living rooms and a pantry and the first floor had three bedrooms. She also had a stable, piggeries, a wood house, a lean-to used as a cow pen, and a cart shed. She had to get her water from the adjoining common, as no doubt did many of her neighbours. We shall return to the cottagers of this district and their dismal standard of living in chapter eight.

CHAPTER FIVE

$\mathscr{E}$ARNING A LIVING

WORK SEEMED a blessing to some but a curse to millions of others. Craftsmen took great pride in their skills, and the coveted positions of head horseman on a farm, or the leader of a team or gang in heavy industry, gave a man dignity and status in his community. But for most people work was a drudgery, a daily toil of long hours for poor pay, a necessary but tedious and tiring way of obtaining a modest income. The curse on Adam – 'In the sweat of thy face shalt thou eat bread' – had a direct meaning and relevance. The working day commonly lasted from 6 am to 5.30 pm, with half-an-hour's breakfast and an hour's break for dinner. The availability of work was a matter of continuous concern for large sections of the workforce. Dockers and many farm labourers were employed on a casual, daily basis and workers in manufacturing industry were victims of cyclical and seasonal fluctuations in the economy. Oral accounts tell how desperate some families were in slack times, particularly in winter, and what hardship was endured when a man fell ill or was injured. When that happened, membership of a friendly society proved beneficial for a while, and some were able to receive payments from institutional or middle-class charities for working people in distress, but the unfortunate or the insouciant had to turn to the poor law guardians with the ultimate threat of the workhouse. The passing of the National Insurance Act by the Liberal government in 1911 was as welcome as was the provision of old age pensions three years earlier in freeing people from this nightmare.

Seebohm Rowntree had noted how working-class families were particularly prone to hardship at certain points of the life cycle and how the wages of the father were often supplemented by those of his wife and children and by the taking in of lodgers. In 1901 he calculated that average total weekly earnings (including payments by lodgers) per working-class family in York came to 32s.8¾d., though many wage packets fell far short of this. Rural wages were much lower, but free rents and various perks must be taken into account. Women's and children's earnings cannot be guessed at from the information recorded in census enumerators' books, but oral accounts insist that, given the opportunity, working-class women were eager to earn extra money from casual employment and to

A Working Gang, 1894
A group of 27 'pick-and-shovel men', under the supervision of Mr Ames, the ganger, pose for the camera in grounds near Sevenoaks, Kent.

get their children to do likewise. As Raphael Samuel wrote about Headington (Oxfordshire), 'No two families made their livelihood in precisely the same way … Earnings were built up higgledy-piggledy rather than by reliance upon a single weekly wage.'

While many families struggled to keep above the poverty line, towards the end of the nineteenth century the majority enjoyed rising living standards. A 'labour aristocracy' of skilled workers earned higher wages than the bulk of the semi-skilled and unskilled workforce. At the same time as real wages rose, allowing families more to spend on consumables, the price of food and raw materials from abroad fell noticeably as Britain benefited from its empire. The reduced cost of sugar, for example, enabled manufacturers with an eye for new markets to make fortunes out of confectionery. In Halifax in 1890 John and Violet Mackintosh started a novel blend of traditional English butterscotch toffee and American caramel and quickly built a profitable business. In Sheffield George Bassett's confectionery business was so successful that he was elected mayor of the borough in 1876; the celebrated Liquorice Allsorts were a new line in 1899. Many other branded foods and what are now regarded as traditional English meals, such as egg-and-bacon breakfasts and fish-and-chips suppers, became common only in the closing years of Victoria's reign.

This rise in working-class standards of living was matched by increased leisure. Normal weekly working hours fell from 60 or 70 in the mid nineteenth century to 53 by 1910, though in certain occupations the working week remained much longer. During the late 1880s and the 1890s the unskilled working classes became better organised and more effective in their demands for higher wages and fewer hours. The London Dock Strike of 1889 ushered in a period of great industrial struggle, including the first national coal miners' strike in 1893. Far fewer strikes occurred during the reign of Edward VII, even though real wages fell as prices rose more quickly than earnings, but a new wave of major strikes broke out in 1910–12 before industrial conflict was brought to an end by the outbreak of the First World War.

During the nineteenth century the typical business organisation was still the family firm. The Staffordshire pottery industry provides a good example, for although it became factory-based it was neither amalgamated into large concerns, nor extensively mechanised. When the Second World War began, more than two-thirds of the firms in the pottery industry still employed fewer than 200 workers. Small firms gloried in their traditional skills and regarded mechanisation as unnecessary, and much work was contracted out to semi-independent workers. The same picture was true of the Sheffield cutlery and tool industries and the metal crafts of the Birmingham and Black Country districts. Even in heavy industry, firms often stuck to a particular line of business. Most of the Lancashire cotton mills, for example, either spun yarn or wove cloth, which in turn was sent to an independent dyer and finisher.

Nevertheless, the rise of steam-powered factories and huge enterprises such as shipbuilding or the manufacture of armaments was a prominent feature of the Victorian age. Company towns and industrial villages were dominated by a mine or a quarry, an ironworks or a textile factory, which was almost the sole place of employment, while the workers' houses and the few public buildings and amenities were often company-owned. Machines, factories and power were the key elements in innovation and the growth of productivity and factory methods became increasingly dominant after 1880 as Britain remained a world leader in industrial production. During the reign of Edward VII the national economy stayed essentially sound and flexible. In 1914 Britain's share of world trade in manufacturing amounted to 31 per cent, the largest in the world.

Many of the country towns also prospered, albeit on a less dramatic scale, during the second half of the nineteenth century. Even if their livestock markets declined, their trades, shops and professional services expanded and their populations grew. Horse-related crafts flourished and

Normal weekly working hours fell from 60 or 70 in the mid nineteenth century to 53 by 1910, though in certain occupations the working week remained much longer.

nearly every country town had a few small industries, such as a brewery or an agricultural engineering works. At Woodstock (Oxfordshire), for example, in 1900 the glove-making firm of R. & J. Pullman employed about 60 people in a factory and 150–200 sewers in the neighbouring villages. Local studies often show that Victorian small towns and villages were far more self-sufficient than their successors. Their peculiar trades, family firms, particular topography, and buildings erected with local materials in the vernacular style gave each of them a distinctive character, which is much more muted nowadays, when every market town has shops with plate-glass windows and garish signs announcing the same household names. In the later years of Victoria's reign many of the old country crafts disappeared in the face of mechanisation, though in every village a core remained. Rural by-employments, such as the plaiting of straw bonnets, the making of leather gloves or the hand cutting of files declined to the level of quaint survivals as machines produced similar goods far more cheaply and much more quickly. Corn milling, that ancient and essential rural industry, changed dramatically in the 1880s, when roller grinding, coupled with a huge rise in wheat imports, led to the construction of giant flour mills in London, Liverpool, Hull and other ports and to the gradual decay of country wind and water mills. The pace of change was far slower in the market towns than in the new industrial districts, but change they did and some appeared vibrant even on market days.

The 1901 Census Returns

Historians have long been attracted by the information on occupations that is provided by census returns. The statistical reports on each census and the enumerators' books for particular places have both been used to good effect. But the information that is recorded in the 'occupation' column is frequently unsatisfactory. It usually takes no account of dual occupations or by-employments, nor of activities carried out at different times of the year, while much of the paid work done by women and children was unrecorded because of its irregular nature. Other contemporary sources, for example directories or wills, sometimes described a person's occupation differently from the census return, and of course some people took on different jobs as they grew older. Even descriptions such as 'agricultural labourer' or 'general domestic servant' disguise the variety of tasks that were performed. When comparing the occupations that were recorded in different censuses, we need to know whether the instructions as to what should be written down had been changed since the previous census. A man who was once described as an agricultural labourer might be returned next time as a shepherd, though he had always looked after sheep. Considerable amounts of editing by government officials were necessary to standardise the occupational entries for the published reports. We should be aware of all these difficulties, but not weighed down by them, for the census returns are a mine of information about how our ancestors earned a living.

The report on the 1901 census noted that the number of occupational headings, which had varied from census to census and had been 347 in 1891, had been augmented to 382. Thus coal and shale miners were, for the first time, separately classed as 'hewers', as 'other workers below ground' or as 'workers above ground'. Those involved in the manufacture of iron and steel were separated as working in 'blast furnaces', in 'puddling furnaces and rolling mills', in 'steel smelting and founding', in 'iron founding' and in the manufacture of specific articles. Jobs in the textile industry were similarly differentiated. This is helpful to family historians in providing more precise details of what an ancestor did for a living.

The 1901 census for England and Wales enumerated 12,134,259 males and 13,189,585 females over the age of 10. Of these, 83.7 per cent of the males and 31.6 per cent of the females gave information about their occupations. The proportion of occupied females was noticeably higher in urban than in rural districts, especially among widows. The highest proportions of females in paid work were generally found in the textile districts of Lancashire (notably in Blackburn), the West Riding of Yorkshire, Cheshire and the East Midlands. No fewer than 13 of the 15 county boroughs in which the proportions of occupied women and girls reached 40 per cent or more were important textile centres, the two exceptions being Bournemouth and Bath, both of which had an unusually high number of domestic servants. The number of persons who were unoccupied or who provided no information about their work amounted to 1,977,283 males and 9,017,834 females. Of these, 287,742 males and 82,777 females were classified as retired or pensioned, but the bulk of the 'retired' who were under the age of 45 and about one-quarter of retired males and one-half of retired females over 45 were inmates of asylums. Clearly, most people kept working as long as they could, usually out of sheer necessity. The absence of a large population of healthy, often prosperous retired people is one of the most marked contrasts between then and now.

The absence of a large population of healthy, often prosperous retired people is one of the most marked contrasts between then and now.

Farming

By the second half of the nineteenth century more English and Welsh people lived in towns than in the countryside. Yet many counties retained their old rural characters and agriculture was still a major employer. Thomas Hardy's great novels about a vanishing way of life were published during the prolonged agricultural depression of the last three decades of the nineteenth century, when cheap, imported American cereals forced many British farmers into bankruptcy. The variety of farming countrysides that Hardy depicted so vividly in the context of 'Wessex' experienced very

mixed fortunes at this time. When Tess left the happiness of Dairyman
Crick's farm in the lush valley of the Piddle, she entered the much harsher
world of Flintcomb-Ash on the chalk downs, where swedes had to be
picked from the flinty soils and trimmed by frost-bitten hands. The
depression was not general across the whole country and some farmers,
especially those in pastoral districts who reared dairy cattle, did well
in those years. The worst effects of the depression were felt in the
corn-growing parts of southern and central England, in Berkshire,
Buckinghamshire, Herefordshire, Hertfordshire, Huntingdonshire,
Northamptonshire, Nottinghamshire, Oxfordshire, Rutland and Surrey.

In 1901 Rider Haggard toured the country, interviewing farmers and
seeing for himself the effects of the depression. In *Rural England*, which
appeared in two large volumes the following year, he reported on each of
the many counties that he had visited. In Cambridgeshire he found that
'where farms are large and corn is chiefly grown, there is little or no prosperity, while where they are small and assisted by pastures or fruit culture,
both owners and tenants are doing fairly well'. Huntingdonshire was
largely a corn county that had 'suffered like all the others where cereals
are grown', but in Northamptonshire 'a certain amount of prosperity' was
evident on the best lands, and Oxfordshire was 'holding its own as well as
most counties'. In Suffolk the owners of land who had no other source of
income were 'practically ruined' and the tenants could only just make a
living, and in Lincolnshire sheep farmers had been made bankrupt
because of the steep fall in the price of wool. The lack of an adequate
labour force was a constant theme wherever he went. Haggard watched
smartly-dressed country girls strolling around Nottingham in an evening
and observed that, 'Everywhere throughout England I have been told that
girls had left the villages.' Having read Rowntree's account of poverty in
York, he was surprised to find that farmers in the surrounding countryside
complained of the lack of labour. 'Surely,' he concluded, 'when such things
can happen there must be something wrong with the state of England.'

As the cornlands diminished, so did the number of people employed
on them. In 1870 England and Wales had about 15 million acres of arable
land, by 1891 the amount had fallen to 12,903,585 acres and by 1901 to
12,118,289 acres. Unbroken pastures now stretched more widely across
the landscape, and beef cattle and dairy cows had displaced wheat as the
mainstays of English farming systems. During the last three decades of the
nineteenth century, the number of cattle rose from 4,361,000 to 5,606,000,
whereas the number of sheep fell from nearly 22 million to just over 19
million. The breeds of cattle were less varied than today; in 1908 it was
estimated that two-thirds of British cows were shorthorns and that the
majority of them were grass-fed. By that time, the worst years of the agricultural depression were over. Grain prices stopped going down in the mid
1890s and from 1908 beef prices started to rise. The survivors breathed a

collective sigh of relief at not having gone under like so many of their neighbours.

By the end of Victoria's reign the amount of land devoted to parks, orchards and managed woods was greater than it had been since time immemorial. The area of deciduous woods and conifer plantations had increased to 1,847,351 acres by 1895 and the number of woodmen reached 12,035 at the next census. Coppices covered 30 per cent of the woodland area, but soon imported soft woods and the impact of the First World War would reduce the ancient practices of coppicing and charcoal burning to rare and quaint survivals. Many of the woods that we know so well had a different appearance up to a hundred years ago, when they had far fewer mature trees and much more underwood that was cut for fences, hurdles, brooms, tool handles, charcoal and numerous other purposes after only a few years' growth. This was the working environment that Thomas Hardy's sad figure of Marty South, who made spars in the woods of Blackmoor Vale, knew so intimately. Other types of countryside favoured different woodland regimes. In the uplands and on other poor soils conifers were planted in regular rows, a practice that was considerably extended after the creation of the Forestry Commission in 1919. The 1901 census also noted a considerable increase in the number of nurserymen, seedmen, florists and gardeners; up 20.5 per cent in the previous 10 years to 216,165.

The number of people who worked on the land in Victorian England and Wales, when horse power and hand tools reigned supreme, seems enormous to us now that one man on a tractor can do so much. The report on the 1901 census commented that agriculture ranked third in numerical importance as an employer in the country as a whole, but that in rural districts more than 30 per cent of all males over the age of 10 worked on the land. Farming remained of vital importance to the national economy, though the number of employees had fallen sharply from its peak of 23.5 per cent of the male workforce in 1851 to 9.5 per cent at the end of the century. In many English and Welsh counties mining and manufacturing now provided far more jobs than did farming. In Northumberland, for example, in 1851 agriculture had employed twice as many workers as coal mining, but by 1901 miners easily outnumbered farmers and farmworkers. The 1904 report on the last census acknowledged that employment had been affected unevenly by the agricultural depression, but noted that the decline in the proportion of males engaged in farming had been general throughout England and Wales. The previous census had counted 224,299 farmers or graziers, compared with the 249,431 recorded 50 years earlier, so the number of holders of farms had not declined materially, but the number of farmworkers had been reduced considerably as machinery became more generally adopted and a steady stream of labourers left the countryside in search of higher wages in the towns or overseas. Fewer than half the farmworkers aged 15–24 in 1891 were still farming 10 years later. In the south of England, many had headed for London to work in breweries, for a gas company, on the railways, or as coachmen.

The 1901 census had asked for greater precision in job description on the farms, so comparisons with earlier returns are not easy to make, but in 1851 the total number of workers on farms (excluding farmers' sons under the age of 15 and female relatives of farmers) had amounted to 1,232,576 males and 143,475 females, and by 1901 this figure had been reduced to 715,138 males and 12,002 females. Another way of looking at it is that in 1851 19 out of every 100 men and boys over the age of 10 had worked on farms, but by 1901 the proportion was only 6 in every 100. In the course of 50 years the number of farmworkers had fallen by 42 per cent. All the counties of England and Wales had experienced a decline, but the 1904 report noted the striking fact that, with the exception of Cornwall and Dorset, the reduction in the agricultural workforce in all the counties south of a line drawn from the Wash to the Severn had exceeded 15 per cent during the last decade. The flight from the land seemed irreversible at the time, but it was stemmed during the Edwardian years. In fact, the 1911 census reported a rise in the number of men who were employed on farms.

The highest rate of decline in female farmworkers in the nineteenth century occurred during the 1890s, when numbers fell by a half. Women had long since ceased to work in the eastern corn fields or on the farms of southern England, but elsewhere some still found employment, much of it seasonal or casual. Census returns give little hint of the vital contributions that women made to household budgets at harvest time, but their activities are well recorded in oral accounts. Their wages were important for settling debts that had been run up over winter when little money was coming in.

Life in the countryside was not the idyll that townspeople often imagined it to be. Maude Davies's sociological survey of Corsley (Wiltshire) in 1905–6 showed that many rural families continued to struggle to earn a sufficient living. Corsley was a populous parish, settled in a series of scattered hamlets, with some market gardening, numerous smallholdings and part-time work off the farms, and every cottage had a fair-sized garden for growing potatoes, onions and green vegetables. Twelve of the 34 farmers had a secondary source of income, such as carting coal and other goods. The parishioners were therefore generally better-off than those of Ridgmont (Bedfordshire). Meat was eaten in all but the poorest households in Corsley at least once or twice a week and daily in most homes. Nevertheless, one-eighth of households, including 29 of the 70 labouring families, lived below the primary poverty line and two-fifths of all children had fallen into this trap.

In pastoral areas characterised by small family farms life was often hard, but the spectre of poverty was dimmer than in the arable districts. In

A Woman's Work on the Farm
A woman with two milk pails photographed in 1905 in a Cornish farmyard near Liskeard. The farmer and his wife had recognised different responsibilities in the smooth running of a farm.

Wales family farms were the usual form of holding, and most labour was recruited from relatives or from resident farm servants hired at the annual fairs. An agricultural community in south-west Wales at the beginning of the twentieth century has been the subject of a thorough study by David Jenkins. In 1901 this south Cardiganshire parish of Troedyraur contained 203 occupied houses, of which 157 had less than 30 acres of land. These were in some measure dependent on the other 46. Thirty to 35 acres was the smallest unit that constituted a farm which was capable of supporting a man and his wife without a regular source of supplementary income. The rearing of store cattle and pigs and the keeping of dairy cows for milk and butter were the mainstay of the farming system, but corn and potatoes were also important. Farmers at this level owned their own equipment and a pair of horses. It took two people to run a farm; the man was in charge of cultivation and general labouring, while his wife was responsible for the farmhouse, the dairy and the farmyard. The sale of eggs, milk and butter produced the money that was needed to run the house. Smaller holdings of 15 to 30 acres were known as 'one horse places', where the farmer had to do other jobs in order to earn sufficient income or to borrow equipment. The smallholders with under 15 acres just kept cows for milk and butter, while the labourers who lived in two-roomed cottages had only a garden to cultivate and were engaged by the day or the week, not by the year (as servants were). Altogether, the parish had 2 mansions, 46 farms, 21 'one-horse places', 66 'cow places' and 70 cottages. Many of the farmhouses had been rebuilt since 1850, so the farming system must have been reasonably profitable.

The 1851 census for England and Wales had shown that the ratio of labourers to all farmers was 3:1 and of labourers to those farmers who were employers 5:1. The term 'agricultural labourer' covered a wide variety of jobs and conditions that varied from region to region. The worst conditions were found in south-west England, especially in Devon, Dorset, Somerset and Wiltshire. Rural discontent was much less evident in the north, where the industrial wages that were on offer pulled up those that were paid to the farm labourer, but even there farm labouring was still one of the worst-paid occupations. By the late nineteenth century the drift from the land was such that farmworkers were in short supply. The remaining ones were thus in a better bargaining position, so their wages rose and employment became more regular. Meanwhile, they benefited from falling prices for food, clothing, drink and tobacco, and their wives had more time to cook and bake. In *Brother to the Ox*, Fred Kitchen, a south Yorkshire farm labourer who was born in 1891, recalled that his father was a cowman on the Earl of Scarbrough's Sandbeck estate, getting 17 shillings a week, a free house and garden, and a quart of new milk each day. 'That was the regular rate of pay in those days,' he wrote; 'we lacked nothing.' In 1902 evidence on the wages and expenditure of labourers was

*R*ural discontent was much less evident in the north, where the industrial wages that were on offer pulled up those that were paid to the farm labourer, but even there farm labouring was still one of the worst-paid occupations.

Hop Picking
A hop farm in Worcestershire, 1896. String and wires fastened to poles made from coppiced wood provide the frames for training hops. The man in the foreground is shown tying string to a wire.

collected by the Board of Trade in a detailed survey by 114 investigators. They reported that the average weekly wage of farmworkers, including all extra earnings, was now 18s.6d, nearly three-quarters of which was spent on food, but that wages were supplemented by a cheap or free cottage, by free fuel and drink, and sometimes by other perks.

Unmarried farm servants, who were contracted for a year and lived on the farm, usually sleeping in one of the outbuildings, were a distant memory in southern England by 1900, but the system was still widely used in the north. At the annual hiring fair, workers stood in the streets with a badge on their coat lapels indicating their skills. Female servants were also hired by the year, for their board and lodging and an agreed wage that was paid at the end of their term. Fred Kitchen, who started his working life as a living-in farm servant at the age of 13, wrote, 'To me it always seemed a wretched business, especially for a lad of 13 or 14, to be taken like a sheep or calf to market and sold to the highest bidder,' Stephen Caunce has described the East Riding practice whereby bonds (which were enforceable by law) were agreed between farmers and workers at the Old Martinmas fairs held on 23 November. Work on the farms was structured in a rigid hierarchy, which varied according to local custom from one part of the country to another. In Suffolk the horsemen were the highest-paid and best-regarded workers, but in the East Riding the horses were cared for and worked by the lads, while the labourers handled whatever jobs needed to be done each day. As the horses were worked from 6 am to 6 pm when light permitted, feeding began at 4.30 to 5 am in summertime. The work of a farm servant was graded according to a lad's age and he could expect to move up a rank each year, usually on a different farm. Most lads did not venture beyond the neighbourhood, or 'country', with which they were familiar, but they were not necessarily wedded to farm work if the chance of a different job arose. Fred Kitchen shifted from farm to railway to pit and back to farm during his early years and ended up as a farm labourer once he was married. Northumberland farm servants differed considerably from those further south, for they could be married or single; the single ones signed on for half a year, and few farm servants lived on the farm. Local customs determined how farm service worked. In some areas these practices survived right up to the Second World War.

In 1900 one-fifth of the British corn harvest was still cut by hand. An enormous demand for casual workers attracted groups of migrants into the countryside at harvest time. In 1908 an estimated 45–65,000 East Enders travelled into Kent, for the hop harvest, on special trains from London Bridge. Farmers throughout England depended upon Irish, and to a much lesser extent Scottish, workers for getting in the hay, corn and potato harvests. Much of this movement is recorded only in oral memories, such as those collected in George Ewart Evans's account of the winter work of young Suffolk farmworkers in the breweries of Burton-upon-Trent. So many children worked in the fields at harvest time that August became a school holiday, and some of us who were children in the 1940s and 1950s still think of the October half-term as 'potato-picking week'.

Textiles

By the end of Victoria's reign, far more people worked in manufacturing and extractive industries than in agriculture. In 1901 a total of 1,155,397 people, including the very large number of 663,222 females, were employed in the making or sale of textile fabrics. The best-paid jobs for women were in weaving, then in winding and 'drawing in', followed by spinning. The worst jobs were the heavy and dirty ones in dyeing. Lower wages for spinners meant that many of them were of Irish Catholic extraction. Because of the heat and the slippery floors women and girls worked bare-footed in calico shifts. They arrived home covered in dust and fluff, dressed in their shawls and clogs. Boys too wore clogs (as I did as a child in the 1940s), but men would not be seen in them unless their job demanded it.

From the middle of the nineteenth century until well into the 1920s cotton was Britain's most important manufacturing industry, regularly employing over half a million people and producing a quarter or more of the country's exports. Britain's share of world cotton goods exports peaked at 82 per cent in 1882–84 and much concern was expressed at the close of the century about the falling off of trade. During the 1890s the number of

In 1901 a total of 1,155,397 people, including the very large number of 663,222 females, were employed in the making or sale of textile fabrics.

A Lancashire Cotton Mill
A man and a boy work in the restricted space among the looms of a cotton mill in Nelson, 1906. At that time, the industry was enjoying a period of prosperity.

cotton workers had dropped and imports of raw cotton had fallen nearly two per cent, but Britain's supremacy remained intact. Cotton was still king and in 1901 a total of 196,898 males and 332,233 females were employed in its manufacture. The mill-building boom of 1904–7 was as dramatic as in any earlier period and in 1913 Britain exported a record 7 billion yards of cotton cloth.

In 1901 no less than 85.1 per cent of the workforce in the cotton mills in England and Wales lived in Lancashire, and the rest were found mainly in neighbouring parts of the West Riding of Yorkshire, Cheshire and Derbyshire. The strongholds were the spinning districts of south Lancashire and Cheshire, in towns such as Oldham, Hyde, Ashton, Bolton, Stockport and Manchester, where the suburbs merged into one huge, red-brick conurbation, whose skylines were dominated by tall mill chimneys bearing the factory names. The mills looked very impressive when lit up at night. Some of the smaller towns and industrial villages beyond the heartland of the cotton industry managed to keep their individual character. Colne, for example, remained a medium-sized cotton town whose terraces ran up to the edges of the Pennine moors. Liverpool continued to prosper as the port and commercial centre for the entire cotton region. Between 1850 and 1913 its imports trebled in value and increased more than three-fold in volume, while its exports grew nearly four-fold in value and five-fold in volume. The cotton trade and the flourishing passenger traffic to the United States of America financed an extraordinary expansion of Liverpool's docks, so that the net registered tonnage of shipping using Liverpool doubled between 1890 and 1914. Lancashire had led the way in the Industrial Revolution and was still the most remarkable example of how a county's character could be changed out of all recognition within a few generations.

The cotton industry was distinguished by the size, machinery and work discipline of its major factories, where long hours were worked under close supervision. The noise generated by the clatter of the looms, carding machines and spinning mules, together with the dust and the fumes, is hard to believe today. It was also unusual in that women and girls over the age of 13 formed over half the workforce throughout the second half of the nineteenth century, and even more in Edwardian times, though by 1907 school attendance regulations had forced the employment of younger children to drop to only 3.2 per cent. These proportions varied considerably from place to place, as did working practices and conditions, for Lancashire's cotton towns were fiercely independent and consciously different from their neighbours. Despite the prominence of some enormous mills, on the eve of the First World War the industry was still characterised by medium-sized firms.

Next in importance to the cotton industry came that of wool and worsted. Here, too, women and girls outnumbered men and boys in tending noisy machines in factories large and small. The workforce had peaked at 242,334 in 1891 and had fallen to 209,740 (87,671 males and 122,069 females) by the turn of the century. The industry was as concentrated in the West Riding of Yorkshire, as cotton was in Lancashire, with 86 per cent of the workforce employed there, but within the riding numbers had fallen in the previous 10 years from 209,735 to 181,004. The economies of mill towns such as Halifax – 'a town of 100 trades' – had become increasingly diversified during the second half of the nineteenth century, though the woollen and worsted industries remained dominant. Textile factories had grown considerably both in size and number as steam replaced water as the source of power. By 1901 a dozen leading firms employed 40 per cent of Halifax's textile employees and for the past 30 years Crossley's workforce had numbered 5,000. Future prospects, however, provoked many anxious thoughts. On 24 August 1897 *The Times* reported that, 'It is in Halifax and the surrounding villages that there are made the serges extensively used for knicker-bockers – a woollen weft and worsted warp. Time was when many important continental countries looked to Halifax for clothing of their men-of-war, but one after another have developed industries of their own. Halifax still supplies to some extent the navies of Turkey and Greece and several of the South American republics, China and Japan.' In 1901, however, Halifax's textile trades still employed 19,342 adults and children (11,668 females and 7,674 males). The industry remained a major employer into the third quarter of the twentieth century.

The hosiery industry employed 48,374 workers in 1901, a slight fall of 1.5 per cent over the past 10 years. This branch of the textile trade was concentrated in the East Midlands, with 79 per cent of the workforce in Leicestershire and Nottinghamshire. Powered machines had replaced the old methods of production since the 1870s, so that by 1890 only five per cent of output came from the surviving 5,000 hand frames in small workshops and cottages. Framework knitters no longer dominated the occupational columns of local parish registers. The county capitals were the centres of the industry, but small towns were also much involved; Hinckley, for example, had 20 factories by 1894. The lace industry was concentrated in much the same area. By 1901 three-quarters of the 36,439 workers lived in and around Nottingham and Derby, where lace was principally made by machinery in factories. There, the workforce had grown continuously since 1871, while the numbers in the hand-trades in Bedfordshire, Buckinghamshire and Northamptonshire had fallen from 23,450 in 1861 to 2,350 40 years later. Meanwhile, the silk industry in its ancient provincial centres of Derby, Macclesfield and Leek had declined, even though factories had begun to replace the numerous workshops in the mid-Victorian period. By 1912 Derby had only two silk manufacturers.

The falling-off of trade in the textile industry during the last decade of the nineteenth century had been almost general, but in the Edwardian era production remained strong and accounted for nearly half of Britain's exports as well as supplying the raw materials for numerous workers in the clothing trades.

Mining and Quarrying

The 1901 census counted 640,989 coal miners in England and Wales, as against 513,843 in 1891 and only 183,389 in 1851.

Britain's industrial revolution had been based on coal, the fuel of manufacturing, transport, gas and households, and one of the country's major exports. The mining industry had grown hugely in scale with the sinking of deep mines in the third quarter of the nineteenth century, starting in Northumberland and Durham but soon spreading to the other coalfields as the railway network made them more competitive. When Victoria came to the throne, only a few mines were worked by more than about 50 men, but as deeper seams were reached, so the workforce had grown in size. By 1900 a typical pit employed well over 300 men and boys. The scale of enterprise had changed, but mining and quarrying remained sweat and muscle jobs with picks and shovels. Though mechanisation had transformed the factories, it made little difference to the collier. Even in the regular seams of Northumberland and Durham, the mechanical cutter was not generally used; in 1913 only six per cent of production in the northeast coalfields came from machines. Men worked in their vests and trousers or just in their drawers in the hottest pits deep below ground. Pads were strapped round the knees to prevent them becoming swollen from the constant bending and kneeling on hard floors or in water, and clogs were often preferred to boots. A lamp fixed in the helmet, a 'Dudley' bottle containing water or cold tea, and a 'snap tin' filled with sandwiches completed the attire. A miner's hours of work were definitely shorter than those usually found in factories and other indoor occupations, but the work was heavier, dirtier and more dangerous. Day-workers at the pithead sometimes fared even worse. Arthur Clayton, who was born in 1901 and who spent his working life down south Yorkshire pits, recalled that the worst job he ever had was the one he started at the age of 13, sorting the coal and removing rubbish from the pithead screens in all weathers. Old photographs show that some collieries employed women at the pithead, but they formed only about five per cent of the surface workers.

The 1901 census counted 640,989 coal miners in England and Wales, as against 513,843 in 1891 and only 183,389 in 1851. This figure included the 52,545 who worked above ground, but not the 7,469 owners and managers. The report commented that the number of miners was then equal to 5.28 per cent of the entire male population over 10 years of age. In several counties the proportion was much higher. Glamorganshire had 104,643 coal miners, Durham 98,876, the West Riding of Yorkshire

Sifting Coal, Wigan Junction Colliery
Women did not work underground but were employed at the unpleasant jobs of screening coal, hauling tubs and loading props at the pit brow. Miners pose in the background.

94,110, Lancashire 87,391, Staffordshire 54,296, Nottinghamshire 42,102, Northumberland 35,937 and Derbyshire 25,780; the other 13 counties where coal was mined each had workforces under 10,000. If we include the large Scottish coalfields, we can see that in Britain as a whole the labour force rose from about 40,000 in 1800 to over 1,127,000 in 1913, by which time coal mining accounted for one in 10 of the entire occupied male population. Numbers peaked at 1,248,000 in 1920. Many of us have coal miners on our family trees.

In mid-Victorian times miners were famously mobile, moving from pit to pit and often travelling long distances to other coalfields. The new settlements that mushroomed in the mining districts recruited young men from all parts of the country. The south Wales landscape was altered beyond recognition as thousands of migrants poured into the industrial valleys in search of jobs in the new, deep mines or the iron and steel works. The Rhondda Valley had less than 1,000 people in 1801, but more than 114,000 a hundred years later. As the population of Wales rose from 587,000 in 1801 to over 2 million in 1901, a new type of community was forged in the valleys that was radically different from the farming neighbourhoods in the rest of Wales. The population grew by another 20 per cent during the coal boom of Edward VII's reign, mostly in Glamorganshire and Monmouthshire. The 1911 census discovered that 58 per cent of the Rhondda Valley miners had been born in Glamorgan, 19 per cent in the rest of Wales and 7 per cent in England, and that many others had come from Ireland and Scotland, and even Spain and Italy.

When the coal mining industry collapsed in the 1980s newspapers were full of accounts of the demise of 'traditional' pit villages that were drab in appearance but famed for the warmth of their community spirit. These villages were, in fact, rarely more than 120 years old, often much less. The great majority had been built to high densities in unimaginative layouts wherever a large body of miners had to be housed quickly and cheaply in rural areas. Bereft of amenities at first, they soon acquired shops, pubs, churches and other public buildings, but they were slow to adopt water closets and, before pithead baths were built, miners had to wash in the family's tin bath in front of the fire. Miners did not always live in new pit villages, of course; some lived in the older, nearby settlements and others were housed in isolated rows in the countryside. By the late nineteenth century, young, unmarried miners were still prepared to try their luck in another coalfield, but the family men had become increasingly reluctant to keep moving. When a married man wanted to change pits, he was far more likely to look for one within reasonable travelling distance of his home. Almost always, one or two other pits could be found nearby.

By the end of the nineteenth century coal mining had come to be dominated by powerful employers, whose heavily capitalised firms and companies worked several collieries and employed large numbers of men. The Powell Duffryn Steam Coal Company, for example, had a labour force of over 10,000 men and an annual output of more than 2 million tons. The workforce was divided into three shifts covering both night and day. At the same time, pit villages became more sharply defined as a unique form of settlement, more settled in their population, and more organised into increasingly militant trade unions, which were amalgamated in 1889 into the Miners' Federation of Great Britain. The different coalfields lost many of their peculiarities as the miners became the country's most numerous and distinctive group of workers.

In the other mining industries, by contrast, the workforce fell dramatically as seams were exhausted or foreign competition proved too powerful. The number of ironstone miners, for example, dropped from a peak of 25,879 in 1881 to 17,008 20 years later. Local Cleveland ores still provided 84 per cent of Teesside's requirements in 1883, but by 1913 the proportion had dropped to 60 per cent because of foreign imports. During the late eighteenth and the nineteenth centuries south-west England had been the world leader in copper and tin production. Copper mining and smelting had declined in the face of competition from Chile, other parts of North and South America and Australia, and during the copper slump of the 1860s over 11,000 miners had lost their jobs. Some had moved to Cornwall's clay pits, some to other British mining districts, and large numbers went overseas to North and South America, South Africa and Australia. By 1901 only 789 men worked the copper mines of England and Wales. The fortunes of the tin industry fluctuated widely during the nineteenth and early-twentieth centuries. In Devon and Cornwall the medieval practice of 'streaming' for tin deposited in valley gravels continued well into modern times, alongside the deep mining of lodes of cassiterite (tin ore). New mining villages such as Pensilva were constructed of terraced rows of drab cottages. The mines were notoriously wet and pumps were essential to keep the water levels down. The ruined, roofless engine houses that stand dramatically on moorland skylines and coastal cliffs survive because they had to be built solidly to house the pumping engines. The tin was then smelted in reverbatory furnaces to produce 'white tin'. The recession in the mining industry in west Cornwall began in 1866, forcing many miners to emigrate, particularly to America. The number employed in the Cornish and Devon tin mines declined from 26,814 in 1873 to 6,577 in 1901. Many important tin mines closed in the 1890s, so that by 1900 only a handful were left. A rapid recovery in the price of tin in 1906, however, led to a revival of mining up to the First World War, but the 1920s saw a severe slump.

Meanwhile, the number of lead miners in England and Wales had fallen from 20,030 in 1851 to 4,375 by the end of the century, and countless women and children who had been employed above ground washing and sorting the ore lost their jobs. Numbers plummeted by 48 per cent in the 1880s as seams became exhausted. In 1851 nearly half of Swaledale's workforce had been employed in the lead industry, but the proportion had fallen to a fifth 40 years later. The township of Melbeck lost nearly half its population in the 1880s and Arkengarthdale lost 44 per cent of its population when its mines failed in the 1890s. Other types of mineral worker whose numbers declined included the salt men of Droitwich (Worcestershire) and the 'Cheshire wiches' – Northwich, Middlewich and Nantwich – and the China clay diggers of Cornwall.

The census figures are at their most unreliable when it comes to counting quarrymen and brickmakers. Raphael Samuel has pointed out that the 1891 census for the whole of Britain recorded only 60,000 quarrymen, yet within four years of the passage of the Quarries Act in 1894, no fewer than 134,478 persons were registered as being in quarrying employment. On the evidence of the mines inspectors themselves, even this figure must have represented only about half the total number of those following some kind of quarry-based employment, for quarrymen were usually something else besides, often farm labourers. Brickfield workers must also have been underestimated by the various census returns, if only because of the time of year they were taken. Most yards in mid-Victorian times were 'summer yards' with only a nucleus of workers who stayed all year round. A large influx of seasonal migrants arrived when the brickmaking season began in April, and in the southern brickfields this was also the chief time of year when women and children were employed. Brickmakers and quarrymen had the reputation of being even more uncertain in their settlement than colliers. In the Black Country and on the Welsh coalfields, however, brick-making was largely in the hands of the women.

The most famous quarries were those of north Wales, the largest slate quarries in the world. Penrhyn employed some 2,800 men, who blasted and hacked the slate from huge galleries in the mountainside. The slate quarries and mines at Llanberis and Blaenau Ffestiniog were also major enterprises. Others worked in 50 or more smaller mines and quarries scattered over the hillsides of Caernarvonshire and Merioneth. In the last quarter of the nineteenth century the total workforce in north Wales fluctuated between some 13,000 and 15,000 employees. The industry made enormous fortunes for a few families and dominated the lives of many of the communities of Welsh-speaking north Wales. Welsh blue slates were sent far and wide as a durable and economical roofing material.

Metalworking and Engineering

The ingenious and complex machines and the great variety of manufactured consumer goods that were displayed to admiring visitors at the Great Exhibition of 1851 showed just how rapidly and triumphantly this sector of the British economy had advanced in recent years. Britain's proud, but justified, boast throughout the reigns of Victoria and Edward was that it was the workshop of the world. Incredible quantities of finished goods and of tools to service foreign industries were exported from the metalworking districts to distant parts of the globe. In 1870 the Sheffield cutlery firm of Joseph Rodgers & Son, for example, employed 1,200 workers and had offices and warehouses in London, New York, Montreal, Toronto, New Orleans, Havana, Bombay and Calcutta. By 1901 the manufacture of metals, machines and implements provided jobs for 934,379 males and 54,540 females in England and Wales, a total workforce of nearly 1 million.

By 1901 the manufacture of metals, machines and implements provided jobs for 934,379 males and 54,540 females in England and Wales, a total workforce of nearly 1 million.

Many of these workers were in highly skilled trades, such as the making of surgical instruments, while others, like the nailmakers, had jobs that were repetitive and simple. Skilled or not, most of the craftsmen in the secondary metal trades worked in small- or medium-sized workshops and cluttered smithies in either Hallamshire or the Black Country. Although machine methods were increasingly applied, the old hand skills of the forgers, grinders and assemblers were still prized in the making of the most prestigious articles. Even so, the workshops of the Cradley Heath chainmakers or the water-powered forges of the anvil makers were becoming anachronistic. In 1901 the country's nailmakers numbered 9,943, its bolt, nut, rivet, screw, and staple makers 10,052, its anchor and chain makers 6,376, its needle and pinmakers 4,730 and its steel pen makers 3,296. It was in and around Sheffield, the Black Country and parts of south Lancashire that the major part of the 12,258 tool makers, 9,349 file makers, and 2,133 saw makers were found. Most of the 19,992 cutlers and scissor makers also lived and worked in Sheffield, the ancient centre of the trade. Places with existing supplies of skilled labour, such as Manchester, Leeds and Tyneside, became important centres for machine tools and other kinds of engineering, while London still had large numbers of instrument makers, and from the 1880s the new occupation of electrical engineering was established there, in response to the enormous potential market. Blacksmiths were found in every country town and in numerous villages, and engineering firms in places such as Banbury, Bedford, Grantham, Ipswich, Lincoln and Peterborough were able to compete with Fowlers of Leeds and other specialist makers of agricultural machinery, for they were near their customers and knew their requirements.

The primary production of iron and steel by puddling, rolling, smelting and casting was organised very differently, for these processes required huge capital investment in large works that sometimes employed thousands of men. At its peak in the 1870s the north Staffordshire iron industry had 36 blast furnaces, 400 puddling furnaces and 40 rolling mills, with associated wrought-iron works, but by then it had been surpassed by the new, efficient Teesside furnaces of Bolckow & Vaughan, the Bells, and Wilson, Pease & Company. The north-eastern iron field produced over 2 million tons of pig iron per annum, a third of total British output. Teesside also became a major centre for Bessemer steel under the leadership of Dorman & Long, and by 1913 the north-east was responsible for nearly half the national output. Meanwhile, the great steel works that had been established in the east end of Sheffield after the coming of the railways – Cammell's, Brown's, Firth's, Vickers' and Hadfield's – each employed thousands of workers in the manufacture of high-value special steels and armaments. On one side of the road, Firth's made 'unstoppable shells', on the other Brown's made 'impenetrable armour'. The men worked in small gangs, whose pay and conditions were negotiated by a gaffer. Strength and dexterity were essential requirements when casting steel, and copious pints of beer were consumed to replenish the fluids lost by sweat amid the great heat of the furnaces. By middle age, men were content to take less arduous jobs in the gang and to give way to the youngsters.

The giant iron and steel works attracted new towns, or at least new working-class districts, around them. Other towns, such as St Helens and Widnes, sprang up around the new chemical industries (the alkali trade, dyestuffs, bleach, soap and glass), which grew rapidly and employed 128,640 people by 1901. The pollution that billowed out of the chimneys of the chemical works desecrated the Merseyside landscape, but the penniless immigrants who found heavy, dirty or dangerous jobs there were satisfied with the good wages that they could earn.

The Survival of the Fittest
A *Punch* cartoon of 3 February 1909, alluding to the writings of Herbert Spencer and showing that London has long had a traffic problem.

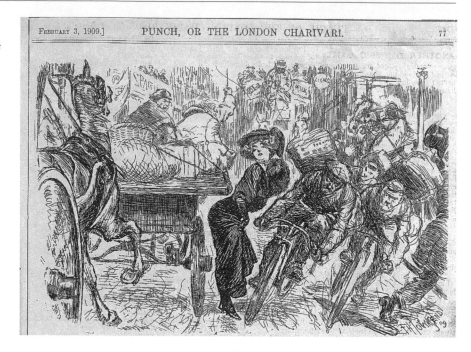

FEBRUARY 3, 1909.]   PUNCH, OR THE LONDON CHARIVARI.   77

Services

The dominant role of manufacturing and mining when the British economy led the world is becoming a distant memory, but even at the height of the Victorian era the service sector was substantial. The number of English and Welsh people who were employed in the large group of occupations that can be grouped together as services rose from 3.3 million (36 per cent of the workforce) in 1851 to 7.2 million (45 per cent) in 1901. The basic consumer industries – those concerned with the processing of food, drink and tobacco – employed over 1 million workers by the end of the century. During the previous three decades Cadbury and Rowntree, Huntly & Palmer, Wills and Player had become household names, but most firms in this sector remained small businesses. The footwear industry, which had traditionally relied on outworkers in Northamptonshire and other villages, also acquired big names, notably Clarks of Street, but in general it was not taken over by machines and factories until the very end of the century. Both the high-quality bespoke trade and village shoemakers who made sturdy boots and clogs continued in their traditional manner.

The enormous amount of new housing that was required as the national population soared to record heights ensured that the numbers employed in the building trades grew from half a million in 1851 to a peak of 1.3 million in 1901. But building remained an industry that was scarcely altered in its organisation and technology before the twentieth century. In the late Victorian period three-quarters or more of building firms employed fewer than 10 workers and half of them had fewer than 5. Work was often contracted out to semi-independent specialists, much as it is today. Unskilled labourers supported the numerous carpenters and joiners, bricklayers, masons, slaters, tilers, plasterers, paperhangers, whitewashers, painters, decorators, glaziers, plumbers, gasfitters, and locksmiths. Their stories are not as well known as those who worked underground or in large factories or steelworks, but they were subject to the same cycles of boom and slump in demand, and in the expanding towns work was usually plentiful.

Another important service industry that had grown substantially was transport. In 1901 those 'employed in the conveyance of men, goods and messages' numbered 1,267,825, of whom only 18,825 were females. They included a quarter of a million postal workers and messengers, who some-how provided more regular and efficient services on their bicycles than we are used to nowadays. We have all come across old postcards with a ¼d. stamp that were delivered on the same day as they were posted. Horse-drawn traffic on Victorian roads increased three- or four-fold, and road transport workers consistently outnumbered railwaymen by more than two to one until the last decade of the nineteenth century. By 1901 half a million people were employed in road traffic, a rise of 38.3 per cent over the previous 10 years. They included 272,300 carmen, carriers, carters and waggoners (not including those who worked on farms), 188,820 coachmen, grooms and cabmen (including 75,355 private coachmen and grooms), 12,479 livery stable keepers, 18,172 in tramway services, 11,974 in omnibus services, 623 motor car drivers and 1,452 others. Urban tramway services had expanded enormously since 1871, when only 63 men had been employed. The number of male carmen, carriers, carters and wag-goners had also increased by a remarkable 60.9 per cent. The rapid growth of horse-drawn omnibuses and trams was such that by the 1890s the London General Omnibus Company was running 860 horse-drawn buses, while its chief rival, the recently formed London Road Car Company, ran a further 275 vehicles. In many provincial cities an electric tram service was running efficiently by the turn of the century, but it was not until the eve of the First World War that the triumph of the internal combustion engine became evident. Meanwhile, between 1891 and 1901 the number of rail-waymen had increased by 48.3 per cent to 353,352. With the opening of the Great Central Railway in 1899 the national network was largely com-plete. The London Underground system, which had started with the Met-ropolitan line in 1863, was also nearly finished. The railways were staffed by a uniformed workforce with regular wages, jobs for life, company houses, pensions and the prospect of promotion to keep them at their jobs.

The number of persons employed in sea, river, and canal transport in 1901 amounted to 132,271, while a further 100,149 found irregular work in docks and harbours. The greatest docks were those of London and Liverpool, but Wales had several great coal ports at Swansea, Newport,

Serving Girl
A domestic servant serves jam
in a Leeds house in 1903.

Cardiff and Barry. Cardiff had scarcely 2,000 people in 1801, but a hundred years later its population had reached 164,000. Ship and boat builders now numbered 86,637, their numbers having risen by 44.8 per cent on the Tyne, Wear and Tees. In the boom years of 1905–7 the Sunderland shipyards built 1 million tons of new shipping. Old photographs show the vast bulk of new ships rising from the docks and blocking out the view at the end of streets of terraced housing. When Edward VII was king, British shipyards built half of the world's tonnage. The fishermen depicted in their traditional dress in Frank Sutcliffe's evocative photographs of Whitby inhabited a very different world from the shipbuilders who lived and worked a few miles up the North Sea coast. Only 23,891 fishermen were enumerated in 1901, but of course many more were away in their boats on census night.

The census returns also record thousands of people with a whole variety of individual skills. These included 149,458 makers of precious metals, jewels, watches and instruments, 14,999 photographers, 13,949 painters, engravers and sculptors, 6,044 actors and 6,443 actresses, 20,605 male and 22,644 female musicians, music masters and singers, and 12,516 male and 948 female performers in sports and entertainments. Another 278,957 skilled and unskilled people worked in the paper, print, books and stationery trades. The number of people who worked in general or local government had increased since the previous census by 37.3 per cent to 198,187, the number of sick nurses, midwives and invalid attendants had risen by 26.8 per cent to 67,269, and the 44,904 police now accounted for one in every 724 of the population. By the end of Victoria's reign, the national workforce was more varied than ever before or since.

Female Employment

Censuses taken in March or April did not record the paid employment of women and children in the summer months and their casual work at other times of the year. Many children began to earn money long before they left school. An investigation carried out in 1908 showed that about one in ten of the country's 2 million schoolchildren worked outside school hours. Oral history accounts commonly speak of girls helping with baby minding and the family washing, while boys ran errands and did other odd jobs. Even according to the 1901 census, nearly one-third of women had regular jobs, almost always in the lower grades. Women could earn a living as teachers or clerks, but they were discouraged from trying to enter the better-paid professions and, of course, they still had no vote at general elections.

Domestic service remained the most common occupation for working-class women. The 1901 census counted 1,330,783 female domestic indoor servants. It has been estimated that one in three women in Victorian

Women could earn a living as teachers or clerks, but they were discouraged from trying to enter the better-paid professions…

England probably served as a domestic servant at some point in her life, mostly between the ages of 15 and 25. The work was demanding, for the hours were long and irregular and the segregated life was often very lonely. If we add other forms of service, the workforce amounted to 1,690,722, or one-eighth of females over the age of 10 in urban districts and nearly one-seventh in the countryside. England and Wales as a whole had 18 female domestic servants to each 100 separate occupiers or families. The highest proportions were found, naturally, in the wealthiest suburbs: Hampstead (79.8 per cent), Kensington (74.9), Great Crosby (72.5), Surbiton (69.7), Ealing (68.6), Weybridge (68.4), Chislehurst (65.7) and Hove (65.3). Altogether, the proportions of domestic servants to households exceeded 50 per cent in 21 urban districts, including 3 in London and 11 in the 4 adjoining counties. A decline of 7.3 per cent during the previous decade in the 15 to 20 age range suggested that the young were beginning to prefer other jobs, but domestic service remained a common form of employment up to the Second World War.

Other women who worked at menial tasks for middle-class urban and suburban families included 111,841 charwomen and 196,141 who washed and laundered. The report on the 1901 census concluded that 40.5 per cent of occupied females were employed in domestic and other servicing, 16.5 per cent in making articles of dress, 14 per cent in textile manufacture, 8 per cent in various other manufactures (such as the 'buffer girls' who had the dirty job of polishing Sheffield silver), 7 per cent as shopkeepers or assistants, 4 per cent as teachers, 3 per cent in services connected with hotels, inns, boarding houses, eating houses, etc., and 7 per cent in other occupations. Only 10,653 males and 26,341 females were employed in hospital and institution service, however. Clearly, the pattern of female employment was very different from that of today.

In 1906 Board of Trade figures showed that half the women in industrial Britain earned less than 10 shillings for a working week of at least 54 hours. The following year a Sweated Industries Exhibition organised by the *Daily News* revealed that in the East End of London women worked 14 hours a day making artificial violets and geraniums for 7d. a gross, buttercups for 3d. and roses for 1s.3d. Putting 384 hooks on cards earned them 1d. and they spent 18 hours at it to earn 5 shillings a week. Matchbox makers received similar pay. In sweated sewing shops machinists made pinafores and babies' bonnets for 2 shillings a dozen, or a gross of ties for 5 shillings.

Dressmaking was a skill that many women acquired, but it was only in the large towns, particularly London, that regular employment could be obtained. About 20,000 women and girls worked in the capital's fashion houses, especially in Oxford Circus, Bond Street and Conduit Street. During the aristocratic 'season' dressmakers and needlewomen commonly worked 12 or 14 hours a day, sometimes more. Shop assistants worked an

In 1906 Board of Trade figures showed that half the women in industrial Britain earned less than 10 shillings for a working week of at least 54 hours.

average of 80 hours a week, and many of them were required to live in dormitories above their work, but by the standards of the time they were not badly off. Every large town and city had acquired at least one department store by the later nineteenth century. Liverpool had its Lewis's, Manchester its Kendal Milne's, and Sheffield its Cole's. London led the way with its Debenhams, Harrods, Selfridges, Whiteley's, Dickens & Jones, Swan & Edgar, Marshall & Snelgrove, the Army & Navy and the Civil Service Stores. By 1900 a dozen London firms had a workforce of over 1,000 and Harrods had 6,000. By the First World War, however, department stores accounted for only 15 per cent of retail trade and multiple- or chain-stores were still largely a phenomenon of the future. The great majority of shops were small, family-run businesses as they had always been. Their character is captured on thousands of old photographs.

The East End of London

Working life in the East End of London was very different from that of the pit villages or mill towns where most men had the same occupations as their neighbours. Here, skilled craftsmen lived next door to men who worked in jobs that required only low skills or just physical labour. Although much employment was classified as manufacturing, most of the workplaces were small-scale and very different in character from the factories of northern and midland England. Though Truman's brewery in Brick Lane, Bryant & May's match factory in Bow, and several manufacturers of jams and sweets near the docks employed large numbers of workers, most businesses had a workforce of less than 20 and thousands of people were self-employed. Typical products included carbonated drinks, cigars and cigarettes, vinegar, artificial flowers and silk cloth. The East End was also the home of the sweated trades of furniture making, footwear and clothing, carried on in modest workshops by a small number of permanent craftsmen and in their own homes by a large pool of casual workers. In Bethnal Green and Shoreditch, upon the decline of the silk trade, furniture making developed rapidly as imported wood became readily available from the docks. Centred on Curtain Road, the trade needed large numbers of sawyers, carvers, gilders, cabinet makers, upholsterers, French polishers and varnishers, suppliers of cane and leather, and knob-makers and horsehair twisters. Nearly all the workshops were small and highly specialised; one would make dining chairs, another small tables, a third bookcases. The work was subject to seasonal demand, and many small firms had to sell at a loss in slack times and lay off their workers when trade got really bad.

Many other crafts and trades were just as seasonal, with regular periods of unemployment. Bootmaking was a common occupation, and the rag trade expanded quickly after the arrival of Jewish refugees from the

Russian empire. The second half of the nineteenth century saw a steady growth of offensive trades in the East End: the manufacture of glue, soap, rubber, tar, and matches. Thick, obnoxious fog discoloured the houses, contaminated the water and caused nausea. Countless other people earned a precarious living by providing goods and services: carmen with horses and carts, stallholders, rag-and-bone men, hawkers, and artificial flower makers. Many women took in washing or went out charring, but the most common trade for women was box making, where a little money could be earned at home and the children could help.

In 1881 the occupations of the 26 male heads of households at 101–139 Gossett Street, Bethnal Green were noted as: silk weaver (4), silk dyer, cabinet maker (2), dining table maker, wood dealer, wood turner, wood journeyman, chair maker, hat stand maker, looking glass picture frame maker, ivory turner, ivory worker, bookbinder, shoe maker, boot finisher, brush maker, cotton winder, dock labourer, dealer, corn merchant manager, licensed victualler, and beer house keeper. Thomas Harvey was described as a wood dealer, even though he was 87 years old and his wife was 86. The varied occupations of the 18 unmarried men and boys (including sons) were: 3 errand boys, 2 clerks, 2 compositors, a chair maker, cabinet maker, table maker, picture frame maker, carver, French polisher, surgical instrument maker, butcher, porter, unemployed warehouseman, and a 'coster-monger and shoe black'. The 21 recorded female occupations (five of which were the same as their husbands') were makers of fancy dress trimmings (3), silk weavers (2), tailoresses (2), tie makers (2), a fancy box maker, a furniture trimmings maker, a needlewoman, a shoemaker, a brush maker, a domestic servant, a mangler, a hawker, a pupil teacher, a corn merchant manager, a general dealer, and an annuitant.

Meanwhile, the occupations of the 83 men and boys who lived a mile or so away at 74–134 Provost Street, Shoreditch varied considerably. Among the 83 men and boys were 3 grainers, 2 cabinet makers, 2 French polishers, a chair maker, a frame maker, and a joiner and fitter. The other tradesmen of Provost Street included 5 painters and a painter's labourer, 2 plasterers, a wheelwright, a smith, a locksmith, 2 metalworkers, a japanner, an engineer, 4 type printers and a compositor, 6 bookbinders, a watchmaker and a watch case maker, a harness maker, 4 boot makers, 2 cork cutters, a brush maker, a cigar maker, a tailor, a shirt maker, a packing case maker, a dyer, a brass moulder, a brace cutter, a bricklayer, and a plumber's boy. Services were provided by a hotel manager, a barman, a waiter, a

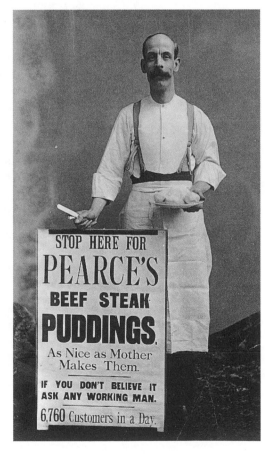

Fast Food
Victorian London was no different from the present day capital in providing quick snacks for busy workers and travellers.

groom, 2 errand boys, a messenger, a portman and 3 porters, a florist, a musician, a newsagent, a general dealer, a gardener, a milkman, 2 sweeps, a warehouseman, a carman, and an engine bus fitter. The other six worked as labourers, one of them as an excavator on the railways. Many of the women also worked in distinctive local trades. They included 12 makers of artificial flowers, 7 milliners, 5 fur sewers, 2 needlewomen, 2 dressmakers, a semptress, a tailoress, a hat trimmer, a boot trimmer, a feather curler, a brace finisher, a bottle labeller, 2 infant-boot makers, 2 box makers, a book folder, a maker of paper bags, a blacking packer, and a worker in a City warehouse, as well as a general shop keeper, a hotel cook, a housekeeper, a domestic servant, 2 laundresses, 2 manglers, and a collar ironer.

In the working-class districts of north London the occupational structure was very different. The occupations of the 20 male heads of household in Gillespie Terrace and a small part of Gillespie Road, Upper Holloway in 1881 were recorded as 4 carpenters, 2 stone masons, 2 carmen (one of whom worked on the Great Northern Railway), a coal porter working for a firm of merchants, a coachman with a private family, a painter, a paper marbler, a clerk and builder, a labourer, a boiler cleaner, a butcher, a gardener, a bookbinder, a school master, and a sealing wax maker. The occupations of the 14 unmarried men and boys were 2 butchers, a foreman builder, a paper stainer, a paper marbler who worked with his father, a cabinet maker, a box maker, a pianoforte maker, a clerk, a coachman (omnibus), a driver of a tramcar, a carman, a stableman or groom on the Great Northern Railway, and a lamp lighter with the same company. The 14 female occupations that were recorded comprised 5 laundresses, 3 dressmakers, 2 domestic servants, a milliner, an upholsteress, a shirt ironer, and a 'school teacher' who was only 15 years old.

Earning a living was often a precarious business in Victorian and Edwardian times. When work was obtained, it was commonly a drudgery and the rewards were meagre. Skilled workers could take great pride in their creations, but everyone else had to console themselves with the thought that working conditions were even worse in many other countries of the world. Opportunities to better oneself were very limited and there seemed no prospect that the curse on Adam would ever be lifted.

CHAPTER SIX

Education, Religion and Leisure

Education

FAMILY HISTORIANS often find that their mid-nineteenth-century ancestors were illiterate and that birth, marriage and death certificates were commonly witnessed by people who signed their names with a mark. Before attendance was made compulsory in 1880 half the children in England and Wales did not go to day school. Large numbers did, however, get a rudimentary education on a Sunday. Once Sunday schools were started by Robert Raikes in Gloucester in 1785 they spread rapidly, so that within 10 years they were providing a basic education for three-quarters of a million children. At their peak in 1906 British Sunday schools attracted over 6 million pupils, or more than 80 per cent of children between the ages of 5 and 14, a truly impressive number. Attendance was particularly high in some of the major cities and throughout Wales. An enormous number of Bibles, magazines, periodicals, sermons, catechisms, handbooks, hymn-books, primers of reading and spelling, and other materials were published for the use of Sunday school scholars. In the days before compulsory elementary education they were crucial in teaching children to read and write and in training them to be orderly, punctual, clean and responsible, but by the end of the century they provided only religious instruction. Often, too, they were the only social and recreational centres for children in the neighbourhood, the ones that organised memorable events such as concerts and picnic trips into the countryside. Their's was the world captured so accurately by Arnold Bennett in his early novel, *Anna of the Five Towns* (1902). The 'National' day schools of the Church of England and the 'British' day schools of the Nonconformists, which grew out of the Sunday school movement in the first two decades of the nineteenth century, gradually became the major providers of regular elementary education in towns and rural districts alike, but in Victoria's reign they could not keep pace with the rapid growth of population. A secular system, paid for out of the rates, had to be introduced to complement the schools run by the churches and chapels. Very soon, these new schools became the chief providers of elementary education.

At their peak in 1906 British Sunday schools attracted over 6 million pupils, or more than 80 per cent of children between the ages of 5 and 14, a truly impressive number.

The Education Act of 1870 introduced the election of local school boards with power to build and manage schools where the provision by the two voluntary bodies was inadequate. The threat of losing control of their tenants' children stimulated many Anglican squires to improve the educational opportunities of the poor by building or rebuilding a National school before a local board could take over responsibility. Government funding was made available for church schools to improve their facilities, just as it is today, so they remained a vital part of educational provision, except in districts where they were unable to compete with the brand new board schools. In the largest cities the splendid Victorian Gothic board schools that were erected to cater for over a thousand pupils each remain some of the finest public buildings of that era. By 1892, for example, Sheffield had 23 such schools, including 4 with over 1,500 pupils, each designed in a variety of 'English Domestic Gothic' styles. In town and countryside alike numerous board schools remain in use as infant and junior schools to this day. The school that I attended as a boy and which provided my parents with all their formal education was originally a board school which opened in 1879. Once schools were provided, attendance was made compulsory and visits by government inspectors ensured adequate standards, although these were not achieved overnight. In 1876 less than half the population of England and Wales (46 per cent) lived in districts where school attendance was at least nominally compulsory, and the countryside lagged far behind the towns, but in 1880 all children were compelled to attend school up to the age of 10. Fees for poor children were paid by the local boards from 1876 until all fees were abolished in 1891. The leaving age was raised to 11 in 1893 and to 12 (except for those employed in agriculture) in 1899. As with all Acts, there was a time lag between what was intended and what happened, but in the long term the establishment of board schools had a revolutionary effect on elementary education. By 1893 nearly 95 per cent of newly married couples were able to sign the marriage register. The ability to sign one's name was a much prized achievement, although many people were no more literate than that.

The activities of these new elementary schools are well recorded in local and national archives. Board school records, which are kept at county or county borough record offices, together with whatever records have survived at individual schools, often include school log books and admission registers which name the child and give the date of admission, the father's name and address (and sometimes the mother's name), the child's date of birth, the name of his or her previous school, and the date of leaving. Some registers also record when a child left school and his or her destination. The National Archives

Playground Drill
Boys at Milton Board School, Kent, 1903. Co-ordinated exercises were a regular part of a school's curriculum.

has copious records of schools from 1870 onwards, which give the names
and assessments of pupils in examination schedules from 1872 to 1904,
listed alphabetically by county, then place. Other records at the National
Archives include the reports and recommendations of Inspectors on the
returns made in 1870 by local authorities about population size, school
accommodation, enlargements, closures, and elections of School Boards in
towns and villages, but not in boroughs. Leaving certificates (from 1908)
and school photographs, showing children grouped in classes outside or
seated in rows at their desks, are more likely to survive in individual family
collections, though an increasing number are being copied by local
libraries and record offices.

The upper and middle classes shunned such schools in favour of private
education. Public schools were so named because they were open to
anyone whose parents could afford to pay, though in practice this excluded
the great majority of the public and applied only to boys. The emergence
of a sizeable middle class and the coming of the railways attracted boarders from long distances, so that the nine big public schools that had been
established by 1860 – Eton, Harrow, Winchester, Shrewsbury, Westminster, St Paul's, Merchant Taylors', Charterhouse and Rugby – were soon
followed by many more, but the hundred or so public schools at the end of
the century varied greatly in rank and prestige. Their role was avowedly
social rather than intellectual; they trained boys to behave like gentlemen,
to fight hard but lose gracefully, to become leaders but at the same time to
work in teams and remain loyal to friends. This exclusive social group,
imbued with the values of courage, good form, leadership and the Christian virtues, went on to careers in responsible positions in government, the
church, the army and the navy, in Britain and in far flung parts of the
Empire. Meanwhile, their sisters were educated close to home. Few girls'
high schools and boarding schools were founded before the 1880s and
1890s.

In Victorian times, working-class children had little chance of progres-
sing beyond the elementary stage. Although some scholarships were available for the poor and able, secondary education in grammar schools was
mainly for the middle classes. In the later years of the nineteenth century,
however, some local school boards, especially those in the northern industrial towns, founded higher-grade schools, which were secondary schools
in all but name, for working-class pupils. Some of the best voluntary
schools also became higher-grade elementary schools. Meanwhile, the
Technical Instruction Act (1889) allowed the newly-established county and
county borough councils to provide a variety of teaching, from elementary
work to post-school training for trades and crafts, and technical institutes
and 'night school' classes were introduced in response to growing competition from Germany and America. During the last decade of the nineteenth
century many a grammar school took advantage of grants from technical

education committees to employ more staff and to provide buildings and equipment for science teaching. These ancient schools now offered a much wider curriculum and some of them soon began to admit girls.

The board schools and the improved voluntary schools (including a rising number of Roman Catholic schools in some industrial districts) had an enormous influence on the lives of boys and girls in Victoria's later years. Children received a basic training in reading, writing and arithmetic and some knowledge of the wider world, they were taught how to behave, and they did not have to go out to work at quite so early an age as their parents had. But the old practice of half-time education lingered on in the textile districts of Lancashire and the West Riding of Yorkshire, where child labour in the mills rose steadily in importance from the middle years of the nineteenth century to the mid 1890s. This practice was defended, not only by some factory inspectors, but also by trades unionists and civic dignitaries, on the grounds that it made children alert and dexterous and prepared them for the world of work. From 1890 onwards, however, the National Union of Teachers and the medical profession led a successful campaign, arguing that half-timers lost all their aptitude for study and retarded the progress of the rest of the class, their growth was stunted and they were more likely to succumb to a variety of physical ills, which marred them for life. The report on the 1901 census observed that during the previous decade some important Acts had come into force, which had restricted the employment of children of school age, notably the Elementary Education (School Attendance) Act (1893) and the Amendment Act (1899). Their most important effect had been to raise the minimum age at which children could be employed, either totally or as 'half-timers', to 12 years. Although some of the restrictive provisions remained optional, with much being left to the discretion of the local school authorities, the number of half-time scholars had dropped from 173,040 in 1890–91 to 74,468 10 years later. Many counties had no half-timers; by far the largest numbers were in Lancashire, Cheshire and the West Riding of Yorkshire.

The proportion of people who could not sign the marriage register other than with a mark fell from 194 to 25 per 1,000 among men and from 268 to 29 among women.

According to the returns of the Board of Education, 36,207 males and 113,597 females taught in English and Welsh elementary day schools in 1901. Pupil teachers, whose minimum age had been raised to 14 in 1877, still outnumbered the adult assistants who were employed by the board schools. The system lasted until 1906, by which time three-quarters of elementary school-teachers were women, who earned an average wage of £75 a year. Whereas in 1871, when board schools were first being built, the country had on average one teacher for every 67 persons aged between 3 and 20, by 1901 the figure had fallen to one for every 50. During the same three decades, the proportion of people who could not sign the marriage register other than with a mark fell from 194 to 25 per 1,000 among men and from 268 to 29 among women. The new system was reaping benefits.

Seebohm Rowntree's survey of York in 1901 noted that no school board had been established there until 1889 and that free elementary education had been introduced nationally two years later. By 1901 York possessed 21 free elementary schools and 8 elementary voluntary schools that were not free (7 Anglican and 1 Wesleyan). Attendance averaged 88 per cent of the enrolment in the board schools and 84 per cent in the voluntary schools. The system of 'half-timers', so prevalent in the nearby West Riding mill towns, was unknown in York. Rowntree thought that the local board schools were conspicuous, well-planned buildings, with ample playgrounds, but that the voluntary school buildings were old, and in most cases poor; some of them were situated in narrow streets with hardly any playground. Under the government's new code the obligatory subjects taught in York's schools were reading, writing and arithmetic, with drawing for boys and needlework for girls. In addition, one of the 'class subjects' mentioned under the heading of 'optional subjects' had to be taught to Standards 1, 2 and 3 by means of object lessons. The optional subjects – all of which were taught in York's board schools – were singing by note, recitation, English, geography, elementary science, history, and (for girls) domestic economy. The top classes were taught elementary science, French and drill, with cookery for the girls and manual instruction for the boys, and swimming and life-saving classes were held at the Corporation Baths. Religious instruction in the board schools was unsectarian. Each morning, the whole school assembled in the central hall, the children marching in to a school band (whose instruments were not provided out of the rates). After they had saluted the headmaster and teachers a hymn was sung and some simple prayers said, then the children went to their classrooms for half-an-hour's religious instruction based on selected parts of the Bible. The board's regulations stated that in all departments the teachers were expected to bring up the children in habits of punctuality, of good manners and language, of cleanliness and neatness, and also to impress upon them the importance of cheerful obedience to duty, of consideration and respect for others, and of honour and truthfulness in word and act. In 1900 almost all the classes had been marked 'excellent' in religious instruction by the diocesan inspector. The leaving age at York was 14 unless the Labour Examination (based on Standard VI) had been passed and the Labour Certificate obtained. About 10 per cent of the pupils left when they were 12 or 13. The curriculum was typical of that in the country as a whole. Children wrote morally elevating maxims into their copy books, chanted their multiplication tables, learned a little about the outside world, were taught to be upright citizens and were chastised for bad behaviour and poor work.

Some of the elected school boards, particularly in the rural districts of England and Wales, failed to provide a satisfactory standard of elementary education and were slack in enforcing attendance. Meanwhile, by the end of the century some rural voluntary schools were receiving as much as 90 per cent of their income from public funds. The time seemed ripe for a new, wider administrative structure that would ensure consistent standards, control appointments, provide professional advice for local managers, and make sure that children went regularly to school. After a keenly-fought battle over the future of voluntary schools and the financial help that they required, the system was completely reorganised by the Education Act of December 1902, when responsibility for providing elementary, secondary and technical education was given to local educational authorities run by county and county borough councils under the direction of a central Board of Education. From 1903 the 'board' schools became 'council' schools and 330 local education authorities replaced the 2,559 school boards. The Elementary School Code issued by the Board of Education in 1904 provided the rationale for the educational system until the 1960s.

Local education authorities, under the guidance of the Board of Education, now began to extend provision for secondary and technical education. Growing numbers of children had been 'staying on' at elementary school or 'going on' to a 'higher grade' school since the raising of the school-leaving age, but now secondary education was to be firmly rooted in the grammar school tradition. After 1902 most of the grammar and girls' high schools were financed and controlled by local authorities and were invigorated by an injection of public funds. As a result, grammar schools trebled in number, from 491 in 1904 to 1,616 in 1925, and pupil numbers rose from 85,358 to 334,194 in the same period. Local private schools gradually withered, but the public schools and some major grammar schools remained outside the state system.

The annual reports of the educational committees of the local authorities during the reign of Edward VII provide much detailed information about the building of new schools, the struggle to reduce class sizes and enforce attendance, and plans to provide special schools for handicapped children. Some authorities pressed ahead determinedly but others were more relaxed in their approach. As late as 1916 my father was allowed to leave school at the age of 12 because my grandfather had just died and he was now looked upon as the breadwinner. After the First World War, the Education Act (1918) raised the school-leaving age to 14 and finally closed the loopholes that had allowed roughly half the children in elementary schools to leave early. By then, education had become firmly established as a right rather than a privilege.

Schools also played a vital social role through nourishment and medical services. Under the Education (Provision of Meals) Act (1906) school canteens provided free meals from rates. Soon afterwards, the Education Act (1907) placed local authorities in charge of the health of schoolchildren and established a medical service which looked for vermin infestation,

A Ragged School
Dinner time at 12 o'clock for 250 poor children at Camberwell Ragged School and Mission, 1901. The children were told to bring a spoon.

ringworm, impetigo, scabies and defects of vision, hearing and speech. Doctors and nurses discovered that one-sixth of pupils were so underfed, verminous or suffering from defective teeth, skin or eyes as to be incapable of benefiting educationally from their time at school. They found that children from overcrowded homes were likely to be on average 10 pounds less in weight and five inches less in height than those who lived in better working-class houses and that middle-class children were even bigger. The annual report of the Chief Medical Officer of the Board of Education in 1912 showed that 18.6 per cent of the children examined in Dorset, 12.7 per cent of those in Gloucestershire and 12 per cent of Somerset children were suffering from the effects of inadequate diet. But the situation was even worse in towns, where the percentage rose to 31.4 in West Hartlepool and 26.3 in Norwich. Old photographs show that children from the poorest families went barefoot in summer and relied on charities for boots to go to school during the rest of the year. Their clothes were either hand-me-downs or were bought second-hand at cheap sales. In 1894, England's first medical inspector, Dr James Kerr had found that a third of the 300 children he had inspected in Bradford had not taken off their clothes for six months. In Gloucestershire nearly one-quarter of elementary schoolchildren examined in 1908 suffered from head infestation, in Oxfordshire about one-fifth. The nose and throat were key problem areas and teeth were notoriously uncared for.

Only a very small proportion of the population proceeded to higher education. On the eve of the First World War just 22,234 students attended English universities. Less than a thousand of these came from grant-aided secondary schools. In *Jude the Obscure* (1895) Thomas Hardy had memorably described the frustrations of an able working man who was unable to gain admittance to an ancient university, but the number of new institutions that were offering degrees was growing. At the beginning of Victoria's reign only Cambridge, Oxford, London and Durham had university status; by 1914 the new 'civic' or 'red-brick' universities or university colleges included Birmingham, Bristol, Exeter, Liverpool, Manchester, Newcastle, Nottingham, Reading, Sheffield, Southampton, and the three colleges of the University of Wales at Aberystwyth, Bangor and Cardiff. Meanwhile, the Workers' Educational Association had been founded in 1903. The profession that was most open to working-class people was that of teaching, which paid modestly but offered status in the community. Although in 1902 only 55 per cent of teachers had attended a training college of any kind, seven years later C. F. G. Masterman was of the opinion that teachers were 'taking up the position in urban districts which for many years was occupied by clergy in rural districts'.

Religion

The sole national census of religious worship in England and Wales was that taken in 1851. Its findings made disagreeable reading to members of the Established Church, for they showed that well over half the population of the country did not attend any form of religious service at all and that, of those who did attend, about half preferred a chapel service to one held by the Church of England. In Cornwall, Wales, parts of the midlands, the West Riding of Yorkshire, the north east and some other parts of England the proportion of Nonconformists was higher still. The Church of England's strength lay south of a line drawn from the Wash to the Bristol Channel, though even in these southern counties Dissent had a firm foothold.

The Nonconformist sects did not have much in common, apart from their opposition to the Church of England. They ranged in doctrine from evangelical fundamentalists to Unitarians and in organisation from the Salvation Army and the centrally-organised Wesleyans to locally autonomous groups such as the Congregationalists. Some sects had a particular appeal to certain types of people; farm labourers, for example, were attracted to Primitive Methodism, in whose chapels their trades union leaders got their first experience of public speaking as lay preachers, while the Methodist New Connexion attracted the urban, industrial poor and acquired a reputation for political radicalism. But people from all social classes became Methodists of one sort or another, and during the second half of the nineteenth century chapel architecture reflected the increasing prosperity and respectability of many congregations. The great majority of Nonconformists belonged to one or other of the main groups, whose histories went back into the seventeenth or eighteenth centuries. Family connections down the generations often determined which chapel a person attended, and the pattern of settlement could have a decisive influence on the spread or suppression of Dissent. The squires of estate villages could effectively prevent the building of chapels, unless they themselves were Dissenters or sympathetic towards them. On the other hand, large parishes served by just one medieval church were particularly prone to Nonconformity, especially where new industrial settlements had mushroomed in recent years far from the parochial centre. The Pennine parish of High Hoyland, for example, was served by its ancient parish church in a hill-top hamlet, but in the valley below by 1851 the new textile settlement of Clayton West had chapels for the Wesleyans, Independents, Particular Baptists, Methodist New Connexion and Primitive Methodists, and 150 members of the new Wesleyan Reform met in Aaron Pierce's warehouse. The siting of Nonconformist chapels took little account of the old parish boundaries.

Nonconformist chapels had been built in impressive numbers during the first half of the nineteenth century. The Wesleyans had only 825 chapels in 1801, but 11,007 50 years later; the number of Baptist chapels had risen from from 652 to 2,789; and those of the Congregationalists from 914 to 3,244. The Anglicans fought back by founding new churches and creating new parishes in the expanding towns and by building hundreds of mission rooms, but during the second half of the century the Nonconformists too built anew, usually on a more impressive scale than before. In Lincoln, for example, during the 1870s and 1880s chapels were erected by the Wesleyans, United Methodists, Primitive Methodists, Congregationalists, Particular Baptists and General Baptists, and other Methodist and Congregational chapels were opened on the outskirts of the town. In Brighton, about the same time, 11 new churches and chapels were built to accommodate residents and holiday-makers alike. All were of architectural importance and Sir Charles Barry's sparkling white St Peter's church was particularly noteworthy. In north-eastern England during the second half of the nineteenth century Stockton got 19 new churches and chapels, Darlington 20, South Shields 30 and Sunderland 40. Two-thirds of the churches, chapels and mission rooms ever built in Halifax were constructed between 1867 and 1901. In 1851 Halifax had 25 churches and chapels, in 1900 four times as many. The Sunday School Jubilee Sing at the Piece Hall in 1890 attracted 30,985 participants from 93 Nonconformist Sunday schools within Halifax's huge ancient parish. These comprised 9,882 Methodists of all hues – 5,923 Wesleyan, 3,678 United Free Church, 3,366 Methodist New Connexion, 2,245 Primitive – and 6,472 Congregationalists, 2,593 Baptists and 1,010 others. No members of the Church of England were present, but as 17,498 had enrolled in Halifax

Deanery in 1889, the continued strength of all forms of organised religion is evident.

During the first half of Victoria's reign the countryside as well as the towns had seen a major effort to improve the country's stock of ancient parish churches. For example, between 1840 and 1876 just over half of Dorset's 300 parish churches were either restored or rebuilt. Later restoration work was much more sensitive than these early efforts, which met with fierce criticism from those who mourned the loss of much that was old and valuable. Throughout the nineteenth century the Church of England favoured neo-Gothic styles of architecture. By 1890 most of the great Victorian Gothic architects – Pugin, Scott, Street, Butterfield – were either dead or near the end of their careers, but the Gothic style continued to dominate church architecture into the twentieth century, notably in the new cathedrals at Truro and Liverpool. The tradition was carried on by J. Ninian Comper (1864–1960), who did a vast amount of church restoration or addition and who built a considerable number of new churches. The growing numbers of Roman Catholics also favoured Gothic, the style of the fifteenth Duke of Norfolk's great church at Arundel, built by 1873 to match the 'medievalising' of his castle, but the Roman Catholic cathedral at Westminster (1895–1903) was built in Byzantine style. During the second half of Victoria's reign even some of the wealthier Nonconformists turned to the Gothic style instead of the previous classical designs or the early, barn-like buildings, though poorer congregations still had to make do with plain brick boxes or even 'tin tabernacles'. The continued vitality of organised forms of religion is apparent from all this building. Gothic churches and a wide variety of chapels are essential features in our images of Victorian towns and villages.

In 1881, after discussions at the Church Congress, several provincial newspapers organised local censuses of religious worship in order to compare the results with the findings of 1851. It quickly became apparent that in many places the spate of new building had failed to match the rise of the local population. In Nottingham, attendance at church and chapel had gone up from less than 24,000 to nearly 47,000, but 30 years of church building had not checked the decline in the proportion of worshippers to under 26 per cent of the population. In Sheffield, services at the 50 Anglican places of worship attracted 34,152 attendances and the 149 other services and meetings brought in another 55,024, but this meant that only 12.37 per cent of the borough's population went to the morning service and only 17.75 per cent went in the evening. Similar results were obtained in many other parts of the country. Overall, attendance in the working-class districts of large towns did not average more than 20 per cent. Countryfolk could be equally obstinate in staying away from church or chapel. Flora Thompson observed that at Juniper Hill (Oxfordshire) few adults went to church between the baptisms of their offspring, but then her hamlet had no place of worship and the committed had to walk to the next village for a service. Evangelists were at work in the countryside as well as the towns, however. Old photographs bear out Thomas Hardy's assertion in *Tess of the D'Urbervilles* that texts from the scriptures were painted on gates and stiles to catch the eyes of the rural population.

Though church-going was only a minority interest, most people nevertheless thought of themselves as Christians and taught their children to pray. Enormous numbers of children in England and Wales attended Sunday schools, which were by far the largest form of voluntary association, though most left as soon as they started to work. It has been argued that the late Victorian period was the point in British history when religion attained its greatest social significance. It did this not merely through attendance at services but by its dominance of organised leisure and the formation of social policy. The chapels, in particular, were the local centres of social and communal life, with a wide range of social activities on offer: The Boys' Brigade (1883) or The Church Lads' Brigade (1891), men's fellowships, women's guilds, choral societies, football, cricket and other sports clubs were all based on a chapel or church. The Band of Hope, founded in Leeds in 1847, had over 3 million members under the age of 16 by the end of the century. Their meetings in chapel halls combined the earnest advocacy of teetotalism with entertaining songs and sketches. Up to the First World War the lives of countless English and Welsh people were continually associated with church, chapel and Sunday school. Many of our ancestors shared the intense fellowship of chapel life, based on a regular weekly and seasonal round of meetings. Old

A Sunday School Procession
The Whit Friday procession of Manchester's Roman Catholic Sunday School scholars arrives in Albert Square. The Protestant Sunday Schools paraded on Whit Monday.

photographs show how religious festivals remained great community events, particularly Sunday school anniversaries and the Whit walks and open-air sings of the north of England. Sundays were kept as quiet and uneventful days of rest, when the only sounds in the streets were those of hymn singing from the churches and chapels. The chapels promoted the idea of a Pleasant Sunday Afternoon, presided over by the minister and begun with a short prayer and a hymn, but then given over to an address by a layman on a secular subject, followed by songs and music. When, in 1896, Parliament voted to allow the Sunday opening of art galleries and museums, religious bodies were outraged.

Figures for the whole of Britain in 1901 show that Nonconformists still outnumbered the members of the Established Church.

Figures for the whole of Britain in 1901 show that Nonconformists still outnumbered the members of the Established Church. The Church of England had 2,796,000 members, the Church in Wales 141,008, the Scottish Episcopal Church 116,296 and the Church of Ireland 296,000. The Church of Scotland (a Presbyterian organisation) had 661,629 members, other Presbyterians and Congregationalists numbered 1,283,499 and Baptists 1,945,128. The Methodists had 728,289 members in England, 33,926 in Wales, 8,191 in Scotland and 27,745 in Ireland. No membership figures were available for Roman Catholics, whose numbers had risen considerably since the Irish had arrived on the mainland after the potato famine, nor for those who attended Jewish synagogues.

The 1901 census for England and Wales enumerated 25,235 clergymen of the Established Church, an increase of 4.1 per cent during the previous decade, compared with a rise of 11.9 per cent between 1881 and 1891. Roman Catholic priests (including monks) numbered 3,088, an increase of 23 per cent, and ministers of other religious bodies numbered 11,572, an increase of 15.1 per cent, compared with only 3.3 per cent between 1881 and 1891. The relative numbers of ministers of the Church of England to the rest varied considerably across the country. The census also recorded 10,096 missionaries, scripture readers and itinerant preachers, 6,219 nuns or sisters of charity, and 6,206 church officers, giving a total of 62,416 people who were connected with the clerical profession. But by 1901 clergymen could no longer take for granted the esteem and deference which had been normal at the beginning of Victoria's reign. George Sturt recalled a tale of his gardener that summed up the new attitude: 'Bettesworth was "huckin' about" in his garden when the curate passed by from church. He stopped an' he says, "Bettesworth, I wish this 'ere Sunday work was done away with altogether." I looked at 'n an' I says, "Well, sir," I says, "if it was, I dunno what in the world 'd become o' you."'

Two censuses of church and chapel attendance were taken in York by Seebohm Rowntree and his investigators in March 1901. On 17 March 6,964 attended the morning service and 7,666 went in the evening, but these figures include those who went to both. About two out of every three worshippers were working-class people. Those who attended the evening service of the Church of England comprised 1,164 males and 2,128 females; the Nonconformist congregations were divided between 1,442 males and 1,303 females. Roman Catholic worshippers numbered 648 males and 879 females, and the Salvation Army attracted 68 males and 34 females. A week later, on 24 March, the census takers counted higher attendances of 9,485 at the morning service and 10,006 in the evening, but as York's population in 1901 amounted to 75,812, the highest attendance was only 13 per cent of the city's inhabitants.

Lady Florence Bell's survey of Middlesbrough, published in 1911, noted that the Church of England had 9 churches and 6 mission rooms, the Roman Catholics had 3 churches (one of them a cathedral; for the population contained large numbers of Irish immigrants) and the Nonconformists had 34 chapels, i.e. 2 Congregational, 6 Baptist, 1 Society of Friends, 3 Presbyterian, 1 Unitarian, 9 Wesleyan, 3 Methodist New Connexion, 5 Primitive Methodist, 2 United Methodist Free Church, and 2 Plymouth Brethren. The town also had 2 Salvation Army missions, 1 Church Army mission and 1 Spiritualist Association. Bell's assistants counted 7,234 men, 8,360 women, and 6,598 children attending church or chapel on a typical Sunday. In other words, about 70,000 of Middlesbrough's 97,000 population did not attend any form of worship. 'It was not that the Church of God had lost the great towns,' said Bishop Winnington-Ingram in 1896, 'it never had them.' A census carried out by the *Daily News* in 1902–3 showed that in the upper working-class areas of London just over 16 per cent of the adult population attended divine service and that in the poor districts of the capital the figure sank to well below 12 per cent. Some poor people attended three or four different church services in order to receive charity. Elsewhere, those worshippers who were uninterested in doctrinal differences went to a different place of worship in the evening from the one they had attended in the morning.

Nevertheless, millions of people still attended church or chapel every Sunday, often two or three services a day. Membership and regular attendance were still normal among the middle classes, whose womenfolk spent a large part of their time in charitable activities for the sick and the poor or in support of missionary efforts. In Salford the year 1901 saw the opening of a new Roman Catholic church, the reopening of an Anglican Church Army hall, the laying of foundation stones for a Wesleyan chapel and a Primitive hall and classroom, a gathering of 6,000 people under temperance banners in Peel Park, a summer open-air sing that attracted a crowd of 7–8,000, and the annual Sunday school picnics by omnibus and train into the countryside.

Dissent triumphed throughout Wales. The evangelical movement transformed Welsh culture, glorifying rhetoric and the singing of hymns. The old parish churches (most of them small and poor by English standards) declined as centres of community life as the chapels took over.

During the third quarter of the nineteenth century huge new chapels, bearing names such as Bethesda, Ebenezer, Mount Pleasant and Zion, were erected in the industrial valleys and in the market towns, while hundreds of smaller buildings served rural communities. By 1901 south Cardiganshire, for example, had a place of worship for every 186 people. The great revivals of 1904–5 swelled the number of worshippers, so that by 1906 Wales had about 1,500 churches and chapels, 80 per cent of them Nonconformist. The Established Church attracted 193,000 members, the Methodists 189,000, the Independents 175,000, the Baptists 143,000, the Wesleyans 41,000 and the Roman Catholics 65,000. Nonconformists outnumbered Anglicans by three to one. They formed about 40 per cent of the total population in five Welsh-speaking counties, but only 20 per cent in the border counties of Flintshire and Monmouthshire. The Liberal Party, which spoke for the Nonconformist interest, dominated Welsh politics in the late-Victorian and Edwardian era. In both England and Wales the struggle between church and chapel was one of the great political issues of the time.

Leisure

Rising incomes and cheap imports put more money into the pockets of working-class people, and shorter working hours allowed them to spend some of it on leisure activities. By the late nineteenth century a distinctive working-class culture had emerged in the towns, based on a sense of neighbourhood and mutual support, especially among women, and leisure activities centred on the churches and chapels or the public house and spectator sports like football. A pride in skilled or manual work was matched by a desire to have a good time. In the countryside, however, traditional recreations had been largely abandoned as droves of farmworkers left the countryside. Parish feasts disappeared, country fairs declined in vitality and old customs and festivities were neglected. Recording them before they went for ever seemed a vital priority for members of the folk-lore movement. May Day had been taken over by schools and made into a children's holiday, and Victorian squires and clergy had turned the disorderly harvest suppers into respectable tea parties with speeches. From the 1860s many parishes had a day of harvest thanksgiving with a special church service known as the harvest festival. By the end of the century this had come to be regarded as an important 'traditional' event in the church calendar.

During Victoria's long reign the English invented the modern forms of soccer, rugby, cricket, tennis, boxing, horse-racing, mountaineering and skiing, and pioneered walking and cycling as pleasurable pastimes. The fashion for organised, competitive games spread from the public schools throughout the Empire. The English also invented modern tourism with

Thomas Cook's package tours. In towns and villages throughout the country choral singing, brass bands, music concerts, Gilbert and Sullivan operettas, and both professional and amateur theatre flourished as never before. Commercial popular entertainment was provided by music halls and seaside resorts, while quieter forms of recreation ranged from visits to libraries, museums and art galleries, recreational parks and zoos to membership of antiquarian, natural history and philosophical societies. Looking back on his youth in the reign of King Edward, J. B. Priestley wrote:

> Consider what Bradford had to offer us – three daily papers and a weekly; the Subscription concerts on Fridays, the Bradford Permanent series on Saturdays, and superb choral singing almost any night; two theatres, two music halls, two or three professional concert parties; an Arts Club; a Playgoers' Society; one football club that had won the FA Cup not long before; several fine old pubs from the *George* in Market Street to the *Spotted House*, each easily reached from the band concerts in Lister Park.

Outside a London Public House
Two couples pose for George Sims, *Living London* (1901). Urban pubs were open from 6 am to 11 pm and at 2d. a pint beer could cost as little as a pint of milk.

But many scorned these attractions and spent their time in the local pub, 'the quickest way out of Manchester'. Beer remained an essential ingredient of leisure for most working-class men, and even at work it was a common practice to send for jugs of ale from the beerhouse or 'off licence'. In 1876 it was calculated that an astonishing 34 gallons of beer per head for every man, woman and child in Britain was consumed each year. Drunkenness was the most common cause of family arguments and of misery in working-class homes. Many an otherwise decent family drifted downwards through poverty to total want because of the excessive drinking of the father. The number of pubs that were available in the towns varied considerably from place to place. In Lancashire, a return of 1895 showed that Manchester had 600 licensed houses per 100,000 inhabitants, and that Rochdale and Salford were not far behind, but that Oldham, Bury and Burnley had far fewer and Nelson had only 123. Much of the growth of Nelson and Burnley had taken place after the tightening up of licensing regulations in 1869 and 1872, which had allowed magistrates to refuse new licences and to suppress some existing ones. Between 1872 and 1901 the ratio of drinking places to population fell from 1:200 to 1:300, nearly all the closures being beerhouses rather than pubs. This number compares with 1:668 by 1961. Even so, pubs were available

everywhere and were open most of the day and until midnight in London.
The late-morning opening and 'afternoon gap' were not introduced until
the First World War. A bill to close pubs on Sundays was approved for
Wales in 1881 but rejected for England. In most parts of Britain, especially
Scotland and Wales, however, Sunday remained a frustrating day for those
not inclined to attend the services of church or chapel.

In 1908–9 magistrates sent 62,882 people to gaol for drunkenness.

Although the amount of alcohol that was consumed began to fall from
the 1870s, drunkards were still a common sight in both the towns and the
countryside and drink was a principal cause of poverty. In 1908–9 magistrates sent 62,882 people to gaol for drunkenness. The Nonconformists led
the Temperance movement by forming Bands of Hope, whose members
signed the pledge to remain teetotal, and by promoting Temperance halls
as rival attractions to the pubs and music halls. In 1900 England and Wales
had about 102,000 public houses, despite the recent enforced closures.
The Liberal government's attempt to reduce the number of pubs by
another third was defeated in the House of Lords after fierce resistance
from the Conservatives and the brewers. England and Wales had nearly
6,500 breweries at the end of the nineteenth century, but their beers were
sold locally and the customer did not have a wide range of choice. An epidemic of arsenic poisoning between the summer of 1900 and early 1901
caused over 70 deaths and created much concern about adulterated beers.
However, dilution rather than additives was usually the main problem: one
in five samples tested at that time had been watered down and sometimes
salt had been added for flavour and to stimulate thirst. At twopence a pint
beer was cheap. In *The Temperance Problem and Social Reform* (1900),
Rowntree and Sherwell estimated that every male drinker consumed on
average 73 gallons of beer and 2.4 gallons of spirits a year.

The respectable middle classes never stepped into a pub, but did their
drinking at home or in gentlemen's clubs. Bottled beers had become
increasingly popular in the late nineteenth century, though they were
more expensive than draught beers. Many pubs were undoubtedly cheer-
less drinking dens, smelling of stale liquor, but others were warm and wel-
coming. Old friends could always be found there and clubs were provided
with congenial meeting places. Seebohm Rowntree acknowledged the
social attractiveness of York's pubs, many of which were places that offered
a cheerful and musical atmosphere on a Saturday night. In the late 1890s
Charles Booth found that many London pubs were quiet and orderly and
that 'while there is more drinking, there is less drunkenness than for-
merly'. Lady Bell thought that in Middlesbrough they were practically the
centres of the workmen's social lives. Wages were paid at the end of the
week, so that 'from Friday 'til Monday it constantly happens that a man is
half incapacitated by drink'. Children fetching beer in jugs from pubs for
their parents were a frequent sight in the towns. In the countryside, men had
little other than the local pub to turn to for a change from the domestic

fireside. But Flora Thompson remembered that low wages meant that the farmworkers of Juniper Hill had to make their half pints last all evening.

Music halls grew out of pubs, where their original purpose was to get people to buy drink. They flourished so much in the second half of the nineteenth century that lavish new theatres featuring stand-up comics and singers of sentimental ballads and humorous songs were opened in all the major towns. The age of the yearning or frustrated 'pop' song had not yet dawned. When the Salford Palace of Varieties was reopened in 1901, the general manager, Sam Higham, was reported to have been in good form with his song, 'Where was Mabel when the band struck up?' and his new sketch, 'John Bull', which 'fairly brought down the house'. By 1875 London had more than 300 music halls and the leading performers were stars. Ten years later, Marie Lloyd from Hoxton made her debut in the Eagle, in City Road. Cheaper halls and singing saloons, which charged threepence rather than sixpence or a shilling, were found in the back streets. All the large industrial towns had music halls and popular theatres offering melodramas, and many acquired palatial new or rebuilt premises in the 1880s and 1890s, some of which seated several thousand people. In the early 1890s the average nightly attendance at the 35 largest London music halls was estimated at 45,000 and over another 500 halls, most of them small and ephemeral, offered entertainment elsewhere in the capital

A Day at the Fair
A crowd of people of all ages enjoy a Punch and Judy show at a Hereford fair in 1898.

city. Music halls continued to attract working-class and lower middle-class audiences until the cinema became the new popular form of entertainment.

Funfairs had attracted large crowds in parts of London since the 1820s and had soon spread into industrial and market towns across the country. The St Giles's Fair at Oxford and the Nottingham Goose Fair became famous across a wide region. By the last quarter of the nineteenth century, when steam roundabouts and steam organs had become part of the attraction, many old rural feasts and hiring fairs had been converted into pleasure fairs. The disorderly behaviour associated with these fairs led to calls for their suppression. Thus in 1881 *The Salisbury and Winchester Journal*, reporting on the 9–10 September fair in Church Square, Fordingbridge, which was visited by 'Bartlett's steam circus and swing boats, as well as by several lesser shows', commented that, 'We think we are expressing the wishes of a great many of the inhabitants of this town when we hope that this will be the last "holding of the fair", as it is undoubtedly a nuisance and a disgrace.' The fair returned the following year, but its days were numbered. The British people, on the whole, were becoming more polite and better-behaved; attending shows and concerts, and becoming members of numerous clubs and societies. Even the large crowds at football matches were orderly.

The Victorians praised the virtues of work and took great pride in their skills. The long hours but relaxed approach to how time was spent at work, punctuated by days off such as the 'Saints Mondays' of many old crafts, had been largely replaced by the discipline of the works or factory. As the pace of work became more intense, shorter working hours were introduced in many trades, but most people were too tired after a long day's work to think of 'leisure activities'. A welcome improvement in 1850 was the introduction of a half-day holiday on Saturdays. The day holidays which were given to bank clerks in 1871 closed the banks and so quickly became public 'bank' holidays. Slowly, working people acquired greater opportunities for regular recreation and leisure and a wider choice of how to spend their increased earnings. The coming of the railways changed the whole concept of what a holiday should be. Families could now travel cheaply on a day-return to a seaside resort. Extended holidays at the seaside were much rarer, however, and were largely confined to workers in the Lancashire cotton industry, where by the 1890s factories found it efficient to close everything down for a fortnight during the summer 'Wakes' weeks.

Some of the Victorian seaside resorts were planned by aristocratic landowners. Eastbourne was already a fashionable watering place by the early nineteenth century, but after the opening of a branch railway in 1849 it was developed in fine style by the Duke of Devonshire. Its new Town Hall and St Saviour's church, its white and pillared Grand, Burlington,

Claremont and Queen's hotels, its pier, its glass domes and elaborate ironwork, and the wide, handsome boulevards of Devonshire Place and Cavendish Place gave it an air of opulence and grandeur. Some of the streets were named after Derbyshire villages near Cavendish properties, such as Baslow and Bolsover. Further along the coast, Bexhill's late Victorian and Edwardian appearance is the result of the initiative of the De la Warr family. On the east coast, the character of Skegness was transformed after the railway arrived in 1873, when the Earl of Scarbrough developed a resort to cater for the tastes of the working classes of the East Midlands.

Much of the surviving architecture in English and Welsh seaside resorts dates from their golden years in the late Victorian and Edwardian period: hotels and boarding houses, churches, shops, theatres, promenades, bandstands in public gardens and piers that enabled visitors to promenade over the sea and spend their money at a variety of shows. Brighton and Margate were the major resorts in the south, but Blackpool became the greatest working-class attraction of all, once it was opened up by the railways. By the mid nineteenth century skilled and supervisory workers in the cotton industry were taking advantage of cheap fares to spend holidays at Whitsuntide or the Wakes (the traditional holiday when church floors were re-covered with fresh rushes). John Walton has described how, by the 1870s, many cotton workers enjoyed unpaid summer holidays lasting three days beyond the weekend, and during the 1890s a new tradition of a full-scale 'Wakes Week' holiday was established in most of the Lancashire mill towns. By the 1890s towns like Burnley and Blackburn were almost deserted during their holiday weeks, as shops closed and churches and chapels held combined services for the remnants of their congregations. This was a distinctive cotton town phenomenon, for even the West Riding textile districts followed a long way behind. Blackpool was attracting 3 million visitors a year by 1900, 4 million by 1914. Its pier, tower and great wheel date from the 1890s. Blackpool could justifiably claim to be the world's first specialised working-class seaside resort. Meanwhile, the inland spas and hydropathic centres such as Cheltenham, Harrogate, Ilkley and Matlock continued to attract a wealthier, more sedate clientele. They too benefited from the railways. The Lake District offered more energetic holidays, as well as pleasant boat trips, but before the age of the motor car it remained a remote and generally quiet part of the country.

For most of the nineteenth century the vast majority of working-class people walked to work or to the shops. Countryfolk might use a carrier's cart or one of their own to get to market, but most people were used to walking long distances. In the major cities public transport facilities changed dramatically at the end of the century and it became possible to get to sports grounds and other centres of entertainment quickly and cheaply. In 1898 English cities had just over a thousand miles of tramways

In 1903 London had 3,623 horse buses and only 13 motor buses; by 1913 it had 3,522 motor buses and only 142 horse buses were left.

for horse-drawn trams; by 1914 the network was three times as large and cheap fares on the electric trams enabled working-class people to live in suburbs away from their place of work and to get to football grounds and other centres of entertainment. The motor engine provided another stimulus to public transport. In 1903 London had 3,623 horse buses and only 13 motor buses; by 1913 it had 3,522 motor buses and only 142 horse buses were left. London's overhead and underground railway expansion in the last three decades of the nineteenth century assisted the growth of the suburbs and the decline of the centre. At the same time, long-distance rail journeys were becoming quicker. By 1900 the journey from London to York had been reduced to 5 hours and that to Edinburgh to 8½ hours.

Victorian society relied heavily on the horse for transport, both in the towns and in the countryside. By 1870 the United Kingdom had about 120,000 privately-owned large carriages and 250,000 light two-wheelers. Old photographs show royal visitors arriving in horse-drawn carriages, and civic events being celebrated by gaily-decked horses drawing newly-painted carts and waggons. On 1 May 1901 the inhabitants of Salford watched the annual procession of the corporation's carts and horses, led, as usual, by the fire engines. Alderman Shaw was reported as saying that he did not believe the plans to draw the fire engines by motor car or electric car would ever succeed; there was nothing so reliable as a horse. But Dunlop's invention of the pneumatic tyre in 1888 and the introduction of petrol-driven cars seven years later heralded a new era of private transport. The motor car was the supreme status symbol of the Edwardians. By 1904 the United Kingdom had 24,201 motor cars, a third of them in London. The car was widely regarded as a dangerous nuisance by those who did not own them, for they churned up the unmetalled roads, frightened horses and were a threat to lives. Thomas Hardy, a keen cyclist who distrusted cars, wrote, 'It is a disagreeable way of getting about the country, I think, and always gives me the back-ache the next day.' The middle-class vogue for week-ending in country cottages was made possible by the railways and the motor car. The cheap bicycles that became available in the 1890s were greeted with enthusiasm by all classes and by women as well as men. London alone had 274 cycling clubs affiliated to the Cycling Association by 1902. Cafés and tea-rooms spread beyond the suburbs into the countryside to cater for the cycling boom and for the rambling clubs such as the Sheffield Clarion Ramblers (founded 1900), which introduced working-class people from the smoky industrial towns to the pleasures of moorland scenery.

Saturday half-holidays provided the opportunity for organised sport at both the professional and the local, amateur level to flourish on an unprecedented scale. Soccer matches were soon attracting weekly crowds of 20,000 in the large towns of northern and midland England, where skilled workers were earning higher wages. Football teams were drawn from the neighbourhoods of the grounds, just like amateur clubs or the rugby teams of northern England and south Wales. The Football Association, founded in 1863, began its popular cup competition in 1872, but control of the professional sport was grasped by the Football League, founded in 1888 by 12 clubs from the midlands and the north. Football had become such a popular spectator sport by 1901 that the Cup Final at Crystal Palace that year (a 2-2 draw between Tottenham Hotspur and Sheffield United) attracted a record crowd of 110,820. Rugby matches also attracted large crowds on Saturdays in the industrial towns of Yorkshire and Lancashire. In 1885, for instance, a match between Swinton and Bradford was watched by 10,000 spectators. In northern England the game became a professional sport in 1895 with the creation of the Northern Rugby Union, known later as the Rugby League. By that time, rugby union had become the national sport of Wales. The County Cricket Championship, which began in 1889, was another crowd puller that helped to foster county pride and fierce loyalties. Large crowds also turned up to watch organised athletics meetings, cross-country races and boxing matches, and thousands of young men were not just spectators but active participants in sports, and local leagues featured teams from works, pubs and chapels.

Horse-racing also attracted the crowds and betting was a well-organised business. Although race weeks at places such as Doncaster were traditional holidays for working men, the railways had increased their popularity. Derby day, of course, had become one of the most important social events in the country. Horse-racing was one sport that could unite aristocrats and labourers, and betting was the only way that working men thought they could obtain money without having to earn it. In 1890 uniform starting prices for every race were telegraphed all over the country and all attempts to ban off-course betting proved ineffective. Mid-day racing sheets attracted the fascinated attention of millions, but an obsession with betting on the horses could have dire social consequences. By the eve of the First World War gambling had replaced drunkenness as the worst social evil. In 1913 the *Salford Reporter* complained that it had become customary for a crowd of two to three hundred men and youths to assemble on Sundays in a public place to gamble away their wages in open disregard of the police.

Many of the rich devoted huge amounts of time to country sports. The shooting of grouse began on 12 August, that of pheasants in the autumn, and sporting landlords set aside four days a week for seven months of the year riding to hounds. In *The Memoirs of a Fox-Hunting Man* (1928) Siegfried Sassoon recalled the dedication and enthusiasm with which the sport was followed in the Edwardian period, with regular 'meets' in recognised hunting districts. The best hunting country was in the midland 'shires' – Northamptonshire, Leicestershire and Nottinghamshire. The shooting of game was even more popular and, with improved guns, the

Football had become such a popular spectator sport by 1901 that the Cup Final at Crystal Palace that year attracted a record crowd of 110,820.

Ladies' Golf
The Devon Ladies' Golf Team, winners of the Cup played for at Sunningdale in 1903. Golf was becoming increasingly popular amongst the English middle classes and had recently been taken up by women.

size of bags increased prodigiously from the 1880s. In December 1913 seven men (including King George V and the Prince of Wales) shot 3,937 pheasants, 3 partridges and 4 rabbits in a single day's shoot on the Burtley beat at Beaconsfield. In August 1913 nine guns shot 2,843 grouse on Broomhead Moor in the northern part of the Peak District. The game-keepers who were employed by the owners of shooting estates acted as country policemen whose job it was to keep the public off the grouse moors and out of the woods where pheasants were reared. The country-man's attitude was that poaching was a justifiable activity, if risky, but not theft. The 1901 census recorded 16,677 gamekeepers, an increase of 20.7 per cent since 1891 and 60 per cent since the 1860s. In Norfolk, Suffolk and some other predominantly agricultural counties gamekeepers out-numbered rural policemen.

By the First World War, however, many gentlemen were spending less time hunting and shooting and were turning instead to the less-costly pas-time of golf or were wintering abroad where expenses were lower. Golf, of course, was an ancient game in Scotland, but England's oldest club was The Royal Blackheath, founded in 1766. Most of the clubs surrounding London in the late nineteenth century were modern. The game received a great boost to its popularity as a townsman's recreation after the introduction of the rubber-covered ball in 1908. Middle-class women, too, were taking up golf, together with tennis, croquet and the new enthusiasm for cycling, and a craze for ping-pong swept the country in 1901.

At the close of the nineteenth century technical change was catching the popular imagination and was the subject of H. G. Wells's books, *The Time Machine* (1895) and *The War of the Worlds* (1898). In 1899 Marconi successfully transmitted a message from France to Chelmsford, and in 1901 sent a wireless telegraphy signal across the Atlantic, but as yet few people used the telephone or any form of electrical devices and the cinema's great age lay in the future. Before the invention of the 'wireless' and the 'gramophone', the only mass entertainment in the home was the newspaper. Most homes took a Sunday paper and perhaps a local weekly. *Old Moore's Almanack* and the penny periodical *Answers* (founded in 1888 and soon selling a million copies a week) provided short accounts of 'remarkable occurrences and curious information' for the newly-literate masses. George Newnes' *Tit-Bits* and Lord Northcliffe's *Daily Mail* were written in a simple style to cater for this market. By 1900 the English read more newspapers than any other nation. *Lloyd's Weekly News* sold 1 million copies in the 1890s, and so did the *Daily Mail* for a brief moment at the height of the Boer War. Their circulation rises were achieved by spectacular competitions offering cash prizes or pensions for life. Even so, in 1910 daily papers were read by less than one-fifth of adults, and most homes took newspapers only on Sundays. Except in periods of national crisis or celebration, the working classes showed little interest in any event other than horse-racing that occurred beyond their neighbourhood. Although the British were the most literate nation in the world – a mere five per cent of adults were illiterate – no other forms of reading were usual. The public libraries lent less than two books per person a year. In Middlesbrough, Lady Bell estimated that only one in four families read books as well as papers. In most working-class homes the only books on show were those obtained as Sunday school attendance prizes. Up-to-date information was often available to children only from the enormous number of illustrated cards in cigarette packets, which they collected and swapped.

During the second half of the nineteenth century the centres of major towns and cities ceased to be residential areas and became retail and entertainment districts instead. Rising incomes created mass-markets for cheap foods supplied by Maypole Dairies and the Home and Colonial Stores, the patent medicines of Thomas Holloway, and the branded soaps and scouring powders – Pears, Sunlight, Vim, Brasso – which kept houses and their inhabitants clean and made fortunes for entrepreneurs such as William Lever. Working-class co-operatives were often securely founded by the 1860s, and from the 1880s their success was assured. They

Hammersmith Provision Store, 1901
Multiple stores offering goods at cheap prices and at convenient times were transforming the nation's shopping habits. Some were open from 7 am to 10 or even 11 pm.

Hammersmith Provision Store, 1901
Multiple stores offering goods at cheap prices and at convenient times were transforming the nation's shopping habits. Some were open from 7 am to 10 or even 11 pm.

increased their membership 30 times between 1863 and 1914 and their turnover even more. The famous chain stores – Marks & Spencer, Boots, Sainsbury's – had humble origins and most provincial towns had their family firms which remained rooted in the neighbourhood. Department stores such as Selfridges, Liberty, Swan & Edgar, and Debenhams, grew quickly from the 1870s, using advertising, display and amenities to attract the continuous trade of mainly middle-class customers. Some West End shops and stores stayed open until 8 pm or even 10 pm, but this meant a working week of up to 84 hours for their assistants. Before the First World War, however, the small, family shops that are featured in so many old photographs still accounted for 80 per cent of the nation's retail trade. Most shopkeepers still lived over or behind their shop. The late-Victorian and Edwardian period was the heyday of the little corner shop, especially in the manufacturing towns of midland and northern England. Only a few of the multiple stores had branches throughout the country before the First World War. Most were concentrated in and around London or in particular parts of the north.

The industrial towns and cities of the north of England were transformed into shopping and entertainment centres in the last quarter of the nineteenth century. Sheffield's central streets were widened to twice their medieval width to accommodate the new electric trams and to allow the erection of large shops and department stores, notably that built by John Walsh in 1900 of steel and glass exposed on the ground floor but masked by stone on the upper storeys. In Halifax, increased consumer spending encouraged a much more sophisticated retail trade. Simpson & Sons offered furniture for the whole home in a five-storey showroom, all linked by elevator. The Halifax Borough Market was opened in 1896 by the Duke and Duchess of York. Designed in a French Renaissance style, it claimed to be 'among the very finest in the country'. It housed 19 shops and a pub on its outer perimeter, and 43 shops and over 100 stalls under its domed interior of glass and iron construction. Under the same roof, the fish market contained 16 lock-up shops inside and 6 on the outside.

But Leeds could justly claim to be the shopping centre of the north. It too improved the width and appearance of its central streets. In the 1880s Alexander Monteith's Grand Pygmalion became the borough's first department store, employing 200 assistants on four floors. From the late 1870s middle-class shops were gathered together in attractively-designed arcades: Thornton's (1878), Queen's (1888–9), Grand (1896–8), Victoria (1898), County Arcade and Cross Arcade (1898–1903). Retail outlets which depended entirely or mostly upon working-class custom were suitably diverse, ranging from street hawkers to the Leeds Industrial Co-operative Society, which in the late 1890s had 70 shops, mostly situated in the working-class industrial suburbs. The Leeds City Markets of 1902–4 consisted of a hall with 18 shops fronting the main roads and an open area inside that was occupied by stalls and surrounded by small shops. Its upper storeys housed a hotel, a restaurant and billiard, coffee and club rooms. The central streets were thronged with traffic. A count made on Briggate in January 1898 revealed that during a 10-minute period, from 8.20 to 8.30 am, 2,306 pedestrians, 3 omnibuses, 10 tramcars, 3 four-wheeled cabs, 6 hansom cabs and 2 post mail carts passed by. In 1909 the *Leeds Shopping Guide* claimed that, 'No City in England can boast a more wonderful transformation than that witnessed in Leeds during the past two or three decades.'

The closing years of Victoria's reign saw a striking change in the personal appearance of English men and women. The new enthusiasm for cycling and games favoured shorter, less restricting clothes, while rising incomes meant that women, especially in London, could try brighter and lighter fashions. Well-to-do men began to wear lounge suits instead of morning coats, and many abandoned top hats in favour of bowlers in winter and straw hats in summer. Frock coats and top hats were still worn by London gentlemen, however, and were brought out of the wardrobe by others on Sundays. Middle-class men in the Edwardian era turned increasingly to tweeds and grey flannels, but old photographs of street scenes show working men in cheap, ready-made clothes, and a 'billy pot' or a flat cap on nearly every head. Some agricultural labourers in parts of Oxfordshire still wore smocks at the end of the nineteenth century, but in general a working man's clothes no longer gave an obvious clue to his occupation. Meanwhile, women's dress had become much freer. The bustle went out of fashion about 1890 and soon afterwards whalebone corseting and wasp waists followed them into oblivion. From the 1880s a separate blouse and skirt was common, but the well-padded appearance of women's clothes was continued with the fashion for 'leg-of-mutton' sleeves. In the 1890s bloomers (for cycling) and long knickers replaced thick petticoats. Both the weight and the volume of under-clothing were reduced drastically and soon skirts were worn higher off the ground. Changing fashions in hair styles necessitated a complete change of hat. In mid-Victorian times the hair was plaited and coiled in a knob at the back of the neck and bonnets were tied under the chin, but from the 1880s the hair was brushed forward from the back of the head and massed on the top in the French style and so hat-pins had to be used. Edwardian ladies wore large feathered hats and few people ventured outside without something on their head. Old photographs show working-class people dressed in drab cloth, often shiny through long wear, but by the early years of the twentieth century a real improvement was evident in the quality of people's clothes, brought about by higher wages and the availability of cheap, ready-made garments.

CHAPTER SEVEN

EMPIRE AND NATION

Empire

THE BRITISH EMPIRE was the largest the world had ever known;
one where, in the popular phrase, 'the sun never set'. In 1901 it covered
about 12 million square miles, equal to more than one-fifth of the land
surface of the globe. It was already large by 1861, when it covered 8 million square miles, but over the next 40 years it increased in size by 50 per
cent, mainly through acquisitions in Africa. By the end of Victoria's reign,
the British Empire covered over 4 million square miles in North, Central
and South America, 3 million in Australasia, another 3 million in Africa,
and 1.75 million square miles in Asia. The United Kingdom itself covered
just 121,089 square miles.

Roughly estimated, the population of the British Empire in 1861 had
been 175 million, but by 1901 it had reached over 400 million. Of these
vast numbers of people, more than 300 million lived in Asia, about 45 million in Africa, some 7.5 million in America, over 5 million in Australasia,
nearly half a million in the Mediterranean, over 150,000 in islands in
British seas, and 41.5 million in the United Kingdom. In all, 1,674,000
natives of the United Kingdom resided in British colonies, dependencies
or protectorates (including in all cases the army, navy, marines and merchant
seamen); nearly 900,000 of them in Australasia, 390,000 in Canada, about
220,000 in Africa, about 97,000 in India and about 32,000 in Gibraltar and
Malta. Figures for South Africa were not available in 1901 because of the
Boer War and in that year the West Indies could not afford a census. At
the same time, natives of the United Kingdom who were living abroad, but
not in the dependencies or colonies, were either enumerated or estimated
at 2,791,403 in the United States of America, 34,892 in France, 26,849 in
Argentina, 16,793 in various parts of the German Empire, 8,768 in Italy,
7,759 in Spain, 5,235 within the Russian Empire, 5,096 in Belgium, 3,898
in Switzerland, 3,639 in Chile, 3,480 in Austria and Hungary, 3,287 in
China, 2,766 in Egypt, and 2,278 in Portugal. The British had spread far
and wide.

Much of the Empire had been acquired during the last quarter of the
nineteenth century, with the 'opening-up' of Africa, but India was still the

*In all, 1,674,000 natives of the
United Kingdom resided in
British colonies, dependencies
or protectorates...*

The British Army in India, 1897
A battery gun team in the Southern Division of the Royal Artillery pose near Quetta with their elephants.

prized possession. Lord Curzon, Viceroy of India from 1899 to 1905, believed that, 'As long as we rule India we are the greatest power in the world. If we lose it we shall drop straight away to a third rate power.' His Indian Museum at Kedleston Hall (Derbyshire), which displays his 'Eastern Collection', including relics and memorials of the Delhi Coronation Durbar in 1903, shows what a vivid and romantic impression India had made on him. Imperialism had become the policy of all the Great Powers from the 1880s and was at its height at the turn of the century, when the popular mood was jingoistic. All the British political parties had imperialist wings and, when Joseph Chamberlain became Colonial Secretary in Salisbury's cabinet in 1895, what had hitherto been a low-ranking office was elevated in status. Chamberlain regarded the colonies as 'undeveloped estates' whose resources should be exploited for the benefit of all. Nevertheless, by 1901 trade derived from the vast territories that had been annexed since 1880 amounted to only two per cent of Britain's total trade, a negligible proportion of the whole. By 1901 the major white colonies – Canada, Australia and New Zealand – were already internally self-governing. The rest, including the sub-continent of India, were ruled directly or indirectly from Britain.

Every part of the Empire was represented at the celebration of Queen Victoria's Diamond Jubilee in 1897, when Chamberlain brought the colonial leaders, chieftains and exotically-dressed troops to parade through the streets of central London. From then on, every great royal occasion was set in an imperial context, and royal visits to provincial towns and cities were stage-managed to promote the monarchy as the symbol of unity. Central London was re-fashioned as a mighty imperial capital during the closing decades of the nineteenth century and the years leading up to the First World War, with magnificent institutional buildings and enormous offices, grandiose hotels and lavish theatres. Thomas Collicutt's Imperial Institute at South Kensington (1887–93) and Aston Webb's Victoria and Albert Museum, were both designed in a mixed style that was typical of the public buildings of the early 1890s. Norman Shaw's New Scotland Yard, the police headquarters on Victoria Embankment (1887–90), used a mixture of Baroque and Scottish baronial styles in a strong, free manner. Baroque quickly became the accepted style for major public buildings, notably The Old Bailey Criminal Courts (1900–6), the Government Buildings in Parliament Square, Westminster (1898–1912), and The Admiralty and The War Office, Whitehall (1898–1906), each of them full of civil servants and clerks working from 9 am to 5 pm. From about 1906 Baroque was replaced by a more chaste classical style introduced from France. The Mall was laid out as the one truly grand, processional avenue in London, leading from Trafalgar Square under Admiralty Arch (designed by Aston Webb in 1909 and originally crowded with offices for the Royal Navy) towards Buckingham Palace, which Webb refronted in 1912–13. The King Edward VII Galleries at the British Museum (1904–14) rounded off this impressive collection of imperial buildings. Other major structures which helped to give a new dignity to the capital city included such diverse structures as the Coliseum Theatre (1902–4), the Ritz Hotel, Piccadilly (1903–6), the Piccadilly Hotel (1905–8), the Palm Court lounge, Waldorf Hotel (1906–8), the Royal Automobile Club, Pall Mall (1908–11), Selfridges department store, Oxford Street (1907–9 and later) and the Methodist Central Hall, Westminster (opened 1911). London fashions were followed in many parts of England and Wales, with the building of Cardiff City Hall (1897–1906) and notable town halls at Colchester (1897–1902), Stockport (1904–8), Lancaster (1906–9), and other major buildings in Edwardian Baroque on a large scale, such as the Royal Naval College, Dartmouth (completed 1903), the Ashton Memorial in Williamson Park, above Lancaster (1904–9), and the Mersey Docks Building (1903–7) and the Liver Building (1911) in Liverpool.

British people took for granted their superiority over foreigners, especially the coloured inhabitants of the colonies. Cecil Rhodes spoke for many when he said, rhetorically, 'Ask any man what nationality he would prefer to be, and ninety-nine out of a hundred will tell you that they would prefer to be an Englishman.' A feeling of loyalty towards one's country often degenerated into a contemptuous attitude towards foreigners. Ideas of racial superiority promoted by Social Darwinism fostered the belief that

Victoria Embankment
The mile-long curve of the embankment was a great triumph of Victorian engineering that was constructed over the mud-flats of the river. It eased congestion along the Strand and provided a riverside walk with fine views of some of London's most imposing buildings.

black people were inferior beings who were totally different from Europeans. The widely-accepted image of black Africans was that of exotic and savage inhabitants of the 'Dark Continent' who needed to be civilised and taught Christian beliefs and virtues. It was thought that foreigners could never compete with British manufactured goods because they were not clever enough. The popular press was loud in its praise of the Empire and Britain's imperial mission. In 1896 Harmsworth launched the *Daily Mail*, which sold at one half-penny and soon achieved a circulation of 700,000. The *Mirror*, the *Sketch* and the *Daily Express* followed soon afterwards and adopted a similar tone.

This belief in racial superiority was common even among the poorest of the English. In *In Darkest London* (1889) Margaret Harkness, the novelist who wrote under the pseudonym John Law, described the typical 'loafer' or semi-criminal street scavenger:

> Among the foreigner lounges the East End loafer, monarch of all he surveys, lord of the premises. It is amusing to see his British air of superiority. His hands are deep down in the pockets of his fustian trousers, round his neck is a bit of coloured rag or flannel, on his head is a battered cap. He is looked upon as scum by his own nation, but he feels himself to be an Englishman and able to kick the foreigner back to his 'own dear native land' if only Government would believe in 'England for the English' and give all foreigners notice.

Anti-immigrant feeling among the London working class led to the formation of the Band of British Brothers in the East End in 1901. Similar attitudes were commonplace among those who had emigrated from Britain. Although native leaders were often valued by the governing classes, the ordinary indigenous people were treated with contempt. Nor was it just a matter of displacing the Aborigines or Maoris. When the Commonwealth of Australia was formed on 1 January 1901 by a federation of the six colonies a 'White Australia' policy was adopted to prevent immigration from Asia.

Contemptuous attitudes towards the natives is only part of the story, however, for Imperialism was driven by idealism as well as the desire for profit. In 1894 Lord Roseberry proclaimed that the British Empire was 'the greatest secular agency for good the world has seen'. Although the Empire was based on self-interest and the machine gun, its advocates claimed that it was driven by a moral purpose, a God-ordained duty to colonise backward parts of the world. Rudyard Kipling captured this mood in 1898 when he wrote, 'Take up the White Man's burden / Send forth the best ye breed / to serve …' His 'Land of our birth, we pledge to thee / Our love and toils in the years to be' quickly became a much-used school hymn. Kipling was widely acknowledged as the 'Poet of the Empire', who wrote in ordinary language in a style that imitated old ballads and hymns. His adventure story *Kim* (1901), a vivid picture of life in India, and his numerous children's stories made him hugely popular with ordinary readers. Although he was sneered at by some other literary people for his 'vulgarity' and 'jingoism', he became the first Englishman to receive the Nobel Prize for Literature. Kipling was a complex man who, despite his attachment to the Empire, refused all state honours. He was preoccupied with the thought that the British Empire would one day fade like the Roman one had. It was no coincidence that Roman Britain fascinated both scholars and the general public alike at the time when the British Empire covered so much of the world.

Men on the left of the political spectrum had much the same attitude before a more sombre judgement took hold after the Boer War. George Bernard Shaw, for example, wrote *Fabianism and the Empire* (1900), a Fabian booklet that defended imperialism as the means of progress. Magic lantern shows that depicted imperial travel and missionary work popularised the ideal of selfless service and a common pride in the Empire, no matter how lowly a person's status might be. J. E. C. Weldon, the Bishop of Calcutta, was not alone in thinking that the British Empire was 'divinely ordained'. Imperialism appealed to all sections of society and the growing numbers of 'lower-middle' class people in the towns and suburbs were amongst its staunchest supporters. But government policies were not accepted uncritically. When Mary Kingsley followed her best-selling *Travels in West Africa* (1897) with *West African Studies* (1899), a strong attack on the Crown Colony system as a waste of life and money and a destroyer of African social institutions, her views received a lot of support.

The 24 May 1902 (the anniversary of Queen Victoria's birthday) was officially designated as Empire Day, to be celebrated throughout the British Empire as a means of training school children in good citizenship. Although it did not receive official recognition as an annual event until

1916, it was observed eight or nine years earlier in schools in Burnley, Blackburn and Wigan and in other parts of the land. Entries in school log books refer to the singing of songs such as 'Soldiers of the Queen', 'Hearts of Oak', and 'There's a Dear Old Flag to Fight For'. Military music was popular and youth organisations imitated military discipline. The Boys' Brigade, which was founded in Glasgow in 1883 and which spread into England in the 1890s, had as its object, 'The advancement of Christ's kingdom amongst boys and the promotion of habits of obedience, reverence, discipline, self-respect and all that tends towards a true Christian manliness.' The Boy Scouts (1907), which grew out of Colonel Baden-Powell's army experiences in the Boer War, placed less emphasis on discipline and religion and more on outdoor pursuits. It soon became the most popular youth organisation of all.

The Boer War

The end of the nineteenth century saw the Empire overstretched and under-defended, but until the South African war began in October 1899 the extent of this problem was not generally appreciated. Everyone assumed that the Boers would soon be crushed. On 16 December 1899 *The Salisbury and Winchester Journal* reported the departure of reserve troops for South Africa: 'Fordingbridge was the scene of an enthusiastic demonstration on Monday last, the occasion being the departure of seven young men from the town and neighbourhood, reservists of the Wiltshire regiment. The men were due to leave Fordingbridge by the 11.47 train to Salisbury, but shortly after nine crowds began to gather, and at 10.30 the vicinity of the Bank was a dense throng of spectators.' Led by a band, the men marched to the market place, where they were each presented with gifts to the value of £5 from a collection that had been organised by 'a working man named Harris'. After hearty cheers, 'the vicar offered prayers, the crowd repeating the Lord's prayer', then the men were carried shoulder high to the station. As the train left, the band played the National Anthem. Such scenes were repeated throughout the land.

It was widely expected that the soldiers would be back home for Christmas, but the war dragged on for two-and-a-half years. The War Office reckoned that the 365,693 imperial and 82,742 colonial soldiers who fought in the war suffered more than 100,000 casualties of all kinds and that 400,346 horses, mules and donkeys were 'expended'. The financial cost of the war to Britain was over £200 million. Yet it turned out to be a humiliating experience for the British and a clear signal that the limits of imperial expansion had been reached.

In 1880–81 the Boers had gained independence for Transvaal and Orange Free State in all matters except foreign policy, but the subsequent discovery of the vast Witwatersrand gold field tempted Britain to get them back by forceful means. Military invasion was justified on the grounds that the Boers' new wealth would make them too powerful a neighbour, possibly in alliance with Germany, but most foreigners saw Britain as the aggressor. When the German kaiser sent the Boer president a telegram of congratulations on repelling the infamous Jameson raid, British hackles were raised. It seemed a simple matter to enforce authority over a small army of farmers, but the Boers surprised everyone in the first months of the war by advancing deep into Natal to hold several British garrisons under siege. Only in May 1900 did the weaponry and sheer size of the British army begin to turn the tide. By then, the names of Ladysmith, Kimberley and Spion Kop had become etched deep into the minds of people back in Britain. The most famous name of all, however, was that of Mafeking.

A British garrison under the command of Colonel Baden-Powell in this small town in the north-east corner of Cape Province lay under siege from a superior force for 217 days before it was relieved on 17 May 1900. As the news that disaster had been averted spread throughout Britain, crowds took to the streets to celebrate in jingoistic fervour. Just how widespread or solid the feeling was remains a matter of controversy, but *The Times* was in no doubt. It reported that the inhabitants of poor districts took particular delight in the celebrations, claiming that:

> the news was received with extraordinary enthusiasm in East London and Saturday was generally observed as a holiday. The Whitechapel and Bow roads were a mass of flags and bunting, while all the tramcars and omnibuses flew flags … a large body of working men with flags and banners perambulated the Bow Road, singing patriotic airs, while hundreds of cyclists wearing photographs of Colonel Baden Powell formed into procession and paraded the principal thoroughfares of Poplar and Stepney.

The Salisbury and Winchester Journal noted that:

> Fordingbridge was not behind its neighbours in showing its joy at the relief of the beleaguered force. In a very short time the town presented quite a holiday aspect – almost every house displaying a flag, whilst festoons of flags were numerous. The Master of the National School and Mr Dutton organised a procession of their scholars, many of them in uniform and carrying large toy guns, others carrying flags. They paraded the town, singing 'Soldiers of the Queen', 'The Handy Man', and 'Rule Britannia', stopping at various places and giving cheers for the Queen, Baden Powell, Lord Roberts, etc. The scholars dispersed at the Bank after singing the National Anthem. In the evening the Volunteers paraded the town, fired volleys in the market place, and burnt an effigy of Kruger. The Union Jack floated on the church tower and the bells rang a merry peal. The Crown Hotel displayed an effective motto, 'Mafeking', in red, white and blue.

By October 1900 the Transvaal had been largely reconquered and the Conservative government took advantage of military success and their

Return of the Veterans
The homecoming of local soldiers who fought in the Boer War is celebrated at Builth Wells.

opponents' divisions to call a snap election, which quickly got dubbed the 'khaki' election after the colour of the soldiers' uniforms. The Conservatives were returned with a 134 majority over the Liberals and the Irish Nationalists, but as the Liberals got 2 million votes against the 2.4 million of the Conservatives a lot of people had clearly not been swayed by Chamberlain's opinion that a vote against the government was a vote for the Boers. The war was far from over, however, for the Boers conducted effective guerrilla warfare. As they did not wear uniforms, they could quickly revert to their role as farmers. Lord Kitchener's answer was to herd noncombatant Boers (mainly women) into unhealthy 'concentration camps' and to burn their farms systematically. In June 1901 Campbell-Bannerman, the Liberal leader, shocked the jingoists but touched a sympathetic cord among many others when he publicly attacked these policies as 'methods of barbarism' that were unworthy of the British Empire. When the last Boers surrendered in May 1902 at Pretoria most Britons were heartily fed up with the war. Little satisfaction could be gained from victory over 'a tiny rabble'. The army's poor performance had come as a shock and for a while the nation underwent a period of self-examination and a marked cooling of aggressive imperialist attitudes. The British Empire was no longer simply a source of national pride and pleasure. The jingoistic mobs went quiet, but few turned to the opposite extreme of pacifism. The emphasis on imperial expansion was now replaced by a concern for imperial unity, consolidation and defence. In Kipling's famous phrase, the war had taught Britain 'no end of a lesson'.

The mood of self-examination focused on the physical deterioration of the men who had volunteered to fight, only to be rejected on medical grounds. In Manchester out of 12,000 men offering to serve in 1899, some 8,000 were rejected straight away and only about 1,200 were accepted as being fit in all respects, though the army measurements had just been reduced to the lowest standards since the battle of Waterloo. In 1903 the government set up an Inter-Departmental Committee to examine the poor standard of health in war recruits. They found that during the 10 years from 1893 to 1902 as many as 34.6 per cent of volunteers nationally had been rejected on medical examination, besides an uncounted number, known to be very large, who had not been thought worth examining. The figures were even higher in the large, industrial towns and cities. The findings were rightly thought to reflect ill-health in childhood. A stunted, rickety appearance was seen to be the result of inadequate food, not enough sunlight in the polluted towns, insanitary conditions and low wages, rather than neglect by ignorant or indifferent parents.

The middle classes were dismayed by the hard evidence of life in the slums, their shocked reaction often being expressed in emotional terms such as the ghetto, the abyss, or the jungle and to the slum dwellers themselves as 'inferiors'. Jack London spoke for many of them in *The People of the Abyss* (1903), where he looked on the urban poor as the 'inefficients' of society. One extreme solution that was much discussed was that of eugenics. Another, which was expressed by William Booth, the Salvation Army general, in his book *In Darkest England and the Way Out* (1890) was forced emigration. Dr Thomas John Barnardo (1845–1905), who had been providing homes for destitute children in the East End of London since 1870, was another who saw emigration to Australia and Canada as the only hope for the poor. In complete contrast, the social reforms advocated by Booth and Rowntree formed the basis of the Liberal programme. Winston Churchill, soon to be a Liberal, was deeply impressed by Rowntree's study of poverty in York, and his recent memories of reporting the war in South Africa moved him to remark, 'I can see little glory in an empire which can rule the waves and is unable to flush its own sewers.' At the 1906 election he proclaimed, 'The cause of Liberalism is the cause of left-out millions.'

At the end of the Boer War it was clear that the empire could not be expanded further and that the less-exciting policy of consolidation must now be pursued. From 1903 Joseph Chamberlain championed the cause of imperial preference, which aimed to unite the Empire by levying lower tariffs on imports from the colonies and protectorates than on those from other countries. He was met with fierce opposition from people who thought that Britain's interests were still best preserved by its traditional

East Kent Buffs
A group of Volunteers
photographed at Sittingbourne
in 1901 as an 'Active Service
Squad'. Conscription into the
British Army was not introduced
until the First World War.

policy of free trade. Despite the ignominy of taking so long to defeat the
Boers, the Empire continued to attract dedicated and idealistic men and
women to serve in far-off lands in the belief that they were civilising the
world and making it a more progressive and peaceful place in which to
live. This idealism needs to be remembered as much as the distasteful,
braying jingoism that celebrated the relief of Mafeking and which ulti-
mately contributed to the catastrophe of the First World War.

The Army and Navy

By 1911 the population of the British Empire had reached 416 million, of
whom 344 million were coloured. The largest and most dispersed empire
the world had ever known was dependent on the Royal Navy as much as
the Army. Yet Britain did not introduce conscription into the armed
services until well into the First World War. The army and the navy relied
on volunteers and those who wanted to pursue a military career. Over half
the volunteers were working-class men, and more than half of these were
skilled workers. Some sought adventure, but many were driven by poverty
and unemployment to seek security. As Sir Ian Hamilton observed in
1911, the statistics showed that 'each year about three-fifths of the recruits
for the Regular Army enlisted between October and March', when work
was short in industries such as agriculture and building. The number of
working-class volunteers for the Boer War continued to grow even though
the war became less popular. Robert Roberts' wry observation on his
Salford neighbours who had been soldiers in the outposts of the empire
was that, 'Their experience seemed to have gained them little beyond a

contempt for lesser breeds, a love of family discipline and a passion for hot pickles.'

Ever since the battle of Waterloo, wars involving British soldiers had been fought in far distant lands. The Crimean War of 1854–56 was the only major campaign against a European power, and that was fought a long way from home. Men who enlisted in the army expected to travel the world and to spend years of their service in India. Thomas Hardy's poem 'Drummer Hodge', written during the Boer War, captures the feeling that war was something that happened on foreign soil, in remote parts of the world. It was not until the First World War was fought in the Flanders mud and the sounds of battle were heard in southern Britain that armed conflict lost its air of distant romance.

If an ancestor who served in the army was not an officer, you may have difficulty in finding him in the archives unless you know the regiment in which he served, for military service records were kept by the regiment and were not deposited centrally. An old photograph of a soldier in military uniform might help to identify his unit. From 1881 certain regiments of the British Army were allocated to particular counties, for example the Lancashire Fusiliers. At the Family Records Centre deaths registered during the Boer War name a man's regiment. The key sources at the National Archives for someone looking for a soldier who served in the Boer War are the pension records in WO 97 or First World War Army Service records if they continued to serve. A few regiments are covered by the depot description books in WO 67 which run on to 1908. Working-class recruits could not expect to rise beyond the ranks of the non-commissioned officers. To be 'an officer and a gentleman' was synonymous. Siegfried Sassoon's *Memoirs of a Fox-Hunting Man* recalls how a young man who had been educated at a public school and who spent much of his time 'riding to hounds' automatically became an officer despite his lack of military experience. The English class system was nowhere more obvious than in the armed services.

The 1901 census enumerated 112,822 men who were serving in the Army at home and 55,416 men in the Royal Navy and Marines. The entire Army amounted to 441,935 men, an increase of 219,076 or 98.3 per cent since the previous census, mainly because of the war in South Africa. The officers and men serving abroad included 25,534 who were born beyond the United Kingdom. The total number of men in the Royal Navy had increased 70.9 per cent to 90,559. The official report on the census noted that in the Navy service commenced at an earlier age and continued to a later age than in the Army. A total of 18,913 men served in the Royal Marines, an increase of nearly 40 per cent.

Although it was entirely dependent on volunteers, the British Army had become a large one that had to be provided with substantial barracks in southern England. The small and remote village of Aldershot was

The 1901 census enumerated 112,822 men who were serving in the Army at home and 55,416 men in the Royal Navy and Marines. The entire Army amounted to 441,935 men, an increase of 219,076 or 98.3 per cent since the last census...

transformed into the country's chief military centre, famed throughout the Empire. Aldershot's population rose modestly from 494 in 1801 to 875 in 1851, then during the Crimean War it grew rapidly, reaching 16,720 in 1861. By 1901 it had soared to 30,974. To the north, the barracks and training establishments at Farnborough turned a small village of 477 people in 1851 to a busy settlement housing 11,500 people 50 years later. The Royal Military Academy at Sandhurst became the major training school for officers and in 1895 the War Office bought a large area of Salisbury Plain for army training and manoeuvres. The number of men who volunteered for army service fell after the Boer War but rose again from 1908 to pass a quarter of a million. The First World War saw an astonishing surge in numbers, with 2.5 million men, from all social classes, enlisting in the first 18 months, before the introduction of conscription.

By 1900 the volume of British foreign trade was over six times higher than it had been in the middle of the nineteenth century. When allowance is made for the great rise in the population, this increase in trade still amounted to about three times per person. Food, drink and tobacco accounted for nearly half Britain's imports, raw materials about a third, and manufactured goods the remaining one-fifth. Britain paid for its imported food by exporting the goods that it had made. About two-thirds of British export earnings came from manufactured goods, principally Lancashire cotton. By 1905 over 6 million yards of cotton pieces were exported each year. In 1907 textile exports earned the country £180 million; by 1913 this figure had risen to £200 million. Britain's share of world exports of manufactured goods amounted to over 40 per cent in the second half of Victoria's reign, and though the proportion fell to about 30 per cent in the Edwardian period this was still an impressive performance. Britain also benefited from the wealth generated by the City of London, the greatest financial centre in the world.

At the end of the nineteenth century half the ships on the high seas were registered in Britain and about a third of the world's trade was controlled from there, but the growing might of Germany was being watched anxiously and a naval race for supremacy between the two had begun. HMS *Dreadnought*, launched in 1906, heralded a new era in the construction of heavily-armed and armour-clad battleships. Naval shipbuilding was a specialised area in which most northern shipyards could not compete effectively. The Royal Navy dockyard at Portsmouth was in a class of its own. The town's population was already large in 1801, at 33,226, for Portsmouth had long been a major naval centre. During the next 50 years, the houses in the ancient narrow streets of the old town were turned into slum dwellings as the population rose to 72,096. Military establishments and naval depots, garrisons and barracks spread around the old settlement from the 1860s and 1870s, so that by 1880 Portsmouth was the most heavily defended town in Europe. Alongside the naval quarters came more and more hotels and communal lodging houses, inns, beer-houses, music halls and brothels. Another expansion of the royal dockyard facilities in the last quarter of the nineteenth century provided shipbuilding, fitting and repair facilities for ever-larger warships. By 1901 Portsmouth's population had reached 188,133.

The two Tyneside giants, Armstrong and Palmer, dominated heavy industry in north-eastern England. During the later nineteenth century the Elswick Ordnance Company that William Armstrong had founded in 1859 became one of the world's leading engineering, shipbuilding and armaments firms, taking over the rival Whitworth company in 1897. In 1900 Armstrong's employed 25,028 workers, but the greatest armoury the world has ever seen was situated in the east end of Sheffield. Vickers, Brown, Cammell-Laird, Firth and Hatfield led the way in manufacturing every type of war material, from the armour-plate of the *Dreadnought* to a soldier's helmet, bayonet and razor, and from the largest naval projectile to the bullet of a rifle. Firms founded at the beginning of Victoria's reign continued to expand on a massive scale into the First World War. Like all the industrial districts of England and Wales, Sheffield was continually enveloped in the smoke that came from home fires and industrial chimneys. J. S. Fletcher, *A Picturesque History of Yorkshire* (1899) provides a vivid description of the city at the close of the century:

> Under smoke and rain, Sheffield is suggestive of nothing so much as of the popular conception of the infernal regions. From the chimneys, great volumes of smoke pour their listless way towards a forbidding sky; out of the furnaces shoot forth great tongues of flame which relieve the sombreness of the scene and illuminate it at the same time; in the streets there is a substratum of dust and mud; in the atmosphere a choking something that appears to take a grip of one's throat. The aspect of the northern fringe of Sheffield on such a day is terrifying, the black heaps of refuse, the rows of cheerless-looking houses, the thousand and one signs of grinding industrial life, the inky waters of river and canal, the general darkness and dirt of the whole scene serves but to create feelings of repugnance and even horror.

Yet this was the place that was famous throughout the world for its special alloy steels and its superbly hand-crafted cutlery. Few of the changes that came about during the second half of the twentieth century were as dramatic and as welcome as the removal of smoke from the urban atmosphere.

Domestic Political Issues

The German threat and the perennial question of Irish Home Rule were central issues of political debate in the Edwardian era, but arguments about imperialism abated after the Boer War and centred on the economic question of imperial preference versus free trade. All the political parties

A political cartoon of 1900, prematurely depicting the death of the Liberal Party. Six years later, the Liberals won a massive majority in the House of Commons.

were staunchly patriotic and even the slum dwellers remained intensely loyal to the nation and to the system as a whole.

The Act of Union (1801) had ended Irish legislative independence by creating the United Kingdom of Great Britain and Ireland. Daniel O'Connell's Repeal Movement of the 1840s had challenged this arrangement and under Charles Stewart Parnell Home Rule became a dominant political issue from the 1880s. Gladstone's dependence on the support of Irish MPs prompted his government to introduce a Home Rule Bill in 1886 that would have granted limited devolution, but his party was split and the Ulster Protestants fiercely resistant. A second bill, introduced in 1893, was soundly defeated in the House of Lords, but the Irish Question remained on the political agenda and more limited forms of self government were considered by both the Conservatives and Liberals. Home Rule came to the forefront of political debate again in the years leading up to the First World War, when another minority Liberal government was dependent upon the support of Irish MPs, but those who were willing to grant Irish independence were thwarted by the determined opposition of the majority of the population in Ulster. When the Irish Free State was created in 1922, it excluded the north-eastern counties.

The issues over which the politicians fought most keenly at the turn of the century were the domestic ones of social reform. Lord Salisbury's Conservative government had been re-elected in 1900 at the height of the Boer War and during a period of full employment. The Tories were increasingly the party of industrial businessmen as well as landlords and they based their elective strength on the middle classes. But even though many men and all women were not allowed to vote, the Conservatives still had to attract between one-third and one-half of the working-class electorate in order to obtain a parliamentary majority. They were particularly successful in doing this in Lancashire, where the native working class were often hostile to the large numbers of Irish Catholic immigrants, who voted Liberal. The Conservatives had just cause for regarding themselves as the 'natural party of government', for the Liberals had not won a parliamentary majority for many years before their handsome victory in 1906. The Liberals claimed to represent the underprivileged members of society and they appealed particularly to the Nonconformists, whose interest in politics regained some of its fervour when the Conservative government provided financial support from the public rates for church schools in 1902–3.

Some 70,000 Nonconformists were prosecuted for refusing to pay their rates when the measure was introduced. The Labour Party was still in its infancy during the Edwardian period. It had been founded as the Labour Representation Committee in 1900, when its first two MPs were elected. The election of 29 Labour MPs in 1906 and 42 in 1910 was widely recognised as an indicator of what would happen once the franchise was extended to all. They formed a vociferous minority who spurred on the Liberal programme of social reforms. The Women's Social and Political Union, founded in Manchester in 1903 by Mrs Emmeline Pankhurst and her daughters, grew out of the Independent Labour Party and at first was a working-class movement. In 1906 the Pankhursts moved to London and the movement became increasingly middle class. Dubbed the 'Suffragettes' by the *Daily Mail* in 1908, the campaigners for 'votes for women' aroused derisive hostility from many politicians but enough excitement and public sympathy to ensure the ultimate success of its goals. The First World War delayed victory, but in 1918 women over 30 were given the vote and 10 years later women over 21 were placed on an equal footing with men, who had achieved universal suffrage in 1918.

The late-nineteenth and early-twentieth centuries saw the Trades Unions become a powerful force for the improvement of wages and working conditions. The upper and middle classes saw them as a revolutionary threat, but the unions had been founded before the rise of socialism and organised working-class politics, and before the First World War most of their members who had the vote supported the Liberals. The masses remained ignorant of socialist doctrine of any kind and remained intensely loyal to the nation and the existing political system. In 1889 the dockers' strike for 6d. an hour – the 'docker's tanner' – had ended in a famous victory that gave a stimulus to Trade Unionism as a whole, but by 1903 few of the 669 trades unions had more than 20,000 members. At first, unskilled workers were the most militant, but their organisation was weak. At the turn of the century, the miners were moderate Liberals and the engineers cautious workmen without political ambition, but within a decade or so they were both in the vanguard of militancy. After 1900 real national wages stopped growing and prices and the cost of living rose. Retail prices increased by nearly a third between 1896 and 1913 and the real value of wages fell by about 13 per cent. In 1901, in the case of the Taff Vale Railway Company v. the Amalgamated Society of Railway Servants, the House of Lords decided to overturn the usual practice since the legislation of 1871 that a trade union could not be sued for damages arising from an industrial dispute. This provocative decision taught the Trades Unions that to achieve their ends they needed to become more involved in politics. The Taff Vale judgement was reversed in 1906 upon the election of a Liberal government. By 1911 British trades unions had a combined membership of 3.1 million, but the great majority of workers remained

The late-nineteenth and early-twentieth centuries saw the Trades Unions become a powerful force for the improvement of wages and working conditions.

unorganised. In the years leading up to the First World War, the working class became far more united and formidable, but the armed conflict in Europe ended all fears (or hopes) that the major strikes of 1910–12 might lead to political revolution.

The physical condition of the nation was the principal concern of the Liberal government that was elected so overwhelmingly in 1906. As early as 1889 G. R. Sims's *Horrible London* had posed the question: 'Is it too much to ask that in the intervals of civilising the Zulu and improving the condition of the Egyptian fellah the Government should turn its attention to the poor of London and see if it cannot remedy this terrible state of things?' The Boer War had taught the British that keeping up their empire had implications nearer home. Ruling a large part of the world could not be done effectively if the army abroad and the workforce at home were weak and stunted, especially now that British supremacy was being challenged by Germany and America. When conscription was introduced in the First World War four-fifths of the recruits were found to have such bad teeth they could not eat properly and less than a third had a satisfactory standard of health and strength. Liberal politicians began to advocate 'social imperialism', a policy of state intervention to strengthen people's bodies and abilities. When added to the Nonconformist conscience aroused by the disturbing reports of Booth and Rowntree, this advocacy inspired the social reforms that were achieved before the First World War. Arnold Bennett was not alone in his musings when he wrote in his journal for 1910, during a stay at the *Royal Oak* at Brighton: 'I am obsessed by the thought that all this comfort, luxury, ostentation, snobbishness and correctness is founded on a vast injustice to the artisan-class.' Yet that offensive phrase 'the quality' was still widely used by the wealthier classes to distinguish themselves from the masses. They fought the Liberal reforms bitterly, but in the end were forced to give ground.

After the Liberals' landslide victory in 1906, which handsomely endorsed the change of government in the previous year, Sir Henry Campbell-Bannerman continued as Prime Minister for another two years, but it was during the premiership of his successor, Herbert Henry Asquith, with David Lloyd-George as Chancellor and Winston Churchill as President of the Board of Trade, that the major reforms were put into place. When the Conservative peers in the House of Lords vetoed Lloyd-George's budget, an election was fought in 1910 on the issue of Peers v. People and the Liberal government returned in triumph, though with a much lower number of MPs. At the close of the Edwardian era the lives of ordinary families seemed to be changing for the better. As yet, they had no inkling of the sheer horror and the enormous casualties that war would soon bring to every town and village in the land.

Foreign Imports and Competition

Looking back over the year 1901, *The Times* thought that three great
events would long be remembered: the death of Queen Victoria, the Boer
War, and (more surprisingly) the world tour of the Dominions by the
future King George V and his wife in the royal yacht, the *Ophir*. The tour
has largely been forgotten, but its inclusion in the list shows how significant was Britain's imperial role at the time. The mood was not entirely
triumphant, however. Not only was the Boer War not going well, there
were ominous signs that America and Germany were overtaking Britain as
the world's foremost economic power. British steel production had been
outstripped by both these rivals. By 1914 the USA had the highest per
capita income in the world.

Concern at the performance of these rivals turned to alarm when
American businesses began to buy up British companies. In September
1901, for example, one of the biggest tobacco firms in Britain, Ogden's of
Liverpool, was bought by the American Tobacco Company, with the inten-
tion of eventually taking over the British domestic market. British manufacturers, led by Wills of Bristol, quickly formed a defensive alliance,

Commemorating the War
In 1903 a large crowd gathered in Nottingham to watch Lord Methuen unveil a memorial for local men who had died in South Africa during the Boer War.

which they launched in December 1901 as 'an Amalgamation of British Manufacturers who have closed their ranks with the determination to hold the BRITISH TRADE to BRITISH PEOPLE. Its aim is to provide the vast smoking public with CIGARETTES and TOBACCOS, unexcelled in quality and made solely by means of BRITISH labour and capital'. This new company, the Imperial Tobacco Company, was the largest in Britain. A war of price cuts and incentive schemes for retailers raged until September 1902, when an agreement was reached whereby the American Tobacco Company withdrew from Britain and the Imperial Tobacco Company pledged not to enter the American market. The two transatlantic giants then set up the UK-registered British-American Tobacco Company to capture the rest of the world trade. Cigarettes had become highly fashionable among all classes of society and were heavily promoted by advertising and incentives, such as cigarette cards. In 1888 Wills had launched their 'Woodbine' brand at five for a penny, and three years later they were selling 84.5 million cigarettes of this type a year. In 1895 only 5 per cent of imported tobacco was made into cigarettes, but by 1914 the proportion had risen to more than 40 per cent.

American wheat had been pouring into Britain since the 1870s and by the end of the nineteenth century American breakfast cereals had found a willing market. These cereals were originally developed as a pure food for the religious sect known as the Seventh Day Adventists, but they were being exported to Britain by the 1890s. The Edwardians could also breakfast on shredded wheat and, from 1908, cornflakes, originally known as Elijah's Manna but branded in England as Post Toasties. Such cereals were less time-consuming to prepare than traditional breakfast porridge and soon became popular. Less enthusiasm was expressed at first for the baked beans that H. J. Heinz, an American firm, had introduced to the American market in 1895. When they were market-tested in Yorkshire and Lancashire in 1905–6, they did not meet with much success. Tinned foods, including salmon, peaches, pears and pineapples, had become common from the 1880s and a limited range of tinned soups and corned beef had also appeared. By 1914 Britain was the largest importer of tinned goods in the world, but tinned foods remained comparatively expensive and many poorer families did not even possess a tin-opener.

The Empire was a major source of cheap food and drink. Tea was perhaps the most spectacular example of a colonial cash crop that was developed within the Empire for a home market. Before 1870 over 90 per cent of Britain's tea was imported from China, but by 1900 China's share of the market had dwindled to only 10 per cent, while 50 per cent of Britain's tea came from India and 36 per cent from Ceylon. In 1901 the average national consumption of tea was six pounds per head, but although tea could be bought as cheaply as 1s.6d. per pound, poorer families were buying only half a pound or less a week. The British had access to an unparalleled range of foodstuffs through its dominance of the seas, whether from the Empire or elsewhere. For example, in 1901 the *London Illustrated News* contained regular advertisements for Cadbury's Cocoa and 'Fry's Pure Concentrated Cocoa' under the banner of 'No Better Food'. In *Plenty and Want* John Burnett concluded that 'by 1914 the world food market was so organised as to place the cheapest wheat and meat, the best fish, tea and coffee on English tables'.

In 1901 the average national consumption of tea was six pounds per head...

$\mathscr{S}$OME ORDINARY FAMILIES

ONCE A FAMILY TREE has been constructed and a family historian has got as far back as he or she can go, at least for the time being, thoughts begin to turn to wider matters: to the nature of the local communities in which our ancestors lived, to the general social and economic history of the country, and to a judgement as to whether our own family's lifestyles were typical or unusual. In earlier chapters we have often quoted the experiences of ordinary families – the sort that do not normally appear in our national history books for none of them was famous or exceptionally good or wicked – because most of our ancestors fell into that category. Their histories shed light on those of many others throughout the land. Here, we shall look at just three families over the whole of the Victorian and Edwardian period, to see how they fared over the generations and to discover whether or not their stories illustrate the wider history of their times.

The Downers and the Sandys; New Forest Labourers

On the Edge of the New Forest

The New Forest that William the Conqueror created as a hunting area in southern Hampshire extends westwards as far as the rich and fertile valley of the River Avon, which winds its way down to the coast at Christchurch. Beyond lie the very different chalk downland landscapes of Cranborne Chase in Dorset and the Wiltshire village of Martin, made famous by W. H. Hudson in *A Shepherd's Life*. The market towns of Fordingbridge and Ringwood, which stand on the banks of the Avon, are the focal points for a distinctive 'country' that lies between the forest and the county boundary. These two towns are now connected by the A338, but their ancient link was the lane that runs along the foot of the slopes that climb up to the commons and the forest. Fordingbridge was the centre of a medieval hundred and of a parish of 6,303 acres. Its spacious medieval church dedicated to St Mary is the successor to the one that was recorded in the Domesday Book. Within the hundred and parish were the forest-edge hamlets and

Fordingbridge-Ringwood 'Country'

The one-inch Ordnance Survey map of 1910 shows the scattered forest-edge settlements on the western edge of the New Forest between the market towns of Fordingbridge and Ringwood.

villages of Bickton, Blissford, Frogham, Godshill, Hale, Hungerford, Hyde, North Gorley, Ogdens, Stuckton and Woodgreen. To the north of Fordingbridge stands Breamore's famous Anglo-Saxon church; to the south lie the parishes of Ibsley and Ringwood, which also included several small forest-edge settlements. The silts and gravels of the river valley were rich in corn and cattle, whereas the hillsides were based on gravel terraces, clays and sands, and beyond stretched the acid heathlands and woodlands of the New Forest. In 1911 Fordingbridge parish contained 2,471 acres of arable land, 2,440 acres of permanent grass, and 723 acres of woods and plantations, and the owners and tenants of smallholdings still had important rights within the forest beyond.

In many ways Fordingbridge was a typical small Victorian market town. In the first half of the nineteenth century the population of the parish grew slowly from 2,335 to 3,096. Over the next half century it fluctuated between 2,925 and 3,222, before reaching 3,164 in 1901. Most of the modest population gains in the market town were offset by losses in the surrounding countryside. By the early nineteenth century Fordingbridge no longer held a weekly market, but its September fair survived and its shopkeepers and tradesmen still served the rural neighbourhood. A railway station was opened in 1865 and within two years a gas works was providing light through 41 street lamps. Joseph Neave & Co. had a baby food factory near the railway station and their fellow Quakers, Samuel Thompson & Co., canvas makers, flax spinners and merchants, had factories at East Mill and West End, where they employed 200 men, women and young people. Beyond the town, Joseph Armfield & Co. of Ringwood had converted the Stuckton iron foundry into an agricultural engineering works and Neave's employed 25 hands, who worked day and night shifts, at the Bickton flour mill.

On the southern boundary of Fordingbridge parish lay the forest-edge settlements of North and South Gorley, both of them collections of farms and cottages scattered along the valley gravels or up the hillside to the east, with no recognisable village centre. When William the Conqueror created the New Forest, Gorley was held by Osbern, his falconer. North Gorley lay in the parish of Fordingbridge until the new parish of Hyde was created in 1855 upon the opening of the Church of Holy Ascension, but South Gorley formed part of the parish of Ibsley. The two settlements and life on the edge of the forest were the subjects of a remarkable book written by Heywood Sumner in 1910, entitled *Cuckoo Hill: The Book of Gorley*. Sumner was an Arts and Crafts artist and fine amateur archaeologist who came to live at Cuckoo Hill in South Gorley in 1901. His comments on the recent loss of population in the district are pertinent to the histories of our two families and to the general desertion of the countryside by farmworkers during this period, when agriculture was depressed and nearby towns were offering brighter opportunities. He wrote, 'There can be no doubt that 100 years ago these hillsides were more thickly populated than they are now.' On a map that he drew of North and South Gorley he marked 35 cottages that had vanished during the previous hundred years, while only 13 new ones had been built. His conversations with local families led him to believe that many of these cottages had been created a few generations previously by squatters who had grabbed a bit of land on the edge of the common:

Here, on a bit of heather waste, he hastily reared a mud-walled cottage. Then he reclaimed the land, made a garden, and then the Lord of the manor stepped in – before the squatter had occupied for twenty years – and claimed rent in token of his over-lordship. The usual custom was to grant such squatters a lease of his holding for three lives at a nominal rent – in consideration of work done in grubbing, building and reclaiming. But mud-walled cottages built in haste will not stand for a long future; and by the time that the three lives had fallen, the mud walls were likewise tottering to their fall.

Landlords knocked the buildings down and converted small holdings into large ones. There is truth in Sumner's statement, but it was too simple a view, for many cottagers left of their own accord in search of higher wages elsewhere.

The smallholders who lived in the mud-walled, thatched farmhouses and cottages were dependent on the common and on their rights in the forest beyond. Gorley Hill Common extended for 91¼ acres and common rights included unstinted grazing for animals, the cutting of bracken and gorse, and the digging of marl and gravel. Wood, peat and gorse were used as fuel, ferns were gathered on horse-drawn carts to sell as litter, holly was supplied to traders, and many smallholders kept a 'bee garden' on the common. The common rights of the Gorley farmers and cottagers were more valuable than their rights in the New Forest immediately beyond. The division between the common and the forest was marked by posts, but otherwise was not obvious. Heywood Sumner wrote, 'The main features of our side of the New Forest are heather uplands, winding moorland streams and scattered woods. The open country is never far distant.' Godshill was once 'covered with pollards, and so much holly was growing upon it that a person might mistake his road', but in 1810 it had been planted with oak and Scots fir. Several other plantations had partly altered the character of the New Forest during the nineteenth century. In 1846, for instance, Hasley Wood had been planted with Scots fir, larch, oak and sweet chestnut. To the east of Godshill Wood broom rape grew among the furze near the road. When furze encroached on the pastures it had to be kept down by controlled fires.

In his *Hampshire Days* (1903) W. H. Hudson wrote:

It must be borne in mind that the Forest area had a considerable population composed of commoners, squatters, private owners, who have inherited or purchased lands originally filched from the forest; and of a large number of persons who reside mostly in the villages, and are private residents, publicans, shopkeepers, and lodging-house keepers. All these people have one object in common – to get as much as they can out of the Forest .... One proof that much goes on in the dark, or that much is winked at, is the poverty of all wild life which is worth any man's while to take in a district where pretty well everything is protected on paper. Game, furred and feathered,

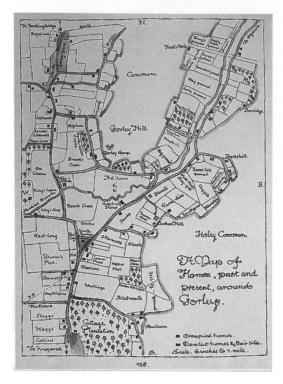

The Book of Gorley
'The map of homes past and present' which Heywood Sumner drew to show how many cottages in North and South Gorley had been demolished in living memory.

would not exist at all but for the private estates scattered through the Forest.

The locals no doubt saw things differently and Hudson went on to say, 'They have, in fact, their own moral code, their New Forest conscience.'

Back in 1792 the New Forest Commoners had reported on the number of commoners and the rights they possessed. Only 8 of the 15 forest 'walks' have surviving returns, so the 2,314 commoners and their 1,526 horses and 2,960 cattle that were recorded represent about half the total. Ashley Walk, on the western edge of the forest, supported 360 commoners, including 30 in Gorley, 63 in Godshill, 19 in Woodgreen, and the rest in numerous other parts of the parishes of Fordingbridge and Breamore. A protracted struggle against the threat of enclosure ended in victory for the commoners in 1877, when the unique value of the New Forest as an area of outstanding beauty and interest was balanced against the traditional rights of the commoners. A new Act recognised that the cottagers benefited from grazing livestock, feeding pigs on acorns and beech mast, digging turfs, and cutting furze and heath faggots (for the local pottery kilns as well as their own fires), and collecting wood to make brooms, charcoal and wooden shovels.

Even so, these common rights were no substitute for low wages. In 1851 local labourers were paid 1s.2d. a day. The empty cottages that Sumner saw were eloquent testimony to the poverty of the farmworkers who had left the district in search of a better living in the rapidly-expanding towns of Poole and Bournemouth or overseas. They had done their best to safeguard themselves against sickness by collective action. Sumner looked at the rules and the account book of the friendly society that had been established at Gorley in 1810 and the banner that had been carried on the fiftieth anniversary. Members paid 2s.6d. entrance fee (raised to 5 shillings in 1860) and another 4 shillings each quarter. In case of illness a man received 6 shillings a week for the first six weeks and 3 shillings afterwards; £2 was paid on death and every member was expected to attend the funeral and had to contribute 1 shilling to the widow. On 21 July 1860, the jubilee day of the society, 105 members were on the roll, but by 1871 membership had dropped to 52. The members' names included those of Sandy and Downer.

The Origins of the Sandys

Sandy is a surname of uncertain etymology that is found in the south-western counties of England. Its distribution pattern shows that it is not derived from the Bedfordshire village of Sandy. It might be from a Norse personal name, but is most likely to be a shortened form of Alexander. The 1817 notebooks of the Revd Henry Comyn, the minister of the New Forest parish of Boldre and Brockenhurst, include the alternative spellings of Sandy, Sanders and Saunders. Two members of the Saunders family were recorded at Burley, near Ringwood, in 1608 and a John Sandy was living nearby at North Ashley in 1665, but we do not know whether or not they were connected with the Sandys who, by the mid eighteenth century, were settled at Gorley, four or five miles away. The New Forest common-ers of 1792 included Stephen Sandy of Gorley and Thomas Sandy of Hungerford, living a few hundred yards from each other, and another Thomas Sandy at Ogdens, a little further on. During the nineteenth cen-tury their descendants continued to live mainly in Gorley and Hungerford or in a few nearby places.

A William Sandy was perhaps the original squatter at Gorley. When he died there in 1779 he was buried at Fordingbridge parish church in an unmarked grave. His widow, Christian, whom he had married in 1744, sur-vived him at Gorley for another 13 years and her distinctive name helps us to link the various branches of the family. Her five children were Mary (who had an illegitimate daughter named Christian), Thomas (who also had a daughter called Christian), George, Moses (who possibly was named after the Moses Sandy who had married at Ringwood church in 1738), and Stephen.

This Thomas Sandy was living at Hungerford in 1792 and died there in 1834 at the age of 81. He had married Susannah Allen at Fordingbridge church in 1774 and they had 9 children in 16 years, 3 of whom died young. Their eldest son, William (c. 1776–1851), was described as a labourer as a young man, then as a farmer, and in the 1841 census as a Hungerford yeoman, so he was clearly earning a sufficient living. Junior members of such families fared less well. The second son, George, remained a labourer all his life, as did his sons, George (Hungerford) and Ambrose (Hyde Lane, Hungerford). This younger son, who earned part of his living as a weaver, was named after Ambrose Kinchington, the husband of his Aunt Christian, and his line continued through his four married sons and six daughters, only one of whom died as an infant, the rest marrying locally. Most of these Hungerford Sandys were farm labourers, but one became a wheelwright; the women included two yarn spinners and a charwoman.

Stephen Sandy (c. 1759–1845), who was living at Gorley by 1792, had married Betty Barter at Fordingbridge parish church seven years earlier. Their five children included a Thomas and a Susannah, who were named after Stephen's elder brother and his wife. Their oldest boy was another Stephen. The 1841 Tithe Award for Fordingbridge parish shows the elder Stephen Sandy (by now a widower, for Betty had died in 1838, aged 73, of 'natural decay') with a cottage, garden, orchard and two small pieces of arable land, covering just over 1½ acres, and the younger Stephen living in the adjacent cottage and garden. Both father and son were owner-occupiers of their cottages and small plots of land on the western edge of Gorley Common, almost at the top of the hillside, a classic position for a squatter to stake a claim. A modern house now occupies the site of the elder Stephen's cottage, but that which had belonged to his son was one of the many whose demolition was noted by Heywood Sumner. The 25-inch Ordnance Survey map of 1897 shows just one cottage on the track up the hill from Gorley Cross to Gorley Common and Gorley Hill.

The elder Stephen lived to the ripe old age of 86, his wife to 72. Stephen Sandy, junior (1795–1873), was 32 when he married 18-year-old Ann Dowding, who had been born at Linwood, two miles away. At the births of their four sons and two daughters, Stephen was a Gorley labourer who signed his name with a mark. The 1861 and 1871 census returns both noted that he was 'kept by the parish of Fordingbridge'. He nevertheless lived 78 years before dying of 'senile decay'. His widow worked as a char-woman until she died at the age of 72, from acute bronchitis. We know very little about them but enough perhaps to get a sense of what it meant to be members of the rural poor of mid-Victorian England.

Gorley in 1881

What had happened to the other branches of the family in the meantime? Had they fared any better? The census returns for Gorley in 1881 record Thomas Sandy, a 37-year-old farm labourer who was born at Gorley, living next door to Ann, Stephen's widow. He was probably the son of Thomas, Stephen's younger brother, and he died before the next census was taken. Thomas's wife was ten years older than he was and had been born a mile away at Frogham; her two children from a previous marriage at Ogdens lived with her. Another branch in 1881 was headed by Stephen and Ann's eldest son, James Sandy, a 50-year-old carter, who had been born at Rockbourne before his parents settled at Gorley. James's son, William Sandy, a 28-year-old carpenter who had been born at Gorley, lived nearby with his wife, a native of Blissford. Five other nearby Sandy households in 1881 were headed by Ambrose Sandy, farm labourer of Hyde Lane; his sons Thomas, farm labourer of Breamore, and Charles, grinder in the flour mill at Bickton; George Sandy of Hungerford, a worker in the yarn factory at Fordingbridge, the second son of Stephen and Ann; and Charles Sandy, a general labourer from Hungerford, son of George Sandy, farm labourer, and grandson of Thomas Sandy, the 1792 Hungerford commoner. Another of Thomas's grandsons, James Sandy, the only son of William, was an 'imbecile' in the Union Workhouse. All the family's movements were confined to the forest-edge settlements that they thought of as their 'country'.

The restricted movements of the Sandys were paralleled by those of their neighbours. Fifteen of the 37 males (excluding sons) in Gorley in 1881 had been born there, another 3 in Fordingbridge, 9 in neighbouring forest-edge hamlets, 3 just across the River Avon, and 7 further away in Hampshire, Dorset and Wiltshire. Five of the 35 females (excluding daughters) had been born in Gorley, another 4 in Fordingbridge, 2 in Ringwood, 13 in forest-edge villages or hamlets, 1 just across the River Avon, and 7 in other parts of Hampshire, Dorset and Wiltshire. The only outsiders were the two schoolmistresses from Surrey and Cornwall and the police constable's wife from Kent. The great majority of the inhabitants of Gorley in 1881 had been born and bred on the western edge of the New Forest. Their movements were as restricted as those of most country people in England and Wales at the time.

The occupations of the 47 men and boys comprised 23 labourers and a cowman, 5 farmers and 2 farmers' sons, 3 carpenters and an apprentice, 3 blacksmiths, 2 carters, 2 bootmakers, a corn miller, a grocer, a publican, a dealer in birds, and a police constable. The women and girls had few regular employment opportunities, for apart from the 2 schoolmistresses only 6 women were said to be employed: a charwoman, glove maker, bonnet maker, nurse, housekeeper, and servant. However, the seasonal nature of other jobs might have been missed by a 1 April census. Girls and young women certainly found employment in the factories of Fordingbridge and Ringwood and others were tempted to seek domestic service in Poole and Bournemouth; just one farmer could afford to keep a servant in Gorley. Nearly every household consisted of just parents and children, with the occasional grandchild; the seven boarders mostly lived in cottages that had no children. Here again, the customs on the edge of the New Forest were those of the English countryside as a whole.

The End of the Century

At the time of the 1891 census, when the effects of the agricultural depression were being felt at their worst, five households of Sandys still lived in the forest-edge villages, though their old cottage in Gorley was occupied by another family. Ambrose Sandy, now 72, lived at Hyde Lane with his wife, Ann, and a lodger (who worked on the roads) and his wife; their five daughters had all married local labourers and craftsmen. Nearby at Hungerford lived Thomas Sandy, a 46-year-old farm labourer, his wife and their two children and Charles Sandy, a 37-year-old dealer, his wife and young son. Charles had been a grinder at the flour mill in 1881 and was a labourer in 1904, when his daughter married a Gorley farmer. Also at

Charles Sandy (1841–1925) and his second wife, Olive. Born in Gorley, he left the countryside to find work at Newtown Kinson on the outskirts of Poole.

Hungerford were William Sandy, a 37-year-old wheelwright, his wife and daughter and a 20-year-old boarder who worked as a farm labourer. William was the eldest son of James Sandy, labourer, the younger Stephen's eldest son. Finally, Fanny Sandy, a 50-year-old widow, was living at Gunville with her son, Thomas. Four branches of the Sandys were still living in Hungerford in 1901 (a farm labourer, market gardener, factory operator and carman) and a carter and his family lived at Bickton. The Sandys were still a numerous 'ordinary family' living in the same 'country' that their ancestors had known for three or four generations. Their way of life seemed immemorial.

But by this time, some of the Sandys had torn up their roots and had left the poverty of the countryside. Charles, the youngest son of the second Stephen Sandy, had married on Christmas Day 1863 at the (Congregational) Lower Meeting House, Ringwood, where he worked in a flax manufactory. He and his brother and sister-in-law, who were witnesses, signed the wedding certificate with marks. His wife, Elizabeth Simmonds, who had been born illegitimately at Burley, in Ringwood parish, gave her occupation as domestic servant and she too was illiterate. Upon their marriage, they returned to Gorley, where their eldest girls, Sarah Anne and Mary Jane, were born, but not long after the 1871 census they joined the growing numbers of countryfolk who left for better-paid jobs in the towns. In 1881 they were recorded at Newtown Kinson, on the northern outskirts of Poole, where their three youngest children had been born. Ten years later, the family were living at Granville Road, Upper Parkstone, but in later life Charles moved back to a cottage in Ringwood Road, Newtown Kinson. He found employment as a general labourer and was described as such in 1910 upon the marriage of his youngest daughter. A photograph taken of him in his seventies, with his second wife, Olive, shows him looking cheerful and well. He benefited from the introduction of old age pensions and lived to the age of 84.

The Origins of the Downers

The Downers were another family who spread themselves along the western edge of the New Forest. They rented their cottages and were even poorer than the Sandys. Their surname had been given to a medieval inhabitant of the Downs, but other southern families had been named in the same way. Downer was a regional name, but not one of single-family origin. Like the Sandys, some of the Downers had probably lived in Fordingbridge parish for several generations. An Andrew Downer had been recorded as the reeve of Godshill and Linwood at the swainmote court of the New Forest in 1635. Thirty years later, Widow Downer of Godshill was exempted from paying tax on her hearth on the grounds of her poverty. At that time, she was the only Downer in Fordingbridge hundred, so perhaps the nineteenth-century Downers in this district were all descended from her.

Local parish records name Downers at Woodgreen from 1699 and at Gorley from 1768. In 1719, for instance, John Downer of Woodgreen and his son Andrew had to pay a £30 bond for the maintenance of a bastard child. The Downers make frequent appearances in the local poor law records. In 1781 George Downer, his wife Elizabeth, and their three children aged between one and four were removed from Kingsworthy back to Fordingbridge, the parish that was responsible for relieving their poverty. Three Downers ended their days in the old Fordingbridge workhouse: the 44-year-old Susannah Downer in 1817, the 87-year-old John Downer in 1831, and the 67-year-old John Downer in 1847.

By the beginning of Victoria's reign, separate families of Downers were established in the forest-edge settlements of Godshill, Woodgreen, Bickton and Gorley. The Tithe Award of 1841 for Fordingbridge parish names James Downer as the tenant of a cottage, garden and small arable plot in Godshill, George Downer as the tenant of a cottage and tiny garden in Bickton, and William and George Downer as tenants of two cottages and a small garden in North Gorley. Woodgreen lay in Breamore parish, to the north of Godshill, and so was not included in this award. The schedule and map enable us to pinpoint William's and George's cottages by the stream on Gorley Green, close to the lane that traverses the valley, where the track down from Sandy's cottage reaches the foot of the hill. The site is now deserted, but grassy mounds indicate the former foundations. The 1897 Ordnance Survey 25-inch map marked the area as Gorley Cross and showed that the two cottages formed one building divided into three sections. Several more cottages were clustered around Gorley Green and alongside the lane as it proceeded in a northerly direction.

The George Downer whose cottage at Bickton was included in the Tithe Award of 1841 was probably the eldest of the six boys and three girls of Andrew (1759–1814) and Sarah Downer of Bickton. In the 1841 census George was a farm labourer, living with his wife, three sons and a daughter, but he died during the following decade and his sons left the district. His younger brother, John Downer, was a journeyman miller and lodging house keeper at Bickton who died in the 1850s. The various census returns show how the composition of a labourer's household could fluctuate over time. John and his first wife, Elizabeth, had lived at Frogham, where he worked as a labourer and had two sons, Henry and William, and a daughter, Martha, who lived only nine months; Elizabeth was buried less than a month later. John and his second wife, Rebecca, had three sons and a daughter, all born at Bickton. Their daughter died when she was a child, so five boys from two marriages were left in the household. In 1851 George

Hicks, John's 19-year-old stepson, a farm labourer born in Gorley, was living with them. The eldest Downer boy, Henry, was a soldier in 1861, a pensioner living with his mother and brothers at Bickton in 1871, and a pensioner lodging with his Hicks relatives in Bickton, near to his brother Andrew in 1881. William, the second son, who was a dairyman in 1851 and a farm labourer 10 years later, died at the age of 35. Andrew, the third brother, was a farm labourer who married the daughter of another Bickton farm labourer; in 1881 he was working as a bleacher and living with his father-in-law, his wife and his three children. The fourth and fifth brothers, James and John, worked in a factory as young men. By 1861 their father had died and all five brothers, together with George Hicks and a lodger, lived with Rebecca, who was described as a 52-year-old agricultural labourer. Ten years later, Rebecca's employment was recorded in the census as 'fieldwork', and living with her were Henry, James, John, George Hicks and a nephew, William Hicks, but by 1881 a great change in the composition of the household had occurred. Rebecca had died and the house was occupied by William Hicks, canvas bleacher, his wife and young son, and their lodger, Henry Downer, by now a 59-year-old army pensioner. Meanwhile, James Downer was married with a family at Hyde Lane and was a foreman at the flax mill, and John Downer was married with a family in Back Street, Fordingbridge, where he worked as a canvas weaver; George Hicks was his lodger. Ten years later, James Downer and John's sons were also working in the local factories. These various members of the Downer family were still living in the 'country' of their ancestors, but they no longer worked on the land.

The James Downer whose cottage on the south side of the village street in Godshill was drawn on the Tithe Award map of 1841 was a 61-year-old farm labourer who lived with his wife, three sons and two daughters. Their eldest son, George, had been born at Woodgreen in 1810 and had married a girl from Godshill Wood. He was described as a farm labourer of Godshill or Godshill Wood when his four boys and a girl were born between 1838 and 1845. After the death of his first wife, George married a widow and moved a mile or so to Frogham. In 1871 he was living at Frogham with his wife, her 82-year-old mother (a dressmaker) and his daughter-in-law. He died there in 1880 at the age of 71. George's line was carried on by his youngest son, Isaac, a Frogham labourer. Meanwhile, James Downer's second son, Charles, who had been born in 1819, set up home at Blissford, where he worked as a labourer. His line was carried on by four sons, one of whom was a carpenter. This branch of the Downers remained prolific but with the same low standard of living on, or just above, the poverty line.

The Downers of Gorley

As we have seen, the 1841 Tithe Award map showed the cottages of William and George Downer, father and son, built onto each other at Gorley Cross. When William died four years later at the age of 77, his death certificate described him as a shepherd who had died of old age. Ann Sandy, from the cottage up the hill, witnessed his death with a mark. In 1851 William's widow, Jane, was a 73-year-old pauper who lived with her eldest son, George, and his family. Her three surviving boys and perhaps her daughter all had families, but her youngest boys, Thomas and William, had died when they were small. George Downer (1808–81) earned his living as a farm labourer and married a girl from Woodgreen. Their two daughters, named (rather surprisingly) Eliza and Elizabeth, were living with them in the cottage at Gorley Cross in 1841, but 10 years later, Eliza had been replaced by George's mother, Jane. In 1871 the cottage was occupied only by George, who was now a widower, and his boarder, Frances Dawkins, a 34-year-old spinster who was kept by the parish. The arrangement enabled George to pay his rent and provided him with a housekeeper.

William and Jane's second son, Charles Downer, married Harriet Barter, a girl from an old Gorley family. Their three sons and two daughters included the unfortunate Caroline, who was described in census returns as an idiot or imbecile. The other daughter, Lucy, was a servant at Fordingbridge parsonage when she died at the age of 32. The eldest boy, Francis, may have died young, but John and Henry lived to become local farm labourers. Their father died at the age of 40, leaving his family in desperate straits. In the 1851 census Charles's widow, Harriet, was described as a 38-year-old general servant, now living in the Fordingbridge Union Workhouse with her five children; the youngest one, Henry, was only nine months old. The workhouse records do not survive, but in the next census Harriet was enumerated as an agricultural labourer, living with her children in a cottage in Fordingbridge High Street. She was still there in 1881, supported by the parish, with Caroline, her handicapped daughter, now aged 33, and with 75-year-old Rachel Barter, who was probably her widowed mother. Her 13-year-old grandson, Frederick, who also lived with her, was probably the eldest child of her son, John Downer, who lived close by with four children aged 12 and under. Families had to make such arrangements when their accommodation became too crowded.

William and Jane's third son, James Downer (1813–90), was living with his parents in their Gorley cottage at the time of the 1841 Tithe Award, but two years later he married Louisa, the 18-year-old daughter of William Dymott, a Stuckton labourer. Both partners and the witnesses signed the certificate with their marks. James was consistently recorded as a shoemaker and at his death as a journeyman shoemaker – one who worked for

Moses Downer stands behind his daughter, Annie, when she married in Holloway, north London, in 1915. The former Hampshire workhouse boy had long since moved to the outskirts of Poole to find work on the roads.

an employer. Their first five children were born at Gorley between 1844 and 1852, but by 1861 they had moved to a cottage at New Holland, on the other side of Gorley Common. Seven of their eight children survived to maturity. They had nearly all grown up and left by 1881, when James, Louisa and their daughter were living at Stuckton, perhaps at his wife's old home. The name Dymott's Cottage is still attached to one of the houses in the village street, close by the Independent chapel. Louisa died there in 1890, followed four years later by James, who had suffered from chronic bronchitis for some years, before lapsing into senility. They were both buried in unmarked graves in the new churchyard at Hyde. The male side of this branch of the family continued only with their eldest son, Thomas, though (as we shall see) the Downer name was also preserved in an illegitimate line.

Thomas Downer, the eldest son of James and Louisa, had little choice other than to become yet another farm labourer. Upon his marriage, he moved to a cottage next door to his parents at Tuck's Hole, New Holland, right on the edge of the New Forest. He and his wife, Jane, had eight sons and five daughters, the eldest of whom died as an infant. In 1871, when he had only two young children, he shared his cottage with his wife's mother and her brother, John Turner. By 1881 the family had moved back to Gorley (perhaps to the Downers' old cottage at Gorley Cross), but not long afterwards, they moved again, to Stuckton, and in 1891 they were living at 1 Lummas Cottage, Fordingbridge. There Thomas and his eldest son found work as agricultural carters, and his younger sons worked as cowboys.

Elizabeth Downer

Thomas Downer's younger sister, Elizabeth, the second child in the family, was born in 1846 at Gorley and by 1861 she was working as a labourer in one of the Fordingbridge factories. Six years later, at the age of 20, she gave birth to an illegitimate child in the Fordingbridge Union Workhouse. He was christened Moses at the parish church and at the time of the 1871 census he was still in the workhouse. Elizabeth, however, was living at her parents' cottage at New Holland and was working as a labourer, perhaps at her old job in the same factory. The poor law guardians took the view that she was able to support herself but not her child and no doubt they came to some arrangement with her over visiting. From 1835 the old Union Workhouse stood in Shaftesbury Street, Fordingbridge, until it was replaced in 1887 by a more commodious building at the other side of the road, which is now incorporated into the infirmary. The children had their own schoolmistress, who taught them in a room in the workhouse, for they were strictly segregated from the children in the National school just across the road. In 1871 the children in the workhouse included Alfred Downer, aged 8, the son of Hannah Downer of Frogham, and his 4-year-old cousin, Moses. Ten years later, the workhouse contained 56 inmates, 22 of them male and 34 female. The master and matron, the schoolmistress and the porter each came from beyond the county's borders. The women included a 76-year-old agricultural labourer, a flax weaver and a domestic servant; the men included a farm labourer, a coachman and a gardener. Amongst the infirm were eight handicapped people who were deaf, blind or 'imbecile'. Moses was still there, now aged 14 and abandoned by his mother.

The workhouse records have been destroyed, so we have to piece the story together by other means. On 9 September 1873, giving her age as 25 when she was actually 27, Elizabeth was married at the new parish church at Hyde to John Turner of Tuck's Hole, her next-door neighbour and the brother of her sister-in-law. Both partners signed the wedding certificate with a mark and her brother, Thomas, and his wife, Jane, acted as witnesses. After the wedding we hear no more of John and Elizabeth Turner. They are not recorded again in local parish registers and they do not appear in the national index of the 1881 census returns for Great Britain. We can only assume that upon marrying they decided to emigrate, leaving Moses in the workhouse.

At the Close of the Century

At the time of the 1881 and 1891 censuses various Downers were living in the forest-edge villages and hamlets of Bickton, Blissford, Frogham, Gorley, Hyde Lane, Stuckton and Woodgreen or in Fordingbridge and Breamore. At the beginning of the twentieth century they were still scattered across the 'country' of their ancestors. They included farm labourers, a laundress, a journeyman carpenter, a painter's labourer, and men who worked at unskilled jobs in a flax mill, a printer's and a gunpowder works.

Several Downers were married at Hyde and Fordingbridge in the years leading up to the First World War, but others were lured away to the rapidly-growing towns of Poole and Bournemouth. One who left the countryside was the young Moses Downer, free at last from the confinement of the workhouse. In 1891 he was a 24-year-old general labourer, living at Ringwood Road, Newtown Kinson, with a wife and two young children. Moses had found secure employment laying out new roads and the promenades along the seafront. He did not move again and died at 400 Ringwood Road in 1950 at the age of 83. His first wife was Mary Jane Sandy (1871–1911), the second daughter of Charles Sandy, who had also moved from Gorley to Newtown Kinson. They married on 30 June 1888 at St Andrew's, the medieval church at Kinson, which was largely rebuilt

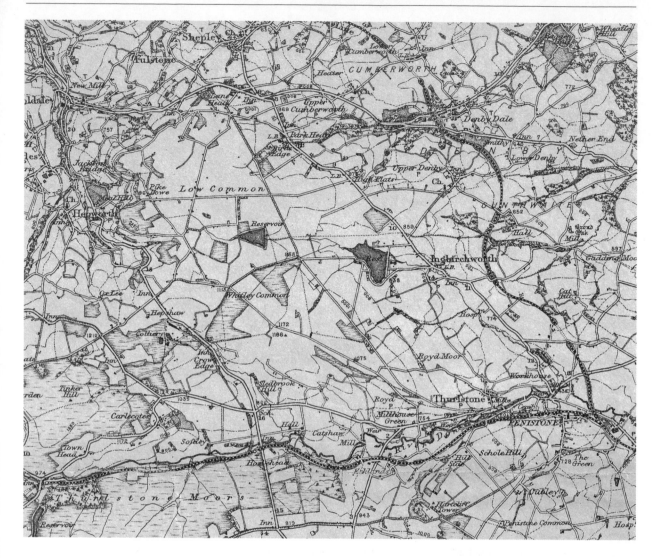

The Thurlstone-Millhouse Countryside
The one-inch Ordnance Survey map of 1908–13 shows the various settlements in the upper Don valley in the moorland parish of Penistone.

seven years later. Mary claimed to be 19 but was two years younger. She kept up the pretence to 1911, when she died while visiting a sister in London. Tottenham hospital must have seemed an unlikely end for a poor country girl born in Gorley.

The Heys of Thurlstone Township

At first sight, the bleak, windswept foothills of the Pennines seem to offer less prospect of earning a living than the attractive slopes and fertile valley on the western edge of the New Forest. But while people were leaving the countryside in their droves in the southern counties, the Pennine hamlets and villages grew in size, for farming was not the only source of employment. The population of Thurlstone, a large moorland township in the western part of Penistone parish, increased from 1,096 in 1801 to 2,018 50 years later and to 2,992 in 1901. Many of the new inhabitants of the township were housed in Thurlstone village or a mile further west at the small, new village of Millhouse Green, but numerous others lived in isolated farmhouses or tiny groups of cottages. The settlement pattern that pre-dated the industrial developments of the nineteenth century is depicted on Thomas Jeffreys's map of Yorkshire in 1772. Jeffreys marked nine mills along the River Don on its course through the old parish of Penistone, but hardly any other buildings on the banks of the river. The older farmsteads, many of whose names were recorded in medieval documents, sought drier land on the spurs that projected from the hillsides. Remoter farms, high on the hills, were created much later, after 6,552 acres of commons and wastes in Thurlstone township were enclosed between 1812 and 1816. Grouse-shooting moors stretched beyond, as far as the county boundary.

The corn mills and fulling mills were ancient features of the landscape, essential items in the old rural economy which was based on farming and the manufacture of woollen cloth, often in combination. Penistone parish lay on the southern edge of the great West Riding textile district and from the fifteenth to the eighteenth centuries its inhabitants had made cheap, coarse cloths known as 'Penistones', which were sold widely, even as far as London. Penistone had a cloth market from 1743 and a Cloth Hall erected 20 years later. The growth of the woollen cloth industry around new or adapted mills in the late-eighteenth and early-nineteenth centuries changed the appearance of the old, hill-top village of Thurlstone. In the early nineteenth century new houses and cottages were built along the valley bottom and up the bank sides, close to the new works.

Further up the valley stood the fulling mill and the adjacent house which gave the new settlement of Millhouse Green its name. The census returns for 1881 record the new owner, William Smith, a 'steel wire manufacturer', who lived close by at Bullhouse Grange. His business must have been profitable, for the house that he built was a substantial one, comparable in size to Plumpton Lodge, the home of the owners of the cloth mill in Thurlstone. Grange and Lodge were two of the favourite house names of newly-rich Victorians. The census returns name 5 wire drawers and 2 female wire scourers in Millhouse, employees of William Smith. The 11 men described as labourers at the steel works, together with the 2 engine drivers and the night watchman, probably worked at Charles Cammell's at Penistone, a couple of miles away. A goit or mill race fed another mill downstream which had started life in the eighteenth century as a paper mill. In the late 1870s the mill had been converted into an umbrella works by William Hoyland, who had been a prominent employee of Samuel Fox, the manufacturer of hollow, steel umbrella frames over the hill at Stocksbridge. In 1881 Hoyland's business was still a small one, employing just

Millhouse Green
Dairy shorthorns are displayed
at Millhouse Show in 1909.
Although increasing numbers of
people found work in industrial
occupations, farming remained
a way of life that was familiar to
all.

three men and eight teenage girls. Half a mile downstream, in 1816 another old fulling mill had been converted into the Plumpton Cloth Mill by the Tomasson family. The mill became renowned for the livery cloths that it made for the royal houses of Europe and for the thick coverings that were needed for coach seats. Three more corn mills, a fulling mill and an oil mill erected in 1740 to crush linseed were fed by the Don as it meandered eastwards through Penistone parish.

During the nineteenth century Thurlstone became an industrial village, though not on the scale of those that were strung out along the Colne and Calder valleys further north. The first processes in the textile industry to be mechanised were the preparation ('scribbling') and spinning of the yarn. As weaving was not mechanised for another generation or two, the mill owners had to build rows of cottages to house the men who wove all the extra yarn that was being spun. These cottages are distinguished by their upper rows of mullioned windows which allowed the maximum amount of light to fall on the weavers' looms. The six-inch Ordnance Survey map of 1854 marks the tenters that stood in the crofts to the rear of the cottages on which pieces of cloth were stretched after they had been returned from the scouring and thickening process at the fulling mill. To 'be on tenter hooks' was a phrase that passed into common speech, though it is rarely heard nowadays. Some of the older farmhouses and cottages in and around the village were also converted for weaving. The old dual economy of the West Riding farming and weaving families that is suggested by this arrangement continued well into Victorian times. Handloom weavers still lived and worked in some of the Thurlstone cottages when the national census was taken in 1881, but they had all gone 20 years later.

In 1901 their successors worked in the Thurlstone woollen mills, the Penistone steel works or the umbrella factory at Millhouse.

Millhouse Green in 1881

It now seems surprising that this moorland district once offered a living
not just to farmers and those who worked in the mills along the River Don
but also to those who were prepared to descend shallow pits to mine coal.
Though few traces of the former collieries survive in the present landscape, coal mining was a common occupation in 1881. The 1854 Ordnance
Survey map marks many 'Old Coal Pits' by the thin seam of coal and
gannister (fireclay) that stretched along the edge of the Pennines from
Sheffield towards Huddersfield. These were all much smaller concerns
than the deep pits which worked the famous Silkstone and Barnsley seams
further east. Millhouse was far removed in character from the pit villages
that were being built at the heart of the South Yorkshire coalfield. It is now
hard to imagine that the tranquil upper reaches of the Don valley offered
so much industrial employment, but in 1881 66 men who lived in Millhouse or in the scattered farmsteads and hamlets further west were
employed at local collieries. Millhouse alone had five coal miners, a beerhouse keeper and coal miner (at *The Golden Cross*), a beerhouse keeper
and colliery viewer (at *The Blacksmith's Arms*), two firemen who operated
the engines which pumped air through the ventilation system, and a colliery blacksmith, all of whom were heads of households. Eleven younger
men were listed as labourers in the coal mines and two boys, aged 13 and
14, were coal trammers responsible for moving the loaded trucks. Girls as
well as boys had done this job in local pits before they were banned from
working underground by an Act of Parliament in 1842. Beyond Millhouse,
fathers and sons in the hamlets or isolated farmhouses often turned to the
mining of coal and gannister for part or the whole of their living. The railways and stone quarries also offered opportunities for employment in
these wilder western parts of the parish. Farm labouring was not a
common occupation, for the typical hill farm was small and did not need
extra hands outside the family, except at harvest time. Sons commonly
worked at industrial jobs until they inherited the farm, and the distinction
between farming and industry was not a sharp one. Life in the countryside
in Thurlstone township was very different from that on the edge of the
New Forest.

In 1881 Millhouse was hardly a village. Its cottages were strung out
around the former green, in Low Millhouse, or as part of Robin Row, with
a few older farm houses nearby. The board school that had been opened in
1879 and the adjoining *Blacksmith's Arms* gave the place some identity
where Lee Lane branched off from the main road. Enough people lived in
and around Millhouse by 1881 to support a blacksmith, a joiner, a grocer,

and a woman who baked bread for sale, but the headmaster and the surveyor to the local board were the only two people to represent the local authority. The West End Primitive Methodists had built a chapel and had started a Sunday school in 1864 on the Thurlstone-Millhouse boundary, but they did not have a resident minister. Old photographs show that large numbers of people, no doubt including many from Millhouse, attended the chapel and Sunday school at Bullhouse, near the colliery. Joseph Bardsley, the long-serving minister there, lived with his wife and two daughters at Moor Royd, within convenient walking distance of the chapel but well away from Millhouse. In the absence of a minister, William Smith of Bullhouse Grange and the newly-arrived William Hoyland were the dominant figures in the new village.

The Hey Family

My great-great-grandfather, John Hey (1781–1855), appears in a list of Thurlstone men who were liable for militia service in 1804 and in a similar list two years later, just before his wedding. He had recently moved from Shelley in the next parish, where his ancestors had lived for about three centuries, and in both lists he was described as a weaver. He spent his working life at his loom in an upstairs chamber at home. Various records in the 1840s and 1850s note that he was a fancy weaver – a man who made waistcoats and other garments with colourful floral patterns. Fancy weaving was the main trade in all the villages south of Huddersfield at that time. John and his wife, Mary Woodcock (1786–1850) of Penistone, had four sons and a daughter. The census returns of 1841 and 1851 record the family in the top cottage in New Street in that northern part of Thurlstone which climbs the hill to Top o' th' Town. The remaining cottages in this part of the village seem to date from the late-eighteenth and early-nineteenth centuries. In 1841 Sarah (a dressmaker) and John (a clothier) were still living in New Street with their parents. Their Uncle Robert and his family lived next door for a time before moving away from Thurlstone. Their mother died in 1850 at the age of 63 from a wasting disease which started in her foot. The census taken the following year recorded the two Johns living together and sharing the trade of fancy weaver. The elder John died in 1855 at the age of 73 and was buried in an unmarked grave in Penistone churchyard. The cause of death was recorded as 'Decay of Nature'. He was the ancestor of all the numerous Heys who now live in Thurlstone, Penistone, Stocksbridge and neighbouring parts of south-west Yorkshire.

John's eldest son was given the unusual first name of Mellin or Melling, perhaps from a surname on his mother's side of the family. Mellin worked in Thurlstone as a groom and in 1834 married Ann Smith, who was born at Bolsterstone, but who was then living in Penistone parish. They had four sons and three daughters. George and John worked in the local cloth mill and Henry (or Harry), the youngest, was a slater and plasterer before he became a publican. Benjamin Smith Hey, Mellin's second son, also started work in the cloth mill, but by 1861 he was a steel temperer in the umbrella hardening shop at Samuel Fox's. He walked the five miles over the ridge to Stocksbridge every Monday morning, carrying a week's rations, and starting early enough to be at work by 6 am. Upon his marriage to Ann Birkenshaw of Thurgoland, a domestic servant in Thurlstone, he moved to Stocksbridge. Their four sons and four daughters included Spurley Hey (1872–1930), an exceptionally talented man who became Director of Education for Rotherham, Newcastle and, finally, Manchester.

Mellin's younger brother, George Hey, my great-grandfather, was born on Christmas Day 1816 in the cottage at Top o' th' Town. He trained as a boot and shoe maker and upon his marriage in 1838 he set up home in the old part of the village at Town Gate Farm. The gable end of his former workshop faces the street, with the farmhouse set further back. By 1871 George was being described as a farmer of 20 acres as well as a boot and shoe maker. Ten years later, the farm had increased in size to 28 acres. He seems to have gradually improved his position in life as he grew older. In 1838 he had married a local girl, Clementina Turner Roebuck (1817–81), the eldest of the 10 children of Enoch Roebuck, a local handloom weaver. Her attractive name (and the harsher-sounding pet form Clemmy) came from her grandmother, Clementina Shaw, and was passed down the family to my father's elder sister.

Clementina Roebuck's birth was recorded at the nearby Thurlstone Particular Baptist Chapel on 17 February 1817, the day that she was born, but she was baptised at Netherfield Independent Chapel the following August. Her parents were not married at Penistone Church until 15 July 1817, though perhaps an earlier ceremony had been performed at the Baptist chapel. The births of two of her younger sisters were recorded 10 miles to the north at Lockwood Particular Baptist Chapel in 1819 and 1822; the other children are known only from later records. George and Clementina had at least nine children and possibly three more. None was baptised at Penistone Church. The Particular Baptist Chapel registers for this period are lost but the Providence Chapel, which was rebuilt in 1828 and again in 1867, was conveniently close for the Heys and the Roebucks. The original meeting place was in a workshop behind some of the cottages at Top o' th' Town and adult baptisms were performed in a stream (and later in the River Don). The attendances at services that were recorded here in 1851 were 33 in the morning, 37 in the afternoon and 23 in the evening. The Baptists and the Wesleyan Methodists were the earliest denominations to build places of worship in Thurlstone. The original Wesleyan Chapel on Work Bank Lane was built in 1793 and was converted into a house when a new chapel was opened on Manchester Road in 1889.

The Hey Family, 1913
At the wedding of Ernest Gray and Clementina Hey, the bride is surrounded by her father and step-mother, her brother Arthur and his wife, Annie, her brother Joseph, and (seated) her half-brother, George, and Arthur's two daughters.

Meanwhile, in 1786 a Sunday School had been built by public subscription at the north end of the village. In the later nineteenth century Church of England services were held at Town End School; St Saviour's Church at the west end of Thurlstone was not opened until 1905. The ancient parish church a mile away at Penistone was used for marriages and burials, but the Heys did not christen their children there.

Thurlstone had become a working-class village with a strong Noncon-formist tradition that was entirely typical of the West Riding textile district. Its houses were clustered into folds and rows, sometimes approached by narrow passages known as ginnels. The Heys and the Roebucks were staunch chapel people. The Biblical names of Clementina's father, Enoch, and her probable uncles, Ebenezer and Hezekiah (woollen weavers all), testify to the convictions of their parents. The Heys had attended Shelley

Independent Chapel before their move. Later, the Bullhouse Independent Chapel replaced the Providence Chapel of the Particular Baptists as the convenient place of worship. It is doubtful whether the nuances of denominational doctrinal differences played any part in the choice of chapel, although the Heys were always Independents or Baptists, not Methodists.

In 1881 the census enumerator recorded six households of Heys in the village of Thurlstone. Mellin had died, but three of his sons were now married. George, the eldest, had left the mill to become a gardener, but he lived in Mill Lane and his eldest daughter was a 'woollen cloth worker'. At Top Mill Lane John and his wife lived with their son, a nephew and John's widowed mother. John worked as a woollen cloth finisher and his wife worked in the mill as a burler, removing knots and other imperfections from the yarn. Mellin's youngest son, Henry, lived at Top o' th' Town and employed two men in his business as slater and plasterer. The families of the elder George and his sons, Noah and George, lived close together in Town Gate. Old photographs show that the street was narrower than it is now, with three-storeyed buildings rising at either side. Regrettably, several of the most distinctive buildings have been demolished. Among them was a three-storeyed structure near *The Crystal Palace Inn* which had a row of 15 weavers' windows under the eaves and another range of windows (later blocked in) on the middle floor. A similar building with a row of ten windows survives near Providence Chapel. In 1881 some Thurlstone men still earned their livings as handloom weavers in buildings such as these.

Clementina died in 1881 from 'apoplexy' and 'paralysis'. It sounds like what we would call a stroke. George died from a heart attack in his cow house on Christmas Eve, the day before his seventy-first birthday. George and Clementina's eldest son, Noah, followed his father's trade of boot and shoe maker and set up home four doors away, while his younger brothers went to work at Plumpton Mill. The second son, Hugh Hey (1843–99), a bachelor who in his adult life lived with his younger brother, George, started work as a boot and shoe maker with his father and elder brother, but the census returns of 1871–91 describe him as a wool sorter, no doubt at Plumpton Mill. Upon leaving school, my grandfather, George Hey (1854–1916), started work as a woollen cloth dresser or finisher at Plumpton Mill. This is how he is described in the census returns for 1871 and 1881 and on his marriage certificate in 1876. The family memory is that he helped to make thick coverings for coach seats. Exceptionally for the Heys, who had always married local girls, both of his two wives came from the south of England. His first bride, Mary Foster (1852–1900), was born near Rickmansworth (Hertfordshire). How she had come to meet a Thurlstone man is not at all obvious, but perhaps she had moved around as a domestic servant.

George and Mary had four children. Until he became a coal miner,

Joseph worked at Bullhouse corn mill, where his Aunty Martha was the wife of Benjamin Goldthorpe, the miller. His father, his Uncle Hugh and his younger brother, Arthur, followed soon afterwards. When Mary died at the age of 47, her tombstone recorded her home as Bullhouse Lodge. This was the substantial house below the hall that Elkanah Rich had built in 1686 for his daughter and her husband. It has been restored and adapted to modern living requirements, so that at first sight it now seems incredible that it once housed the family of the waggoner at Bullhouse Mill. But old photographs show that, like many another ancient house, by the end of the nineteenth century it was suffering from neglect and was far from being the fashionable residence that it had been 200 years earlier. Houses such as this, which had seen better days, were commonly divided into cottages, but this does not seem to have happened to Bullhouse Lodge. In 1901 George was living here with his three children and his second wife, Mary Ann Garland, the daughter of a farm labourer who had left his native Somerset in despair in the 1870s to work at a coke oven at one of the new pits. My father was born here three years later. The family farm at Thurlstone was now the home of George's elder brother, Noah, and his large family.

When we stand back from all the minute pieces of information that we have gathered and look at the broad story of an ordinary family, we learn a great deal about the realities of life in Victorian and Edwardian England and Wales. Of course, we only learn part of the general story, for each family has a different tale to tell. Life on the Pennine foothills or on the edge of the New Forest would have seemed remote to contemporary families in, say, Birmingham or Bristol, London or Louth. But in tracing the histories of our own families we begin to understand how ordinary men and women were affected by general trends in the economy and in society, and in writing their stories we can add a little to the nation's view of its past.

THE 1901 CENSUS FOR ENGLAND AND WALES

BY 1901 THE CIVIL SERVICE had ample experience of taking a national census. The first had been held a hundred years earlier and subsequent refinements had improved the quality of information that was obtained every 10 years. The official reports that followed each census are available in print in public reference libraries, but the census enumerators' books, which provide personal details of each household, are opened to the public only after one hundred years have passed. The enumerators' books from the census that was taken on the night of 31 March 1901 were therefore made available for inspection on 2 January 2002.

The General Registry Office, which came under the Home Office, took over the responsibility for the decennial censuses from 1841. The new poor law unions of 1834 that had been used as civil registration districts from 1837 were the natural choice for census enumeration districts. As the poor law unions were based on market catchment areas they sometimes crossed county boundaries. The census reports therefore summarise information according to 'registration counties', which are not quite the same thing as the ancient geographical counties. Fortunately, this is only a minor problem, but it is worth bearing in mind. Another problem is that later in the nineteenth century some districts had to be changed to take account of population growth; this inevitably makes comparisons over time more tricky.

The enumerator provided each householder with a form, or 'schedule', to be completed for census night (which, from 1841 to 1901, was always a Sunday). The form was collected the next day and help in filling it in was provided where necessary. The information was then transferred to the census enumerators' books (CEBS), which are now available for study on microfilm or microfiche at the Family Records Centre, 1 Myddelton Street, London, or (in the case of the 1901 CEBS) on the internet. Each enumerator was given a week to finish this task, then the completed books were supposedly checked against the schedules by the registrar, then by the superintendent registrar, before they were sent to the census office in London. With few exceptions, the schedules were then destroyed.

Family historians need to remember that the aim of the census

authorities was not to produce CEBS for future genealogical research but
to compile reports about the demographic, occupational and social condition of the whole of England and Wales. These printed reports contain
statistics that were laboriously collated from the information recorded in
the CEBS. The population tables for the townships of every county in each
census taken between 1801 and 1901 are also published in the relevant
volumes of *The Victoria County History*. The primary purpose of the
reports that were published after each census was to provide information
on the size of the population for all the major administrative areas. They
also contain general tables on such matters as migration, occupations, age
pyramids, sex ratios, etc., at national, county or city level.

The enumerators were dependent upon the accuracy of the information that was provided by householders. Notoriously, this sometimes varies
from census to census. Some people apparently did not age 10 years each
decade, some had different names and some had changed their minds
about where they were born. Some individuals were excluded from the
lists of residents because they happened to be away from home on census
night. Children who had been both born and buried since the last census
were obviously not recorded. Movements to and from places might be
missed. Slips of the pen as information was transferred from the schedules
to the CEBS explain other discrepancies. The information must therefore
be treated as cautiously as that from other historical sources. Yet when all
is said and done, what we have is a marvellous series of snapshots of families at 10-yearly intervals throughout the Victorian era.

We need to be aware of possible traps in interpreting the data in each
of the columns in the CEBS, though by 1901 many of the old ambiguities
had disappeared. By then the streets in our towns and villages had been
numbered and most street names had become stable. Households are
therefore easier to locate on contemporary, large-scale Ordnance Survey
maps than they had been in the mid-nineteenth century. The numbering
of houses also enables us to distinguish between different households
within the same building. The 1901 returns also recorded uninhabited
houses and those that were being built. In the countryside cottages had
less need for numbers, and the names of farm houses sometimes changed.
The relation of each member of a household to the the head of the family
is usually clear, provided that the informant had supplied accurate information. One of the most common problems in the earlier censuses had
been the use of the terms daughter-in-law and son-in-law to mean (in
modern terms) step-daughter and step-son. The column headed rank, profession or occupation is the one most used by historians in census analysis,
but the information that was entered often masked the complex ways in
which some people earned a living. Part-time work, especially that of married women and young people who were still living with their parents, was
not normally recorded. We need to be particularly cautious in accepting

the description 'scholar' and we need to ponder concealed seasonal employment, occasional jobs and assistance with parents' work. As Edward Higgs has remarked, 'The statistical abstracts contained in the parliamentary census reports are our principal source for reconstructing the occupational structure of Victorian society. But the statistics are several stages removed from the reality of nineteenth-century society.' Finally, the birthplace noted in the last column might not have been the actual place but the nearest town or the first home that the informant could remember.

The official report on the 1901 census was published in 1904. It began by noting that the area of land in England and Wales was 37,129,162 acres, or 58,014 square miles. The land was farmed in the following manner: corn crops 5,886,052 acres; green crops 2,511,744 acres; clover and grasses under cultivation 3,262,926; flax, hops and small fruit 120,683 acres; bare fallow 336,884 acres; permanent pasture or grass 15,399,025 acres; mountain and heath land used for grazing 3,556,636 acres. The remaining 6,055,212 acres were occupied by woods, plantations, nursery grounds, houses, streets, roads, railways, waste grounds, etc.

Local and family historians need to be aware of the recent administrative changes that were outlined in the report. The Local Government Act (1888) established county councils and county boroughs. Of the 62 administrative counties 15 were identical with the ancient or geographical counties as then existing. East and West Sussex; three Yorkshire ridings; three divisions of Lincolnshire; the Isle of Ely and the Soke of Peterborough became administrative counties; the Isle of Wight was subsequently made one in 1889. The Metropolis, by 1856 and subsequent amending Acts, was also deemed an administrative county. Of 636 registration districts, as constituted at the beginning of 1903, about two-thirds (419) were each situated within a single administrative county, and 22 were each confined within a single county borough.

The Divided Parishes Acts of 1876 and 1879 began the rationalisation of the old ecclesiastical administrative arrangements by disposing of large numbers of detached parts of parishes, and another Act of 1882 caused every detached part of a parish which was entirely surrounded by a single parish to be either absorbed into the surrounding parish or, if its population exceeded 300, created as a separate parish. Nevertheless, many detached parts of parishes were still in existence in 1901.

In 1894 urban and rural district councils were formed to take over the responsibilities of the sanitary boards. By 1901 England and Wales contained 67 county boroughs, 17 other urban districts with populations exceeding 50,000, and 28 metropolitan boroughs, each of which had a population exceeding that limit. A considerable number of urban districts, although technically urban, were distinctly rural in character, being in many cases small towns in the midst of agricultural areas. In 1901 the populations of 215 urban districts were below 3,000; another 211 had between 3,000 and 5,000 inhabitants; and a further 260 had populations between 5,000 and 10,000. The 25,058,355 persons who were enumerated in 1901 in the 1,122 urban districts were distributed as follows: in London (including the City of London and 28 Metropolitan Boroughs) 4,536,541; in 67 county boroughs 9,141,250; in 248 municipal boroughs 4,027,678; and in 806 urban districts other than boroughs 7,352,886.

The census returns for the whole of England and Wales from 1841 to 1901 can be seen on microfilm or microfiche at the Family Records Centre. Local record offices and the main public libraries normally have copies of the returns for the districts they serve. On 2 January 2002 the most extensive archive accession project ever undertaken brought the 1901 returns into people's homes. Researchers with access to the internet, either on their own computers or at their local library or record office, can find the information they want on their screens (at www.census.pro. gov.uk). The images have been scanned from the archival microfilm copy of the returns and a high quality digitised image has been produced. An index, which allows readers to find their way around the records more flexibly and accurately than by traditional means, links directly to the images of the returns. Everyone has free access to the index, but charges are made for viewing the digitised pages of the returns. Record offices, libraries and other institutions, including some family history societies, are able to offer this service through the internet. Finding an ancestor in a census return is far quicker and more convenient than ever before.

$\mathscr{B}$IBLIOGRAPHY

A. Armstrong, *Farmworkers: a Social and Economic History, 1770–1980* (Batsford, 1988)

J. C. Atkinson, *Forty Years in a Moorland Parish* (Macmillan, 1890)

D. Baines, *Emigration from Europe, 1815–1930* (Macmillan, 1991)

J. Bateman, *Great Landowners of Great Britain and Ireland* (Harrison, 1883)

J. V. Beckett, *The Aristocracy in England, 1660–1914* (Blackwell, 1988)

J. V. Beckett, *The East Midlands from AD 1000* (Longman, 1988)

J. Beckett, ed., *A Centenary History of Nottingham* (Manchester University Press, 1997)

Lady Florence Bell, *At the Works: a Study of a Manufacturing Town* (Virago edition, 1985)

A. Bennett, *Anna of the Five Towns* (Methuen, 1902)

J. Benson, *The Working Class in Britain, 1850–1939* (Longman, 1989)

J. Benson, *British Coalminers in the Nineteenth Century: A Social History* (Longman, 1989)

J. H. Bettey, *Wessex from AD 1000* (Longman, 1986)

C. Booth, ed., *Labour and Life of the People in London*, 2 vols, second edition, (Williams and Norgate, 1889–93)

W. Booth, *In Darkest England and the Way Out* (The Salvation Army, 1890)

G. Boyes, *The Imagined Village: Culture, Ideology and the English Folk Revival* (Manchester University Press, 1993)

G. Bourne (pseudonym of G. Sturt), *The Bettesworth Book* (Duckworth, 1920)

G. Bourne (pseudonym of G. Sturt), *The Wheelwright's Shop* (Cambridge University Press, 1923)

P. Brandon, *The Sussex Downs* (Phillimore, 1999)

P. Brandon and B. Short, *The South East from AD 1000* (Longman, 1990)

R. Bullock, *Salford, 1900–1914* (Richardson, 88 Ringley Road, Stoneclough, Radcliffe, Manchester, 2000)

J. Burnett, *Plenty and Want: a Social History of Diet in England from 1815 to the Present Day* (Scolar Press, London, 1979)

L. Caffyn, *Workers' Housing in West Yorkshire, 1750–1920* (HMSO, 1986)

D. Cannadine, *The Decline and Fall of the British Aristocracy* (Yale University Press, 1990)

S. Caunce, *Amongst Farm Horses: the Horselads of East Yorkshire* (Sutton, 1991)

S. Caunce, *Oral History and the Local Historian* (Longman, 1994)

C. Chinn, *They Worked All Their Lives: Women of the Urban Poor in England, 1880–1939* (Manchester University Press, 1988)

P. Clarke, *Hope and Glory: Britain, 1900–1990* (Penguin, 1996)

G. Crossick, ed., *The Lower Middle Class in Britain, 1870–1914* (Croom Helm, 1977)

M. J. Daunton, *House and Home in the Victorian City: Working Class Housing, 1850–1914* (Arnold, 1983)

M. F. Davies, *Life in an English Village* (Unwin, 1909)

A. Digby, *Pauper Palaces* (Routledge & Kegan Paul, 1978)

H. J. Dyos, *Victorian Suburb; a Study of Camberwell* (Leicester University Press, 1961)

R. C. K. Ensor, *England, 1870–1914* (Oxford University Press, 1936)

G. E. Evans, *Ask the Fellows Who Cut the Hay* (Faber, 1956)

G. E. Evans, *Spoken History* (Faber, 1987)

A. Everitt, *The Pattern of Rural Dissent: the Nineteenth Century* (Leicester University Press, 1972)

P. di Felice, 'Italians in Manchester, 1891–1939: settlement and occupations', *The Local Historian*, 30, 2 (2000), pp. 88–104

W. J. Fishman, *East End 1888: A Year in a London Borough among the Labouring Poor* (Duckworth, 1988)

J. S. Fletcher, *A Picturesque History of Yorkshire* (Dent, 1899)

J. Fowles and J. Draper, *Thomas Hardy's England* (Cape, 1984)

K. Gay, *A History of Muswell Hill* (Muswell Hill Local History Society, 1999)

M. Girouard, *The Victorian Country House* (Yale University Press, 1979)

S. J. D. Green, *Religion in the Age of Decline: Organisation and Experience in Industrial Yorkshire, 1870–1920* (Cambridge University Press, 1996)

R. Greenall, *The Making of Victorian Salford* (Carnegie, 2000)

G. and W. Grossmith, *The Diary of a Nobody* (Folio Society edition, 1969)

R. Haggard, *Rural England*, 2 vols (Longman, 1902)

C. Hallas, *Rural Responses to Industrialization: the North Yorkshire Pennines, 1790–1914* (Peter Lang, 1999)

A. Hardy, *The Epidemic Streets: Infectious Disease and the Rise of Preventive Medicine* (Clarendon Press, 1993)

T. Hardy, *Jude the Obscure* (Macmillan edition, 1957)

T. Hardy, *The Woodlanders* (Macmillan edition, 1958)

J. Hargreaves, *Halifax* (Edinburgh University Press, 1999)

F. Heath, *British Rural Life and Labour* (King, 1911)

D. Hey, M. Olive and M. Liddament, *Forging the Valley* (Sheffield Academic Press, 1997)

E. Higgs, *A Clearer Sense of the Census: the Victorian Censuses and Historical Research* (Public Record Office, 1996)

E. Higgs, *Making Sense of the Census: the Manuscript Returns of the Census, 1801–1901* (Public Record Office, 1989)

E. Hobsbawm and T. Ranger, eds., *The Invention of Tradition* (Cambridge University Press, 1983)

C. Holmes, *John Bull's Island: Immigration and British Society, 1871–1971* (Macmillan, 1988)

Pamela Horn, *Education in Rural England, 1800–1914* (Gill and Macmillan, 1978)

Pamela Horn, *The Victorian Country Child* (Sutton, 1985)

Pamela Horn, *The Changing Countryside in Victorian and Edwardian England and Wales* (Athlone Press, 1984)

W. H. Hudson, *Hampshire Days* (Longmans, Green, 1903)

W. H. Hudson, *A Shepherd's Life* (Methuen, 1910)

R. Jefferies, *Hodge and his Masters* (Smith, Elder, 1880)

D. Jenkins, *The Agricultural Community in South-West Wales at the Turn of the Twentieth Century* (University of Wales Press, 1971)

P. Jenkins, *A History of Modern Wales, 1536–1990* (Longman, 1992)

F. Kitchen, *Brother to the Ox* (Penguin, 1983)

P. Laslett, *The World We Have Lost* (Methuen, 1965)

J. Law (pseudonym of Margaret Harkness), *In Darkest London* (The Bellamy Library, 1889)

A. Light and G. Ponting, *Victorian Journal: Fordingbridge, 1837–1901* (Charlewood Press, Fordingbridge, 1997)

D. Linstrum, *West Yorkshire Architects and Architecture* (Lund Humphries, 1978)

J. London, *The People of the Abyss* (Journeyman Press edition, 1977)

H. P. Mann, 'Life in an Agricultural Village in England', *Sociological Papers*, I (1904)

C. F. G. Masterman, *The Condition of England* (Macmillan, 1909)

N. McCord and R. Thompson, *The Northern Counties from AD 1000* (London, 1998)

D. Mills and K. Schürer, eds, *Local Communities in the Victorian Census Enumerators' Books* (Local Population Studies supplement, Leopard's Head Press, 1996)

G. E. Mingay, ed., *The Victorian Countryside*, 2 vols (Routledge & Kegan Paul, 1981)

R. Moore, *Pit-Men, Preachers and Politics: the Effects of Methodism in a Durham Mining Community* (Cambridge University Press, 1974)

J. E. Morris, *The North Riding of Yorkshire* (Methuen, 1911)

A. Morrison, *A Child of the Jago* (Everyman edition, 1996)

T. Pakenham, *The Boer War* (Weidenfeld and Nicolson, 1979)

R. Pearsall, *Edwardian Life and Leisure* (David & Charles, 1973)

C. B. Phillips and J. H. Smith, *Lancashire and Cheshire from AD 1540* (Longman, 1994)

C. Pooley and J. Turnbull, *Migration and Mobility in Britain since the Eighteenth Century* (UCL Press, 1998)

J. B. Priestley, *Margin Released: a Writer's Reminiscences and Reflections* (Heinemann, 1962)

D. Read, *Edwardian England, 1901–15: Society and Politics* (Harrop, 1972)

B Reay, *Microhistories: Demography, Society and Culture in Rural England, 1800–1930* (Cambridge University Press, 1996)

J. Roach, *Secondary Education in England, 1870–1902* (Longman, 1991)

E. Roberts, *A Woman's Place: an Oral History of Working-Class Women, 1890–1940* (Blackwell, 1984)

E. Roberts, 'Working-Class Standards of Living in Barrow and Lancaster, 1890–1914', *Economic History Review*, XXX, pp. 306–21 (1977)

R. Roberts, *The Classic Slum: Salford Life in the First Quarter of the Century* (Penguin edition, 1990)

J. Rowntree and A. S. Sherwell, *The Temperance Problem and Social Reform* (sixth edition, Hodder & Stoughton, 1900)

S. Rowntree, *Poverty: A Study of Town Life* (Macmillan, 1901)

R. Samuel, ed., *Miners, Quarrymen and Saltworkers* (Routledge & Kegan Paul, 1977)

R. Samuel, ed., *Village Life and Labour* (Routledge & Kegan Paul, 1975)

P. Sanders, *The Simple Annals: the History of an Essex and East End Family* (Sutton, 1989)

S. Sassoon, *Memoirs of a Fox-Hunting Man* (Folio Society edition, 1971)

B. E. Shaw, ed., *Frank Meadow Sutcliffe, photographer: a selection* (Whitby, 3 vols, 1974–90)

B. Short, *Land and Society in Edwardian Britain* (Cambridge University Press, 1997)

G. R. Sims, *How the Poor Live, and Horrible London* (Chatto and Windus, 1889)

G. R. Sims, *Living London* (Cassell, 1901)

K. D. M. Snell, *Church and Chapel in the North Midlands* (Leicester University Press, 1991)

K. D. M. Snell, 'The Sunday-School Movement in England and Wales: Child Labour, Denominational Control and Working-Class Culture', *Past and Present*, 164, pp. 122–68 (1999)

H. Sumner, *Cuckoo Hill: The Book of Gorley* (Dent, 1987)

F. M. L. Thompson, *The Rise of Respectable Society: A Social History of Victorian Britain, 1830–1900* (Fontana, 1988)

F. Thompson, *Lark Rise to Candleford* (Penguin, 1973)

P. Thompson, *The Edwardians: the Remaking of British Society* (second edition, Routledge, 1992)

J. Walvin, *A Child's World: A Social History of English Childhood* (Penguin, 1982)

H. G. Wells, *The Time Machine* (Everyman edition, 1935)

H. G. Wells, *The War of the Worlds* (Everyman edition, 1993)

M. A. Williams, *Researching Local History: the Human Journey* (Longman, 1996)

M. Winstanley, 'Women and the Grocery Trade in Britain, 1851–1911' in E. Royle, ed., *Issues of Regional Identity: in honour of John Marshall*, pp. 154–83 (Manchester University Press, 1998)

Picture Credits

While every effort has been made to trace the copyright holders of featured illustrations this has not always been possible because of the antiquity of the photographs.

Chapter One

Diamond Jubilee Celebration (The National Archives: PRO COPY 1/430)
Edensor (Devonshire Collection, Chatsworth. Reproduced by permission of the Duke of Devonshire and the Chatsworth Settlement Trustees)
A Street Group (The National Archives: PRO COPY 1/409)
Cartoon from Punch *6 January 1909* (The National Archives Library)
Amersham (The National Archives: PRO COPY 1/460)
Brodsworth Hall (Doncaster Libraries and Information Services)
Edward VII's Coronation (The National Archives: PRO COPY 1/456)

Chapter Two

A Wedding Group in 1894 (The National Archives: PRO COPY 1/416 pt 2)
Mourning a Loved One (Devonshire Collection, Chatsworth. Reproduced by permission of the Duke of Devonshire and the Chatworth Settlement Trustees)
Advertisement for Abbey's Effervescent Salt, 1901 (The National Archives: PRO COPY 1/181)
Dinner in the Workhouse (George Sims, *Living London*, 1901)
Four Generations at Redruth (The National Archives: PRO COPY 1/430)

Chapter Three

Chinese Graves (George Sims, *Living London*, 1901)
Declaration of Residence for Michael Marks (The National Archives: PRO HO 44/407/B23729)
Russian Jewish Immigrants (George Sims, *Living London*, 1901)
A London General Omnibus (The National Archives: PRO COPY 1/460)
Middlesbrough in 1903 (The National Archives: PRO COPY 1/460)
The Wakefield Family (David Hey)

Chapter Four

Eaton Hall, Cheshire (The National Archives: PRO COPY 1/416)
Muswell Hill (Hornsey Historical Society GH/453/6/PC1)
Children in a Slum Street (The National Archives: PRO 30/69/1663; copyright material from the Ramsay MacDonald papers is reproduced by permission of the executrix of the late Malcolm MacDonald)
Advertisement for Bray's Gas Burners (The National Archives: PRO COPY 1/177)
Port Sunlight (The National Archives: PRO COPY 1/467)
Mud and Thatch Cottages (Hampshire Record Office 33M 84/25/76)

Chapter Five

A Working Gang, 1894 (The National Archives: PRO COPY 1/416 pt 1)
A Woman's Work on the Farm (The National Archives: PRO COPY 1/490)
Hop Picking, 1896 (The National Archives: PRO COPY 1/424)
A Lancashire Cotton Mill (The National Archives: PRO COPY 1/501)
Sifting Coal, Wigan Junction Colliery (The National Archives: PRO COPY 1/445)
The Survival of the Fittest (The National Archives Library)
Serving Girl (The National Archives: PRO COPY 1/460)
Fast Food (The National Archives: PRO COPY 1/404)

Chapter Six

Playground Drill (The National Archives: PRO COPY 1/460)
A Ragged School (George Sims, *Living London*, 1901)
A Sunday School Procession (The National Archives: PRO COPY 1/437)
Outside a London Public House (George Sims, *Living London*, 1901)
A Day at the Fair (The National Archives: PRO COPY 1/435 A)
Ladies' Golf (The National Archives: PRO COPY 1/467)
Hammersmith Provision Store (George Sims, *Living London*, 1901)

Chapter Seven

The British Army in India, 1897 (The National Archives: PRO COPY 1/430)
Victoria Embankment (The National Archives: PRO COPY 1/460)
Return of the Veterans (The National Archives: PRO COPY 1/450)
East Kent Buffs (The National Archives: PRO COPY 1/451)
In Memoriam: the Liberal Party (The National Archives: PRO COPY 1/170 f32)
New-Style Breakfasts (The National Archives: PRO COPY 1/0978 pt 1)
Commemorating the War (The National Archives: PRO COPY 1/460)

Chapter Eight

Fordingbridge-Ringwood 'Country' (The National Archives: PRO ZOS 12/37)
The Book of Gorley (Howard Sumner, *Cuckoo Hill*, 1987)
Charles Sandy (David Hey)
Moses Downer (David Hey)
The Thurlstone-Millhouse Countryside (David Hey)
Millhouse Green (David Hey)
The Hey Family, 1911 (David Hey)

INDEX